Southern Illinois University Press
Series in
Aviation Management
David A. NewMyer, Editor

Aviation Industry Regulation
Harry P. Wolfe and David A. NewMyer
1985   ISBN: 0-8093-1177-1

Aviation Maintenance Management
Frank H. King
1986   ISBN: 0-8093-1210-7

Corporate Aviation Management

Raoul Castro

With a Foreword by
Torch Lewis

Southern Illinois University Press
Carbondale and Edwardsville

Library of Congress Cataloging-in-Publication Data

Castro, Raoul, 1914–
    Corporate aviation management / Raoul Castro ; with a foreword by
Torch Lewis.
        p.   cm. — (Southern Illinois University Press series in
aviation management)
    Includes bibliographical references and index.
    1. Airplanes, Company.   I. Title.   II. Series.
HE9795.C37   1995
658.2′7—dc20   94-7933
    ISBN 0-8093-1911-X   CIP

01 00 99 98   5 4 3 2

Contents

PART FOUR: CONCLUSIONS

APPENDIXES

Figures

Figures   ix

Tables

Foreword

IT WOULD NOT BE NECESSARY FOR ME TO KICK OFF my shoes and socks to count how many pilots in the United States possess as much knowledge about the subject of corporate aviation management as Raoul Castro. If you were to add the requirement that the members of this knowledgeable group had to reduce their thoughts to writing, the numbers would shrink substantially. These sixteen chapters of vintage Castro should be as mandatory to read by corporate pilots and corporate aviation managers as an FAA Airworthiness Directive. They could even be referred to as the sixteen commandments of corporate flight operations.

Raoul Castro did not come by this storehouse of information the easy way. He paid his dues in driving through three decades of the character-building weather of summer and winter in the Great Lakes region long before business jet aircraft appeared on the scene and took all the hair out of flying through thunderstorms in July and icing most of the rest of the time. He has always maintained a high profile in the science of safe flight sharing both his experience and intelligent views on various committees, panels, and forums of the National Business Aircraft Association and other similar organizations. In so doing, Raoul's one dominating precept has always shone through, and that is his firm doctrine that in our business we fly people; we don't fly airplanes.

Come next grass Raoul will complete four decades of dedication to corporate flying. Come graze in his pasture and munch on his wisdom.

Torch Lewis

Preface

GENERAL AVIATION PLAYS A VERY IMPORTANT role in the country's aviation system, with corporate aviation being a critical adjunct with approximately 27 percent of general aviation. Corporate aviation not only provides transportation but also supports related manufacturers and fixed base operators and contributes to an influx of technical personnel into the aviation system. Corporate aviation contributes to tax revenues and employment in city, state, and federal governments.

The need for a source of corporate aviation management information brought about the preparation of this book. *Corporate Aviation Management* is intended as a manual on how to run a successful corporate flight operation and is derived from my aviation experience, my consulting practice, as well as my teaching of management and the contributions of many in the field.

When I was interviewed and hired for my first position in corporate aviation I asked the president of the company if there were any special instructions he had as to how I should run the flight operation, and his retort was, "I want you to run the operation in a business manner." From that day on in 1947 I have been searching for a book that would cover the managerial aspects of this entire field. Numerous pamphlets, articles, and the NBAA Procedures Manual do exist and are very useful. However, none of these covers principles of corporate aviation management or the overall managerial functions involving planning, organizing, controlling, and implementing. The need for such a book specifically written for corporate aviation management was again evident in the seventies when many businesses were disposing of their aircraft and we were asked to manage better, cut costs, or else.

It was never my intention to become an author—I was perfectly happy running the operation and flying thirty hours a month. But as the years went by I realized that a lot of basic management experience, some of which I had put into magazine articles, ought be shared and made available to my fellow pilot managers. I recognize the impossibility of writing to suit all pilot managers whose ability and experience vary over a large range. I also recognize that I had to editorialize in order to tell my story as I saw it. I am bound to talk down to some and up to others; that had to be done to develop a full understanding.

This book is intended to be a practical guide for the executive in charge of the aviation department, the aviation department manager or chief pilot, aspirants to aviation management positions, and teachers and students of aviation management. The book is composed of four parts.

PART ONE: ROLE, DEVELOPMENT, AND FUNCTION OF CORPORATE AVIATION MANAGEMENT

The first chapter provides a description of corporate aviation from the early thirties to the present time. It also covers the role of corporate aviation in the national transportation system. Chapter 2 outlines the evolution of corporate aviation and delves into aircraft management requirements as corporate aviation grew and aircraft became more sophisticated. Chapter 3 examines how corporate aviation managers deal with human and technical relationships and how they can manage them for desired results.

The principles to follow in corporate aviation management to produce an efficient corporate transportation service are discussed in chapter 4. A general discussion of how the aviation department fits into the overall corporate structure is discussed in chapter 5. Chapter 6 shows how trade associations are utilized in the management process.

PART TWO: ECONOMICS

Chapter 7 delves into economics and financial determinants in the acquisition of company aircraft and examines cost/benefit factors, tax implications, and methods used to justify company-operated air transportation. Chapter 8 outlines the various factors to be considered in the selection of the proper aircraft to match the transportation needs of company personnel.

PART THREE: OPERATIONS—
THE SEVEN KEY FACTORS

Chapter 9 delves into the seven key factors of operations and deals with the first key factor, corporate flight operations management. The primary objective of corporate aviation is the transportation of company personnel. Chapter 10 deals with corporate aviation maintenance management, programs, and budgets. Chapter 11 discusses the objectives as they relate to schedule and passenger service. A holistic approach to safety is discussed in chapter 12, which covers corporate aviation safety. A precautionary approach to security is discussed in chapter 13, which deals with corporate aviation security. Chapter 14 explains the reason for having emergency and pre-accident plans. It outlines reporting procedures and the use of forms provided for that purpose. Chapter 15 explains the reasons for training the entire corporate aviation department and methods used to develop training programs.

PART FOUR: CONCLUSIONS

An attempt is made in chapter 16 to predict the future of corporate aviation by using trends and forecasts.

I am anxious that this book be received in the way in which it is offered, that is, to apply sound management principles to the flight department in order to guarantee the acceptance of the corporate airplane as a tool of industry. I recommend and hope that this book will be accepted for its practical procedures and concepts as applied to corporate aviation management and that it can be used to enhance managers' progress and assist in achieving their goals.

Acknowledgments

THE DEVELOPMENT OF THIS BOOK CAME about through the encouragement and help of David A. NewMyer, College of Technical Careers, Southern Illinois University at Carbondale. Henry R. Lehrer, Embry-Riddle Aeronautical University, Daytona Beach, Florida, also provided invaluable help.

Grateful acknowledgment is extended to: Flight Safety Foundation, Inc., National Business Aircraft Association, Inc., Cessna Aircraft Company, National Air Transportation Association, *Interavia: Aerospace Review, Professional Pilot Magazine*, General Aviation Manufacturers Association, Aircraft Owners & Pilots Association, Professional Aviation Maintenance Association, Helicopter Association International, *Business and Commerical Aviation*, and Aviation Data Service, Inc. (AvData).

Other manufacturers that provided material: Learjet Inc. (a division of Bombardier), Beech Aircraft Corporation, Sikorsky Aircraft (a subsidiary of United Technologies), Bell Helicopter Textron, Inc. (a subsidiary of Textron Inc.), Canadair Challenger, Inc., and Gulfstream Aerospace Corporation.

Preparation of this book would not have been possible without the assistance of many individuals: Murray Smith, who offered many suggestions; Frank Dolinski, who not only read the manuscript but helped with the text; Julie F. Rodwell; Carl R. Castro, my son, who made numerous suggestions and did text editing; Jay E. Wright; Fred W. McGowan, who provided insurance information; John Underwood, who provided historical information and pictures; Betsy Franks, who provided artwork; Julia Ann Fischer; Capt. Dom Chiovary; Capt. William R. Forsyth; Capt. Stan Dolinski; Capt. Bob Williams; Virginia Crandell; Clifton C. Stroud II; and Jeff Bocan.

Part One
Role, Development, and Function of Corporate Aviation Management

1

A Description of
Corporate Aviation

The objective of this chapter is to define and describe corporate and business aviation, and to explain the role of corporate aviation as a transportation medium in general aviation.

DEFINITION

Corporate aviation has evolved as a distinct entity within the aviation industry. The terms *corporate* and *business aviation* are often aggregated or used synonymously. Since the first corporate airplane was utilized for the transportation of company executives before World War II, the concepts of business, executive, and corporate aviation have changed, as have the roles of those who operated and flew the first executive airplanes.

Definitions were changed (*Federal Aviation Administration* and *National Transportation Safety Board*) to give such flying activity the proper meaning. The term *business flying* was used to denote the use of an airplane by a company executive in the conduct of his or her business. *Executive flying* was vague and elitist; it gave the impression that all passengers were executives, which was not always the case.[1]

Consequently, a redefinition of basic terminology was required in order to place corporate aviation in its proper context. *Business flying* is defined as: "The use of aircraft by pilots not receiving direct salary or compensation for piloting, in connection with their occupation or in furtherance of a private business." *Corporate aviation is* defined as: "The use of aircraft, owned or leased, which are operated by a corporate or business firm for the transportation of personnel or cargo in the furtherance of the corporation's or firm's business, and which are flown by professional pilots receiving direct salary or compensation for piloting."[2]

WHY CORPORATE AIRCRAFT?

Corporate aviation grew from the need for more flexible air transportation so that corporate personnel could plan their itineraries within convenient schedules. Corporate aviation also provides time-saving direct transportation to remote geographical areas and international locations. An analogous parallel to corporate aviation is the corporate ownership of automobiles and trucks to fulfill a company's ground transportation needs. To a great extent corporate America is dependent on its own transportation systems to transport its employees and its goods and services.

To take advantage of better labor markets, raw material availability, and goods distribution patterns, many companies have developed regional offices or have dispersed their corporate facilities over the country and, in some cases, overseas. The following companies are representative of corporate aviation: Mobil Corporation is a multinational company with aircraft based in various United States cities and in practically every continent of the world. Mobile is a good example of a company that utilizes corporate aviation to provide worldwide transportation for company personnel in every continent where it bases aircraft.

Hillenbrand Industries is another good example of how company airplanes are used. Hillenbrand utilizes its aircraft to transport company personnel to various plants and also to bring customers to its factories for demonstrations of its products.

Companies get involved in the acquisition of aircraft in order to cope with the transportation requirements of the above circumstances. Aircraft are also used as a tool for the realization of company goals and to maintain or increase the productivity and efficiency of employees. Corporations requiring portal-to-portal transportation within a 200-mile radius have selected the corporate helicopter as the most efficient form of air transportation.

American Telephone and Telegraph (AT&T) employs helicopters for travel within a radius of 150 miles from its headquarters. It also operates a number of aircraft that permit personnel to travel to any part of the world. In order to satisfy all travel requirements, the flight department used Travel Interface, a computer software that links with United Airlines' Apollo System, to coordinate between commercial and corporate schedules. Companies that operate their own aircraft have concluded that, despite the relatively higher cost of operating their own aircraft versus other modes of transportation, the practical benefits are seen as worth the difference.

Thus, corporate aviation is playing an integral part in industrial transportation systems. Even though the significance of its role is yet to be widely recognized, corporate aviation may well become the most dynamic transportation mode for industry during the remainder of this century.

In a global sense, the development of a fast and safe transportation system is recognized by multinational corporations as a paramount economic, cultural, and technological force of modern times. The world business aviation fleet indicated by figure 1.1 shows how industry in the Western world is dependent on corporate aviation as the most efficient mode of travel.

THE STRUCTURE OF THE AVIATION INDUSTRY

The basic aviation industry structure is comprised of nine components that serve as elements of support for the whole industry. These elements are all interlinked. This book covers only corporate aviation in detail.

1. *Scheduled airlines* include the majors as well as regional airlines. As an example, the airlines cannot operate without training or airports.

2. *The military* includes the Air Force and the air arms of the Army, Navy, Marines, and Coast Guard. The services have to be included because in many instances the military is involved with civil components.

3. *Aircraft and accessory manufacturers* are the manufacturers that design and build airframes, the accessories as a rule being manufactured by independent contractors or suppliers.

4. *Aviation training* includes primary, advanced, multiengine, and training centers where pilots obtain ratings and recurrent train-

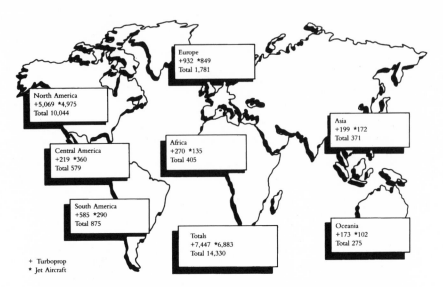

Figure 1.1. World business aviation fleet, showing numbers and locations of turboprop and jet corporate aircraft worldwide, 1992–93. *Source: Interavia: Aerospace Review*, Geneva, Switzerland

ing on specific aircraft. It may also include technicians trained to be able to work on a particular type of aircraft.

5.   *Aircraft marketing.* Today most new airplanes and helicopters are sold by the factory. However, there is a very large market for used large and small airplanes and helicopters.

6.   *The airport system* includes commercial service airports (airline airports), reliever airports, general aviation, and private airports.

7.   *Air navigation system* and air traffic control for civil and military aviation are designed for the efficient use of airspace.

8.   *The regulatory system* includes federal and state regulatory agencies such as the Federal Aviation Administration.

9.   *General aviation,* which the Federal Aviation Administration defines thus: "General aviation is that portion of civil aviation which encompasses all facets of aviation except air carriers."[3]

THE ROLE OF GENERAL AVIATION

General aviation is comprised of four components:

1.   Corporate aviation

2.   General aviation aircraft manufacturers
3.   Fixed base operations (FBOs)
4.   Specialized companies involved in:
    A.   Training
    B.   Aircraft marketing
    C.   Parts and accessories
    D.   Provision of aircraft flight services

1. Corporate aviation is a service that provides air transportation for the personnel of companies that operate airplanes.

2. General aviation aircraft manufacturers build many types of flying machines including rotorcraft, single- and twin piston-engine airplanes, and single- and twin-engine turboprops and turbojets. These are aircraft from 1,500 lb. gross weight trainers to 80,000 lb. gross weight corporate jets. General aviation aircraft are used for training, sport, private transportation, air taxi, and commuter airplanes, etc.

3. Fixed base operations (FBOs) are the service stations of the aviation system. An FBO can be defined as: A service organization located at an airport that provides for-profit services to the aviation industry. Fixed Base Operations (FBOs) can be divided into three areas:

A.   The limited service FBO provides fuel as its main line of service. The FBO may provide passenger services and amenities as a means of attracting business.

B.   The partial-service FBO provides fuel as its main line of service. However, partial maintenance and avionics repair may also be provided, as well as passenger services and amenities.

C.   The full-service FBO provides not only fuel but also a full range of services, including maintenance, airplane outfitting, aircraft painting, avionics installation, etc. In other words, the FBO provides everything required to keep the airplane going from the time the aircraft comes out of the factory green and unfurbished to the time it is put into operation.

Two multibase operators and one single-base operator that supply services to corporate aviation are:

A.   Million Air, a fixed base operator that at present has thirty-two bases in the United States. Some of the Million Air bases provide services in three areas.

B.   Signature Flight Support, a fixed base operator now the largest

FBO chain operator in the United States, provides services in three areas.

C.   Clay Lacy Aviation, a full-service operator with one base in Van Nuys, California. Clay Lacy is a full-service FBO that provides fixed-wing and helicopter charter service, operates aircraft for other companies, and also provides aerial photography work to the film industry.

Specialized companies are involved in providing the following services:

A.   Training pilots from primary instruction through multiengine and instrument ratings
B.   Training aircraft mechanics
C.   Aircraft marketing of new and used aircraft
D.   Parts and accessories manufacturers or dealers for manufacturers
E.   Providing aircraft flight services such as: agriculture, airplane rental, law enforcement, air ambulance, air taxi and charter, offshore oil operations, banner towing, buy-back agreements, fire fighting, etc.

To comprehend the immensity of general aviation, one has to visualize general aviation as a very large service organization, which when examined is found to be involved in many different business activities:

The Aircraft Owners and Pilots Association (AOPA) statistics for 1992, which include all types of flying machines, show that there are over 219,401 general aviation aircraft, of which 6,054 are corporate aircraft, 21,800 business aircraft, and 191,547 other aircraft distributing among the following categories: agriculture, pleasure, law enforcement, air ambulance, training, air taxi, off-shore oil operations, and fire fighting. General aviation in the United States includes over 210,300 aircraft in 1992 and this number is anticipated to grow to over 230,300 by 2000 (see figure 1.2).

THE ROLE OF CORPORATE AVIATION

Corporate aviation is only one of the elements in the aviation industry, but it is a system much larger than many people realize. The National Business Aircraft Association (NBAA) *1992 Fact Book* lists by type aircraft whose primary use is corporate flying, including: 424 single-engine piston, 493 two-engine piston, 1,027 turboprop, 2,299 turbojet, and 561 rotor-craft, for a total of 4,804 active aircraft. Figure 1.3 shows the expected

In thousands

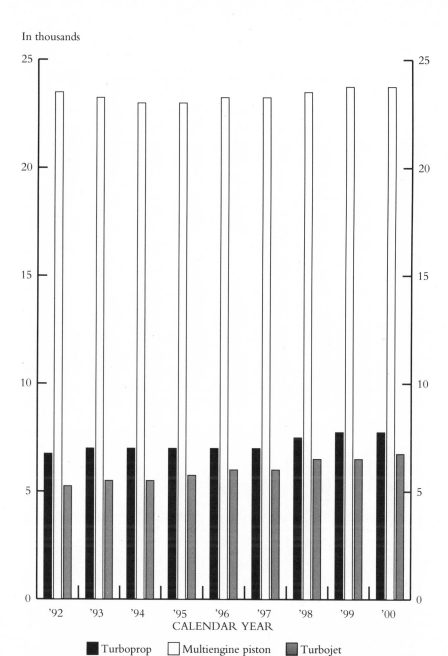

Figure 1.2. Estimated active general aviation aircraft indicating the forecasted growth of the general aviation fleet. *Source: FAA Aviation Forecasts 1991–2002*

In thousands

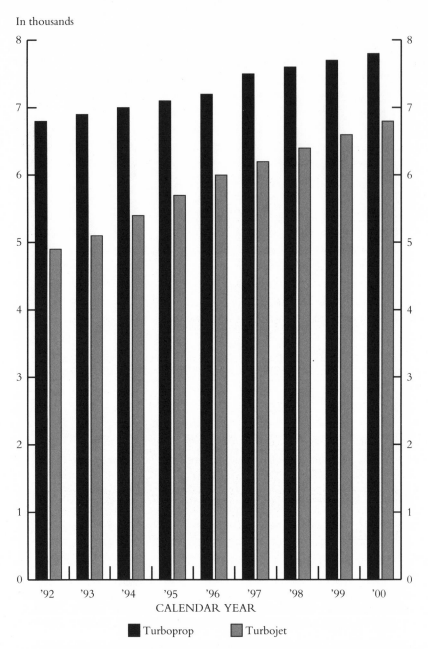

Turboprop   Turbojet

Figure 1.3. Estimated active turbine-powered general aviation aircraft indicating the forecasted growth. Most turbine-powered aircraft belong to the corporate aviation fleet. *Source: FAA Aviation Forecasts 1991–2002*

growth of turbine aircraft by the year 2000. The number of hours flown represents aircraft utilization. Figure 1.4 indicates the increase in the number of hours flown in years listed. The increase can be attributed to better utilization and more aircraft.

From NBAA and National Air Transportation Association (NATA) figures it is calculated that in the United States about 29,140 people are employed by 3,100 corporate flight operations, and about the same number by organizations doing work for corporate aviation.

The use of helicopters (rotorcraft) is increasing as companies learn to utilize the versatility of the machine. Figure 1.5 indicates the expected growth in the number of rotorcraft for the years listed. Figure 1.6 indicates that the trend is more hours flown by virtue of better utilization and more rotorcraft.

As we reach the late 1990s, the corporate airplane appears to be much more of a business tool rather than a fringe benefit. Companies are using aircraft for shuttle service between plants and for customer relations work. NBAA statistics indicate that companies with only one aircraft continue to increase in number. There appears to be a growing trend toward operating the minimum number of aircraft more hours to fulfill the transportation needs efficiently. Companies continue to broaden criteria to allow more levels of employees to use the company airplane. Proponents of corporate aviation argue that company prosperity comes about because of, among other factors, the highly effective use of the aircraft as a business tool.

Opponents generally argue that the reverse is true: corporate aircraft are executive perquisites, which can be afforded by successful companies as an indulgence for top employees and to impress clients. The truth is probably weighted toward benefits the company derives from *proper operation and use* of the corporate airplane. However, there are yet some corporations where the CEO insists on using the company airplane as the Royal Barge. This philosophy is not only detrimental to employees but also unfair to stockholders, as every tool in both a public and a privately owned company should be used primarily for the benefit of the corporation.

Outside of studies made for the FAA by Aviation Data Service (Av-Data) there is little hard analysis available about the economic contribution of corporate aviation. A study conducted for the FAA in 1978 examined general aviation's role in the national economy but did not look specifically at the business benefits to user companies. The economic importance of aviation to a particular company or industry remains elusive, as it does with any other business tool, such as the company computer system or telephone network.

IN MILLIONS (of hours)

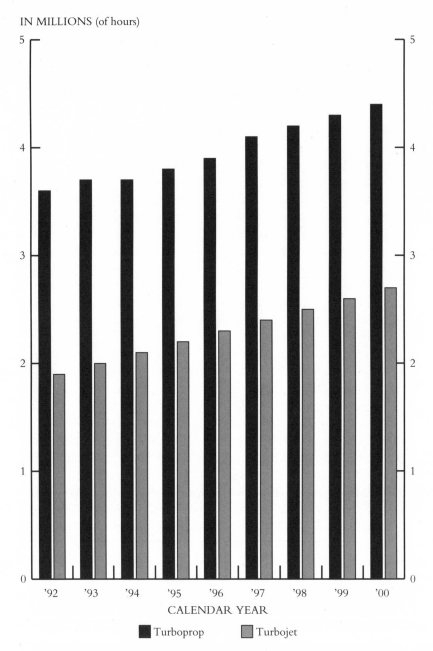

CALENDAR YEAR

■ Turboprop   ■ Turbojet

Figure 1.4. Estimated hours flown by turbine-powered aircraft. The increase in the number of hours flown in the years listed on the forecast probably result from there being more airplanes and better airplane utilization. *Source: FAA Aviation Forecasts 1991–2002*

ACTIVE ROTORCRAFT FLEET (thousands)

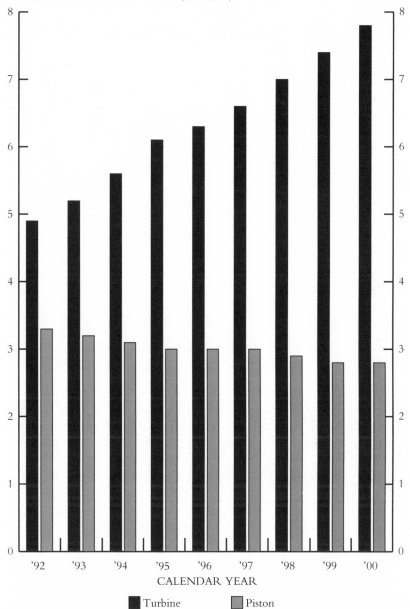

Figure 1.5. The active rotorcraft fleet graph indicates two trends: the increase in the number of rotorcraft being used and the evident switch from piston to turbine power. *Source: FAA Aviation Forecasts 1991–2002*

ROTORCRAFT HOURS FLOWN (millions)

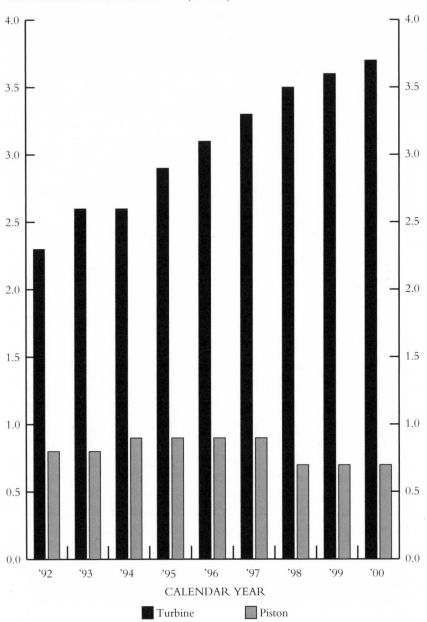

Figure 1.6. The rotorcraft hours flown graph indicates that the trend is to more hours flown by turbine rotorcraft, also an increase in total hours flown as more jobs are found where the flexibility of the rotorcraft can be utilized. *Source: FAA Aviation Forecasts 1991–2002*

TABLE 1.1. *FORTUNE* INDUSTRIAL 500 COMPARISON

	Aircraft Operators	Non-aircraft Operators
Companies	317	183
Employees	10.4 Million	1.6 Million
Net Sales	$2.01 Trillion	$251.7 Billion
Assets	$2.26 Trillion	$201.91 Billion
Stockholders' Equity	$694 Billion	$69 Billion
Net Income	$49.6 Billion	$5.5 Billion
Net Income/Sales	2.5%	2.2%
Net Income/Equity	7.2%	8.0%
Sales/Employee	$192,974	$155,223
Assets/Employee	$216,465	$124,532
Net Income/Employee	$4,762	$3,401

Source: AVDATA, Wichita, KS (1992)

It is worth examining how a company can eliminate an airplane without much trouble, while it would be impossible for a company to dispose of the telephone or computer. Increasingly, however, it seems that efficient corporate airplane usage is parallel in value to that of telephonic systems, including computers. The problem seems to be that up to the present, very few companies really know or want to know how to use the airplane for maximum advantage. NBAA 1993 operational statistics indicate that corporate aircraft are used an average of 304 hours per year, while a corporate airplane can very easily be operated 700 hours per year for maximum utilization.

The best evidence about the value of corporate aviation comes from a series of studies conducted by Aviation Data Service of Wichita, Kansas. These studies have analyzed the nation's top companies, originally the *Fortune* 1000 service and manufacturing companies and, more recently, the *Fortune* 500 industrial companies. In every year since the analysis began, the companies owning corporate aircraft have outperformed the nonaircraft companies, often by significant margins. The number of *Fortune* companies owning aircraft has risen steadily. The aircraft owners, while now only around three-fifths of the *Fortune* 500, include a large percentage of the group's sales, assets, equity, and net income, as shown in table 1.1

CORPORATE AIRCRAFT USES

Airplane operation and/or ownership is not limited to large corporations using jets or turboprops. There are many small- and medium-sized companies that operate beneficially single- or multiengine piston aircraft. Many companies charter airplanes for the transportation of employees or for the transportation of goods and/or materials.

Some corporate aircraft uses are:

Transportation of company executives on company business
Transportation of company personnel on plant inspections
Transportation of clients to company facilities
Transportation of engineers to client facilities
Regular schedule shuttle between facilities
Salesmen transportation
Contractors' site inspections
Door-to-door transportation of company executives with helicopters
Transportation to remote areas with helicopters or STOL aircraft
Demonstration of aviation equipment installed in the aircraft

Corporate aircraft, in many cases, are used not only for executive travel but also for company urgent high-priority transportation, which makes the use of the company aircraft more cost effective by saving time and overnight expenses than using the scheduled airlines. The use of the corporate airplane for customer relations is a prime example of high-priority transportation either to bring clients to the plant or to transport salespeople or technical representatives to customer facilities. Specialty manufacturing firms transport engineers to client facilities for on-site firsthand information about client requirements. Some companies use specially configured cargo aircraft for transportation of parts and machinery (the Boeing 747 that transports the space shuttle is a good example).

The selected uses of corporate airplanes illustrate the diversity of corporate aviation: for all types of companies, all types of industries, and in all areas of the world the benefits are as diverse and numerous as the applications. Many American corporations operate not just one or two aircraft but dozens. In many cases, corporate fleets can be comparable in size to some of the nation's smaller airlines. See table 1.2.

For executives and managers flying on company business, the convenience and time savings are a main concern. Convenience means single-plane service to all destinations, hardly ever a missed flight, and the ability to conduct business meetings and do paperwork in private, or get proper rest while in transit as well as scheduling work. Transportation on demand can also mean the ability to visit several locations in one day, which saves time and avoids overnight hotel and meal costs. Managerial time savings is

TABLE 1.2. SAMPLE—CORPORATE FLEETS BY TYPE

Company	Jets	Turboprops	Helicopters	Total
Chevron	5	6	46	57
General Motors	18	5	3	26
Tenneco	8	0	16	24
E. I. DuPont	12	6	2	20
Occidental	14	2	2	18
Allied-Signal	10	3	2	15
Weyerhaeuser	3	1	9	13
Gannett	4	1	4	9
Henley Group	3	0	2	5
Dresser Industries	4	0	0	4
Potlatch	0	2	0	2
Barnes Group	1	0	0	1

Source: AVDATA, Wichita, KS (1992)

a very important factor, allowing managers to do more of the work they are most qualified to do. The airplane, in this instance, becomes a management multiplier, as existing staff is used more extensively. A large retailer claims high personnel morale and better sales when the stores are visited by the chief executive officer (CEO) and his staff.

THE SCALE OF CORPORATE AVIATION

Corporate aviation as an element of the aviation industry can be summarized with the following data. For example, the National Business Aircraft Association member companies number 3,092 and those companies operate 4,804 aircraft. NBAA nonmember companies operate about 1,250 aircraft. This is an approximate total of 6,054 corporate aircraft flown by professional crews. The number of piston and turbine rotorcraft operated for and by corporations totals 564.

Statistics gleaned from the NBAA *Business Aviation Fact Book* for 1993 indicate that the average number of aircraft operated by a corporation is 2.5. Turbojets are the most widely used type of aircraft, 59 percent of member companies have turbojets, 50 percent have turboprops, and 21 percent use multiengine piston-powered aircraft. Fixed-wing aircraft are used by 83 percent of NBAA members. Four percent of NBAA members use helicopters, while 13 percent use both fixed-wing aircraft and helicopters. Corporate and business aircraft account for over 8 million flight hours per year; of the 8 million hours helicopters account for over 265,000 flight hours per year.

Business-use aircraft (flown by a businessperson in the conduct of his/ her business) number about 21,800 aircraft. This number compares with about 5,000 aircraft in the total United States airline fleet. Personnel employed by corporate aviation: median number of pilots 4.2 per flight department, 1.5 maintenance personnel. Ten point six percent of NBAA aviation departments have more than 20 people, 14.1 percent between 11 and 20 people, 23.4 percent have between 5 and 10 people, 23.5 percent have 3 to 4 people, and 28.5 percent have 1 to 2 persons.[4]

How is Corporate Aviation Different?

The primary focus of a business enterprise is profit, unless it is a nonprofit organization or a corporate aviation department. Corporate aviation provides a transportation service for the convenience of company employees. This service can be compared to the use of computers or the steno pool. The aviation department differs from other company departments in that no direct profit is attributed to its services, the benefits being measured in time saved and personnel productivity. Most corporate ancillary departments are measured by the services they provide rather than by direct profit.

The company's philosophy usually determines who uses the airplanes and for what purpose. This is the probable reason why there are so many types of airplanes on the market. No one type can fulfill all mission requirements, runway requirements, passenger capacity, speed, and so forth. Companies that own one or more aircraft do not necessarily use them in the same way. The way in which companies, both large and small, use corporate aircraft are as diverse as the companies themselves. Some companies operate plant-to-plant shuttles, many corporations use the aircraft for customer relations and others transport personnel to plant inspections. Evidence or the lack of it suggests that very few corporate flight operations are evaluated to determine if they are successfully managed. Consequently, unorthodox management concepts creep into the management of the aviation department, and functions are developed that are not germane to the overall management concepts of the company.

The Role of Corporate Aviation
in General Aviation

Calculations from figures provided by NBAA and NATA indicate that corporate aviation and business aviation make up about 17 percent of general aviation in terms of number of aircraft. However, corporate aviation by the large amounts of fuel and services purchased contributes 60 to 70 percent of the monetary expenditure within general aviation.

Private automobile transportation cannot subsist without the supply of services provided by service stations. Similarly, corporate aviation could not subsist without general aviation fixed base operators providing fuel and other required services. Conversely, fixed base operators would have a hard time making ends meet without the monetary support of corporate aviation. The revenue received by fixed base operators is for fuel and services. The two aspects are closely interdependent. Corporate aviation has contributed to the growth of fixed base operators and general aviation, as evidenced by figures 1.2, 1.3, and 1.4.

The Need for Trained Managers

There is a need for trained corporate aviation managers to direct people. These managers should have writing skills, be able to develop budgets, and control costs. The successful managers perform jobs such as planning, organizing, controlling, and implementing. The less successful are busy doing other things. In the complex business of aircraft operation, the personnel involved, their qualifications, and their motivation toward the fulfillment of their tasks are the factors that control a safe and efficient operation. The study of aviation management becomes an important concern when consideration is given to the fact that human safety and the control of millions of dollars are in the hands of the aviation manager. The success of a corporate aviation department is determined by the proper management of its people and the proper handling of aircraft users.

Notes

1. In the early 1950s the NBAA asked for a meeting with the FAA for the purpose of requesting a number or FAR Part Number such as Part 121

or Part 135. Some corporate operators wanted to report their flights to the airway traffic system as Executive with a number assigned each company similar to the method the airlines use in reporting their company trip numbers. The FAA pointed out that business flying would thus be restricted by additional regulations. At that time executive flying was dropped from the corporate flying vernacular.

2. *Business flying* and *corporate aviation* definitions by the Federal Aviation Administration and National Transportation Safety Board quoted by National Business Aircraft Association, Inc., in a 1985 study of business aviation.

3. *FAA Aviation Forecasts 1993–2004* (Washington, DC: FAA, 1993).

4. *Business Aviation Fact Book*, published by the National Business Aircraft Association, Inc., 1993.

2

Evolution of Corporate Aviation Technology and Progress of Corporate Aviation

This chapter deals with the evolution of corporate aviation. It also covers aircraft and management requirements as corporate aviation progressed and aircraft technology became more sophisticated.

EVOLUTION OF CORPORATE AVIATION

Corporate use of airplanes began with the use of the open-cockpit biplane for advertising purposes. The Curtis Candy Company used a biplane to advertise its candy bars. La Tourraine Coffee Company used an airplane for promotional purposes. The Gulf Oil Company owned a Grumman biplane named *Gulf Hawk*, painted in company colors, which was used to advertise its products at air shows. The *New York Daily News* used a biplane to fly reporters to news events (figure 2.1).

The open-cockpit airplane was not the ideal machine for passenger transportation purposes. Very few open-cockpit airplanes had the capacity for more than two passengers, and exposure to the elements necessitated wearing appro-

Figure 2.1. Waco Co. biplane operated by the *New York Daily News*, 1932–33. *Source*: John W. Underwood, Glendale, CA

priate clothes. Use of the company airplane for executive travel did not actually materialize until a cabin airplane was designed, which could offer some measure of comfort such as constant cabin temperature, comfortable seating, noise insulation, and ease of cabin access. Will Rogers, an early aviation pioneer, proved the reliability and flexibility of single-engine cabin aircraft by using this type airplane to travel all over the North American continent.

The National Air and Space Museum currently displays one of the first cabin-type executive aircraft, the Model CF, built by the Bellanca Company in 1922 (figure 2.2). The Bellanca CF was succeeded in 1925–26 by Wright-Bellanca's WB-1 and WB-2, both prototypes. At the 1925 National Air Races, the WB-1's comfortable cabin created quite a sensation, as did the WB-2 the following year. Charles Lindbergh wanted the WB-2 for his intended transatlantic flight but was unable to reach an accord with Bellanca. So, in desperation, he went to Ryan, which had not yet built a cabin airplane. Ryan was constructing a cabin monoplane, a spinoff of the moderately successful mailplane and progenitor of the *Spirit of St. Louis*.

In 1927, Lindbergh successfully piloted the *Spirit of St. Louis* across the Atlantic, demonstrating many possibilities for aviation in the future. His pioneering feat proved that an airplane could travel great distances and be navigated without reference to the ground for checkpoints, that an engine

Figure 2.2. Bellanca CF, one of the first corporate aircraft. Manufactured in 1922 by Bellanca Aircraft, Wilmington, Delaware. *Source*: John W. Underwood, Glendale, CA

could run for long periods of time, and that a monoplane could be as efficient as a biplane. The WB-2 Wright-Bellanca cabin monoplane was flown across the Atlantic in 1927 sixteen days after Lindbergh. The success of the Ryan and Bellanca monoplanes prompted aircraft manufacturers to begin serious design and production of single-engine cabin monoplanes that could accommodate four or more passengers. Cessna Aircraft Company was just entering the cabin-monoplane business, as were Travelair, Lockheed, and the Stinson Company of Detroit. Stinson was building a four-place cabin airplane for corporate users a full year before the Lindbergh flight. The Stinson airplane embodied several innovations designed to appeal to air-minded executives.[1]

Transportation of corporate personnel actually began with the introduction of the single-engine cabin airplane. Some of the early users of single-engine cabin airplanes were: the Texas Oil Company, which based single-engine cabin Spartan Executives at its regional offices for salesmen use; Wallace Beery, the movie actor, who owned a single-engine cabin DGA Howard; and Phillips Petroleum. In the 1930s, oil companies were

Figure 2.3. Cessna Bobcat, 1939. Manufactured by Cessna Aircraft
Company before World War II as a twin-engine corporate airplane.
A few were purchased by corporations and individuals; then the plane
went into Army Air Force service as the UC-78. *Source*: Cessna Aircraft
Company

the main users of airplanes because the companies required transportation
to places that were virtually inaccessible by routinely available means. Some
of the aircraft used in the thirties were Stinsons, Cessnas, Traverlairs, and
Lockheeds. For twin-engine safety reasons and the requirement for more
power, aircraft companies in the early 1930s, such as Ford, Beech, Lockheed and Cessna, designed various multiengine-cabin airplanes. The availability of relatively comfortable cabin twin-engine aircraft precipitated a
desire on the part of companies to buy airplanes for business transportation.
(figure 2.3) The Timken Bearing Company owned a Ford Trimotor that
was used for executive transportation. The Standard Oil Company, the Cities Service Oil Company, and Nevada Air Explorations operated Douglas
DC-2 airplanes for corporate transportation.

In the late 1930s, there was much activity in the design and manufacture of new twin-engine cabin airplanes specifically built for the airlines.
Lockheed came out with the twin-engine, ten-passenger Electra Ten and
an eight-passenger Electra Twelve that proved popular with several airlines,
amongst them Chicago & Southern Airlines. United Airlines operated the

Figure 2.4. Beech 18, an early corporate aircraft manufactured by Beechcraft starting in 1946. *Source*: John W. Underwood, Glendale, CA

Boeing 247D, a twin-engine, fourteen-passenger airplane. Northwest Airlines put into service the Lockheed 14. American Airlines phased out the Douglas DC-2 aircraft and put into operation the larger version Douglas DC-3. Some corporations purchased and operated airline-type airplanes including the Beech 18, which was designed specifically for corporate use (figure 2.4).

The war in Europe made practically all aircraft design and manufacture turn toward helping the allies in 1940 and for the duration. When the United States entered the war, corporate airplanes became trainers or transports for the services. Civilian aviation had to wait until the war was won for civilian aircraft production. During the war generally available transportation systems were assigned on a priority basis, making routine business travel difficult.

During World War II some companies were able to obtain permission from the government to operate their own aircraft for transportation purposes. After the war ended, the availability of surplus aircraft created a totally new circumstance—an ample supply of both pilots and suitable aircraft. Responding to the availability and relatively low-cost aircraft, many corporations entered into corporate aviation. Some corporations already in aviation expanded their fleets. This activity resulted in a tremendous increase in the number of airplanes operated by corporations. Flight departments became what are known today as corporate aviation departments.

Companies that considered speed more important than comfort had bombers converted to passenger carriers. The Continental Can Company, which wanted coast-to-coast range, had a four-engine B-24 converted for passenger service. International Harvester purchased a converted Douglas B-23 for executive use. Tenneco, Inc., had Martin B-26s rebuilt as passenger airplanes. Some of the bombers that were converted to passenger carriers included the Douglas B-23 and A-26, the Martin B-26, and the North American B-25, as well as the Lockheed Ventura.

The military-transport airplanes that were used for corporate transportation were airplanes that had been originally designed as transports and were again put to that service, such as the Lockheed Loadstar or C-60, Douglas DC-3 or C-47, and the Beech models AT-11 and AT-7. The Beech 18 was upgraded later to the Beech D-18. The DC-3 and the Beech D-18 became the most prominent aircraft in the corporate fleet for a good number of years after the Second World War (figure 2.5).

INTRODUCTION OF JET AIRCRAFT

A corporate jet airplane was not available in the late 1950s when the airlines introduced the jet transport. The lack of a corporate jet airplane left corporate aviation without a modern jet aircraft of speed and one-stop transcontinental range comparable to airliners. The range of most corporate piston airplanes in the 1950s was too short for nonstop flights even between Chicago and Los Angeles. Because the available airplanes were short-range machines, the average company flight was one hour and thirty minutes, or about 300 miles. There was a dire need for an airplane with more speed and range.

In 1960 Grumman introduced the Gulfstream G-1 turboprop airplane, and the Dee Howard Company introduced the piston-powered Howard 500, both airplanes with speeds of around 275 miles an hour and a range just short of 1,500 miles. Lockheed Aircraft Company and North American Aviation offered the United States Air Force and the United States Navy designs for a small jet transport. North American Aviation won

Figure 2.5. Douglas DC-3s and Beech D-18, manufactured, respectively, by Douglas Aircraft and Beechcraft, photographed in 1947. These two aircraft, right after World War II, were the flagships of the corporate aviation fleet. *Source*: Joan Ford, Santa Ana, CA

the contract and flew the military T-39 in 1958. Lockheed was left with the twin-engine jet prototype and no orders. Sensing the need for a corporate jet aircraft, Lockheed decided to introduce the redesigned, four-engine Lockheed Jet Star for the corporate market.

Bill Lear, who had been modifying several piston aircraft, saw the potential for a low-price, small corporate jet aircraft. He started design work in Switzerland with a Swiss engineer but problems developed, and Lear moved the operation to Wichita, Kansas, where he formed the Lear Aircraft Company to manufacture what eventually became the Lear 23 jet.

In the meantime, Bill Remmert, of Remmert Werner, St. Louis, Missouri, convinced North American Aviation to build, for corporate aviation, the T-39 military transport that North American Aviation had been manufacturing for the United States Air Force. North American and Remmert worked out an agreement for Remmert Werner to market the new airplane

Figure 2.6. Cessna Citation VII, a modern corporate aircraft. *Source*: Cessna Aircraft Company

as the Model 40 Sabreliner. Beginning in the late 1950s and early 1960s corporate aviation had the Jet Star, Lear 23, Jet Commander, and the Sabreliner from which to choose. The success of the four airplanes prompted others to get in the act. From Europe came the Dassault Fan Jet Falcon and the DH 125. Grumman Corporation started with the twin jet G-II as a follow-up to the turboprop G-I. Cessna Aircraft Co. offered the Citation series twin-jet aircraft (figure 2.6) and Lear upgraded the model 20 series to the 30 series (figure 2.7). Cessna and Lear became the most popular corporate jets.

Interestingly, in the late 1950s, the use of helicopters became voguish, probably because their use by oil companies to fly to oil rigs proved the flexibility and time-saving ability offered by this type of aircraft (figure 2.8).

Many changes took place as corporate aviation entered the jet and helicopter age: the range of the jets made overseas travel possible, and while the average company flight stage length according to NBAA statistics was still one hour and thirty minutes, that range now equaled 675 miles at jet speed. Over-the-weather flying made travel more comfortable since one could fly

Figure 2.7. Learjet 35A, a modern corporate aircraft with a range of 2,200 miles. *Source*: Learjet Inc. (a division of Bombardier)

above the turbulence. The advent of the jet aircraft with its flexibility and speed suggested to some corporate aircraft operators that such an airplane could be accepted as a business tool that could be utilized to fulfill not only the travel requirements of top management but also the travel needs of middle management.

In this manner, the utilization potential of the jet aircraft could be for the benefit of the whole corporation, rather than as a "perk" for a few top officers of the company. In many cases, progressive company officers conducted surveys regarding the travel habits of company employees to determine whether the company airplane could be utilized for the benefit of the entire corporation. By conducting travel surveys, a company could ascertain which departments could use the company airplane to save time and enhance sales. This focus on flight-department efficiency and utilization continues to be an important theme.

Jet aircraft and helicopters not only brought about greater operating flexibility but also greater administrative responsibilities, creating the requirement for a full-time manager for large-fleet operators and a part-time pilot-manager for single- or two-airplane operators.

Figure 2.8. Sikorsky S-76, a modern four- to eight-passenger turbine corporate helicopter, with a normal cruising speed of 145 kts. *Source*: Sikorsky Aircraft (a subsidiary of United Technologies)

Some administrative responsibilities include:

1. Safety
   Security
   Emergency
2. Operations
   Company manuals
   Procedures
   FAA regulations
3. Financial
   Budgets
   Accounting
   Records
   Reports
4. Ancillary duties
   Insurance
   Contracts
   Purchasing

5. Maintenance
   Technicians
   Accounting
   Manuals
   Stock and ship supplies
6. Schedule
   Passenger service
   Flight records
7. Flight
   Flight crews
   Airports
   Weather
   Flight manuals
8. Training
   Programs
   Manuals

The above activities are the manager's responsibility, performed by the manager and his or her personnel.

MANAGEMENT REQUIREMENTS TO KEEP PACE WITH AIRCRAFT CAPABILITIES

Managing the operation of a single-engine cabin airplane in the early days of corporate aviation was fairly simple. Weather restricted utilization, so there was plenty of time for maintenance to keep the airplane in flying condition. Schedules were flexible and irregular. Records such as log books were simple and did not take much time to complete. The cost of the early corporate aviation operation was charged to transportation or travel accounts. Pilots in that era were not interested in managing, so this situation suited them fine. Some pilots had other jobs within the company such as sales or representing the company products.

As the capability of the airplane increased and utilization improved with such features as night flight, instrument flight, more range, more speed, better runway requirements, etc., managerial tasks increased in proportion. Aircraft mission capability equates with utilization. With modern equipment there is hardly any weather that the modern jet aircraft cannot top, circumnavigate, or fly through. More range permits transcontinental and overseas flights, also multiple short stages without refueling. Speed allows one-day trips, or several trips in a day. Shorter runway requirements permit the use of more airports.

Aviation department management materialized when companies realized that having an aviation-management-oriented person assume full responsibility for the everyday managerial tasks was more efficient than having a nonaviation company manager run the aviation department part-time in addition to managing another company department.

There still are many functions in corporate aviation that need the decision of a high officer in the company. For that reason, the aviation-department manager should report to the CEO, president, or executive vice president of the company.

ROLE OF THE CORPORATE AVIATION EMPLOYEE

As corporate flight operations grew in size, by number of airplanes, and more employees, the manager had to be qualified to manage the size operation he/she was entrusted with. The management skills include the ability to communicate, solving problems, and leadership. The job of the corporate pilot has expanded to include the management of people as well as aircraft. The manager not only has to be a skilled aviator, but just as importantly, must be skilled in working with others, effectively managing all available resources.

With aircraft technology becoming more sophisticated, the demands on corporate technicians become greater. The ever-increasing sophistication of the machine and its circuitry demands that corporate aircraft technicians be trained properly and thoroughly, much beyond the tinkering capability offered by the old vocational school. Consequently, the technician's education must go beyond basic technical training to include the ability to read, understand, and translate complex aircraft technical manuals into final work operation.

For those technicians who strive to become corporate aviation maintenance managers, knowledge of inventory control, maintenance budgeting, cost control, personnel relations, manpower utilization, work scheduling, and other managerial arts are a must. To this day the demands for management skills and technical skills have not abated. Management and technical skills requirements brought into being a sequential process of training for crew members and technicians, which started with "learning by doing," followed by "on-the-job training," and now, career-oriented degrees in aviation sciences. When aircraft operation and maintenance sophistication became too demanding for basic training methods, a curriculum given in a controlled classroom environment had to be established by training agencies, trade schools, aircraft factories, colleges, and universities. Today, academic studies are a prerequisite for technicians and crew members who aspire toward a position in the aviation industry.

TECHNOLOGICAL PROGRESSION OF CORPORATE
AIRCRAFT AS IT AFFECTS PILOTS AND TECHNICIANS

The *open-cockpit* biplane was usually flown by pilots with fundamental flying knowledge. The airplane could be maintained by a mechanic with basic skills, it was a very basic machine, with no systems, either electric or hydraulic, and only a compass for navigation equipment. Engine upkeep and fuselage corrosion were the main maintenance problems, not to mention the fabric coverings of the airframe, wings, and control surfaces.

The *single-engine* cabin airplane was usually designed for cross-country and night flying and required an electrical system to run the lights, navigation, radio equipment, and heater for cabin and cockpit comfort. The airplane had to be flown by a pilot with some cross-country day-and-night navigation training, as well as knowledge of the electrical system. The maintenance had to be performed according to FAA requirements by a licensed Airplane and Engine technician.

Multiengine cabin airplane piloting demands became such that an FAA multiengine rating was established in 1933 to fly that type of aircraft. Because of the possibility of encountering weather on cross-country flights, possession of an instrument rating was required by the FAA. Systems were introduced to operate the retractable landing gear, brakes, flaps, variable-pitch propellers, and fire-extinguishing controls. Table 2.1 makes a comparison of early aircraft with current-generation aircraft emphasizing number of passenger seats, systems, performance, and cost.

With the advent of multiengine aircraft, the need for two disciplines to deal with the complexities became apparent. The complexity of the multiengine airplane and its systems made aircraft maintenance a science that demanded a skilled highly trained new type of technician—the airplane and power plant mechanic. Aircraft dependability required by the emergence of air travel as a mode of transportation made maintenance schedules necessary. Corporations operating airplanes recognized the need for a manager or pilot-manager to assume administrative functions. Multiengine-turboprop aircraft brought about the need for pilots to learn the operation of turbine engines and cabin environmental systems that keep airplane cabins at normal pressure and temperature.

Technicians not only had to learn the operation and maintenance of turbine engines but also the operation and maintenance of the environmental system. Multiengine-turbojet aircraft established the need for new flying techniques. The pressurized aircraft also placed crew members in a new environment: high-altitude flying and high-altitude, over-water flying. The jet airplane is of an entirely different character from any other airplane. Therefore, a pilot has to unlearn many of the procedures that he/she has used in flying other types of airplanes. Maintaining jet aircraft's requires more specialization. Technicians need to consult the airplane's technical manuals more often for information as to how maintenance procedures are performed.

THE PRESENT AVIATION DEPARTMENTS

Among the corporate fleets of the nation, as many as 321 of the largest are owned by *Fortune* 500 companies. But, on the whole, 69 percent of

TABLE 2.1.   CORPORATE AIRCRAFT TECHNOLOGY PROGRESSION

Airplane	Systems—Performance—Price
1. Bellanca CF, 1922: single-engine cabin monoplane, 4 passengers seats	Electrical system for lights, all-fabric covering, speed 80 MPH, range 240 miles, runway requirements 1,600 ft., price $5,000.00
2. Stagger Wing Beech, 1935: Model D17A single-engine cabin biplane, 5 passenger seats	Electrical system for lights, radio navigation, landing lights, gear retraction, starter, all-fabric covering, speed 170 MPH, range 820 miles, runway requirements 2,200 ft., price from $8,000.00 to $18,000.00
3. Douglas DC-3, 1935: twin-engine cabin monoplane, 12 to 24 passenger seats	DC and AC electrical systems, fuel systems, anti-icing system, hydraulic system, propeller system, starters, flaps, all aluminum except control surfaces which were covered with fabric, speed 160 MPH, range 1200 miles, runway requirements 3,500 ft., Price $110,000.00 to $150,000.00
4. Grumman G-1, 1960: twin-engine turboprop cabin monoplane, 9 to 12 passenger seats	DC and AC electrical systems, hydraulic system, fire warning system, fuel control system, environmental system, propeller system, anti-icing system, air power unit, navigation systems, all-aluminum construction, speed 220 kts, range 1200 NM, runway requirements 4,500 ft., starting priace $750,000.00
5. Citation VII, 1990: twin-engine turbojet cabin monoplane,6 to 9 passenger seats	DC and AC electrical systems, hydraulic system, fire warning system, air power unit, environmental system, fuel control system, anti-icing system, emergency systems, air brakes, aluminum and composite construction, speed 409 kts, range 1,808 NM, runway requirements 4,690 ft., price $8,950,000.00

NBAA-member companies operate one or two airplanes. Many smaller companies that have a real need for their own private transportation operate one or two airplanes. Large-fleet operators have, in the past, held the lime-light provided by NBAA and the aviation media. However, NBAA membership growth in the past year is attributed to operators of one or two piston or turboprop aircraft joining the organization. For example: Sorrento Cheese Company, Inc., of Cheektowaga, New York, operates a turboprop Cessna 425; Texas Infinity Corporation of Dallas, Texas, operates a turboprop Mooney MU-2; Sanchez-O'Brien Oils & Gas Corp. of Laredo, Texas, operates two turboprop Beech 200s and a Cessna 210; and Royal Cake Company, Inc., of Winston-Salem, North Carolina, operates a Learjet 24. Reliance Electric owns two Sabreliner 65s that are use primarily for the transportation of customers. Company policy specifies that the customer has priority over the president for the use of the airplanes. The above companies knew the range, speed, or cabin limitations of the aircraft they selected to cover the areas in which they do business. The main concern was selecting an airplane that would best fit their needs for the money they wanted to spend.

It is no longer necessary to obtain a large aircraft in order to have transcontinental range. There are several medium-sized jets that can cross the continent or fly to Hawaii nonstop. Many companies, such as the Whirlpool Corporation, have a requirement for two types of airplanes to fulfill two missions. A high-density passenger shuttle is needed to fly to Chicago's O'Hare Airport and to plants within a radius of 600 miles from Benton Harbor. Two Grumman G-1 turboprops are used for the high-density shuttle and two Falcon 50 medium-size jets transport company personnel anywhere in the United States, Canada, and Mexico, nonstop.

The number and type of airplanes that a company operates usually indicate the work or mission that the aircraft perform. A company in this category is the Arabian American Oil Company (Aramco), which schedules thirty-one aircraft all over the world. The Aramco aircraft list includes an Aero Commander 680W, several DHC-6 De Havilland turboprops, five Fokker F-27s, six G-II Grummans, two B-737 Boeings, a Douglas DC-8, and thirteen helicopters. The companies mentioned in this section exemplify the diversity that is corporate aviation and give some idea of the wide range of management requirements for each operation.

FACTORS AFFECTING CORPORATE AVIATION GROWTH

It was assumed that with the traveling problems that airline deregulation imposed on the business traveler there would be a stampede by corporations to get into the business of operating their own aircraft. This did not materialize because corporate aviation is at present going through a period of transition, caused by such economic factors as taxes, insurance costs, fuel and maintenance costs. Corporate aviation is also being affected by air traffic control restrictions, limited airport access, and buy-outs or mergers. All flight operations are affected. Some operations affected by the transition manage to cope, some go out of existence, and others adjust by changing methods of operation and obtaining more efficient aircraft.

NOTE

1. Conversations with John W. Underwood, aviation historian, Glendale, CA, 2/20/90 and 2/15/91.

3

The Functions and Development of the Corporate Aviation Manager

This chapter examines how corporate aviation managers deal with human and technical relationships day-by-day and how they can manage those relationships to achieve desired results. It also offers information on the skills required and provides ideas on how to obtain education and training for the development of corporate aviation managers.

THE CORPORATE AVIATION MANAGER

The manager has broad authority and responsibility for supervising all phases of the aviation department, including flight operations, maintenance, and scheduling. A corporate aviation manager must have an understanding of his or her department functions and the management skills required to get work accomplished by coordinating the efforts of individuals in his/her operation. Communication skills are required to instill vitality into planning, organizing, controlling, and implementing. Effective overall management, in a word, requires a variety of skills on the part of the manager.

Managing People

Management is a people-oriented discipline. The involvement with the employment and service to people makes management a dynamic study. Management cannot be explained with a simple doctrine. Management can be defined as the art and science of controlling human effort and resources to attain a desired objective in a specific corporate environment.

One author, Franklin Moore, in his book, *Management Organization and Practice*, sees a manager's role this way:

> Everybody knows that a manager doesn't do much. That is, except to decide what is to be done, to tell somebody to do it, to listen to reasons why it should not be done, why it should be done by somebody else, or why it should be done differently; except to follow up to see if the thing has been done, to discover that it has not been done, to listen to excuses from the person who should have done it; except to follow up a second time to see if the thing has been done, to discover that it has not been done, to wonder if it is not time to get rid of a person who cannot do a thing correctly, to reflect that the person at fault has a family with seven children; except to consider how much simpler and better the thing would have been done had they done it themselves in the first place.

The Required Skills of a Manager

Like any other department in a company, the aviation department has to have a manager, or someone in charge, to put management functions into practice. To achieve the maximum safety and efficiency of a department or operation, the person in charge should have at least minimal expertise in the basic skills of management and know how to apply those skills to benefit the department. The quality and efficiency of a corporate aviation department are usually evaluated by the convenience and comfort it can provide for corporate executives. As long as take offs and landings are smooth and relatively on time, passengers and management assume that the most important activities of the operation such as safety, maintenance, training, passenger service, and cost control are also present. Completion of a flight and safe transport of passengers to their destination are only the end results of activities required to make the flight operation successful.

The need to increase employee productivity and maintain flexible travel schedules necessitated the expansion of corporate aviation. Costs of purchasing, maintaining, and operating aircraft have accelerated. These factors and the advent of jet aircraft have precipitated a need for the development of certain basic principles of corporate aviation management. Corporate aviation was traditionally managed according to a collection of fragmented methods developed by practitioners of more general aspects of management. The individual in charge of the aviation department applied his or her own management skills based on past experience, rather than according to a specific principle or plan. Consequently, methods varied extensively from operation to operation, and every corporation had its own philosophy concerning how to use and manage aircraft. What corporate aviation management apparently lacked was a unified, systematic approach and plan to manage the aviation department, according to prescribed management methods.

A case in point to support the unified approach is the situation in which a company chooses to engage an airplane operation management company. This type of company usually operates all the airplanes with one management method (i.e., administration, record keeping, training, maintenance, etc.). There may be some differences in amenities or other non-management functions which the managed company may require, but all airplanes are basically managed equally by the same method. There are some basic principles or plans a manager must use to accomplish his/her overall job.

ASPECTS AND RELATIONSHIPS

In reality, management consists of getting things done through others. Management requires different techniques in order for different tasks to be successful. The most valuable asset a manager can have is his/her ability to learn from every experience he or she encounters. The corporate aviation manager has to be an expert in understanding and handling the technical aspects of his/her job, as well as the human relationships. These quite different skills are required to conduct competently the functions of planning, organizing, controlling, and implementing.

Figure 3.1 denotes the functions and lists the aspects of each function. Regardless of the size, shape, or form of the operation, the chief pilot or aviation department manager has to manage the operation by

FUNCTION	ASPECTS
Planning	Develop objectives Budgeting Develop procedures Develop policies Determine resources
Organizing	Structure organization Select human resources Select facilities Identify work to be performed Update organization to reflect needs Accountability
Controlling	Develop performance standards Measure performance standards Evaluate performance Activities and tasks
Implementing	Determining time sequence Delegate Identify alternate strategies Records and reports

Figure 3.1.   Functions and aspects of management. *Source:* AIMS, Inc., Upland, CA

employing four main functions: planning, organizing, controlling, and implementing. Through these functions, he/she may breathe life into his/her operation by communicating their meaning to the rest of the organization.

PLANNING

Seneca, the Roman philosopher, observed, "When a man does not know what harbor he wants, any wind is the right wind."

Of the four tasks, planning is the primary task of management, and in the case of the aviation manager, he/she must know "what harbor he/she wants." Planning must occur before any of the other managerial functions, because planning determines the nature of those functions. Planning is a great deal more than forecasting, because planning involves the process of choosing an objective, plotting a course, and following that course to the attainment of the objective.

At one time budgeting was considered as planning, but the budget should not be the operating plan, but rather a contribution to the objectives, linking resources directly to results, a listing of proposed expenditures for a specified period, usually one year. The budget serves as a cost-control instrument that must be reviewed and compared with actual expenditures at least once a month. The corporate aviation manager should have an effective planning system that will force him/her to think in an orderly and logical fashion about the course of action to be carried out, in the present and the future.

The development of procedures and policies must be tied to human, facility, equipment, and financial resources—the capabilities of the people or individual who will carry out the work, the facility where the work will be performed together with the equipment to do the work, and the financial resources to cover expenditures. The prime value of planning lies in the thought and analysis that takes place. A written or charted plan is invaluable because it records sound and useful ideas that have emerged from the planning process.

ORGANIZING

When an organization is structured, the founders or executives determine what work should be done to accomplish the proposed plans, who should do it, and how a specific group of people can work together most effectively. Organization involves the arrangement of component tasks so they will get done in the most efficient manner. A sound organization must directly relate the work to be done to the goals that must be achieved. Sound organization evolves from sound plans. The basis for the logical organization hierarchy is related to the plans, the selection of resources, identifying the work to be performed and the expertise of people doing the required work in the proper facility with the proper equipment. The organization and its chart must be updated to reflect the needs whenever necessary. The organizational structure is not an end in itself but another tool in the manager's toolbox. Efficient organization, like quality tools, will contribute to the successful operation.

CONTROLLING

It is a common practice in corporate aviation to have individuals with the title of "Chief Pilot" or "Manager," even though they have no control over their operation. The chief pilot or manager is at the mercy of non-aviation people who really control the activity. In such situations the manager is not managing but coasting. Sometimes, control is lost by the manager because of his/her inability to be accountable and manage to the satisfaction of his/her superiors. Or he/she can lose control by failing to have full knowledge of all aspects of his/her operation. In any case, the operation suffers because people with control normally are not experts in aviation matters. Control is the process of assessing and regulating work as it is being done, and when it is completed.

Control is the key to holding all the people who are involved accountable for the parts they play in the plans that are developed. No plan can succeed without the control of performance standards, reporting systems, and the methods of evaluating and correcting deviations in standards and plans. Carrying out a plan to a successful conclusion means controlling the actions of employees that could have caused a variance in results. In controlling, the manager has to be careful to prevent the danger of letting his or her employees get out of hand or equally in danger if his or her employees beginning to feel a heavy hand. The manager's skill becomes apparent at the point of control. Because one of the goals of effective control is safety, the manager has to develop certain operational standards, and the allowable deviations from those standards. Therefore, his/her leadership style will require stricter discipline, particularly in the area of safety, than the leadership style of other corporate departments.

IMPLEMENTING

Implementing is a means employed by a manager to carry out or achieve a given result. An aviation department continually implements *activities* and *tasks*. It is important that all implementation be planned in an orderly manner, and carried to a successful conclusion. The implementation process involves the identification of alternative solutions and strategies to reduce the discrepancies between what is actually happening and what should be happening. This requires anticipation of the probable consequences of each of the strategies, and the choice of a specific strategy and implementation method. In the conduct of decision making the manager has to take time to answer some questions:

1. What can possibly go wrong?
2. What could cause a problem to occur?
3. What action can I take to prevent a problem?
4. What contingency plan can I use?
5. When should the contingency plan go into action?

A corporate aviation manager must constantly analyze his/her operation to determine what discrepancies are occurring, and why they exist. Experience indicates that many aviation managers fail to analyze and plan effectively, or determine a time sequence before implementing a strategy, thus incurring deficiencies that may be detrimental to the operation.

A manager must develop a record system that will cover all aspects of the operation. Records should not only keep the manager aware of what is happening, but also facilitate making the necessary evaluation of the operation as well as providing information for required reports.

REQUIRED TECHNICAL SKILLS

Technical skills provide the ability to understand the operation's technical relationships, for effective and efficient coordination of the various departments. Technical work is exerted by an individual through his or her own efforts and directly applied to components. For example, an engine mechanic works directly on an engine and an electrician works directly on the electrical system. A maintenance manager maintains airplanes by supervising the technical work of mechanics, electricians, and other maintenance personnel. Supervisors are managing while planning, organizing, controlling, and implementing.

MANAGEMENT LEADERSHIP

Management work is the mental effort a person in a leadership position exerts so as to obtain results from the efforts of other people. In other words, leadership is the "process of inducing an organized group to behave in a desired manner" in an effort to achieve certain goals. "The primary rule of leadership is: lead by example."[1]

Corporate flight operations come in all sizes, shapes, and forms—from the single-engine piston aircraft flown by a single pilot, to the large aircraft fleet utilizing many multiengine aircraft, from an operation shaped to have a number of bases in the United States and abroad, to an operation formed to operate fixed-wing and rotor craft.

Normally, the title for the manager of a small operation is "chief pilot," but when the administrative duties multiply with the addition of crews and a maintenance department, the title is usually "aviation department manager." In this case, the administrative duties are his/her primary responsibility, limiting his/her flying time to no more than thirty hours a month. The small operator with two aircraft or less will have an overlap of administrative and flying responsibilities, and his/her company should understand that he/she will require help in scheduling and paper work. In both cases, the aviation manager should have access to other departments of the company for assistance in such areas as finance, personnel, insurance, and purchasing. The manager must have full authority and responsibility in running the aviation department. Otherwise, as we discussed earlier in this chapter in the section on Control, the entire operation will suffer.[2]

It is important at this point to offer information on the skills required and provide ideas on how to obtain education and training for the development of the professional corporate aviation manager. Although there were a few corporate airplanes before World War II, the postwar period can be characterized as the beginning of corporate aviation. The availability of pilots and airplanes after the war made that possible. The pilots that came back from the war were the persons that established the early corporate aviation departments.

Today corporations expect corporate aviation managers or chief pilots to have the same managerial skills and leadership qualities that other managers of the company possess. Before covering the development process of the corporate aviation manager the competence of the position has to be explained. It must be realized that corporate aviation managers require competence in two skills, technical and human.

THE TWO-SKILL MANAGEMENT CONCEPT

The corporate aviation manager or chief pilot embraces the two-skill concept of management: technical skill and human skill.[3] It is assumed that the corporate aviation manager achieves certain objectives through his or her own effort and the efforts of others. A high percentage of corporate aviation departments operate one or two aircraft, consequently, in that case the manager or chief pilot divides his time between managing and flying. However, the operation being a service-oriented enterprise, his or her human skill becomes very important in dealing with the people he or she comes in contact with.

Technical Skill

Technical skill implies an understanding of and proficiency in specific kinds of activity involving methods, procedures, and techniques. A pilot must be involved in performing his or her own special function of flying an airplane using methods, procedures, and techniques. Maintenance procedures, flight-planning methods, and weather-gathering techniques are also functions of technical skill.

Human Skill

Human skill is the ability to work effectively as a group member and to build cooperative effort within the team one leads. Human skill is primarily involved in working with people. To be effective, this skill must be developed naturally, unconsciously, and consistently; every action has to be demonstrated whether working for or with people. Corporate aviation needs managers that can use their human skill to interact efficiently and effectively, are responsive to interpersonal relationships, and can develop innovative ideas to improve the corporate transportation system.

The following three actual examples are the stages that individuals went through to become corporate aviation managers: *example one*, the development as a manager of an individual in charge of a corporate flight department with technical skills but lacking in human skills; *example two*, the development as a manager of a second officer with some upgradeable technical skills and no human skills; and *example three*, the development as a manager of an individual with no technical or human skills.

It is important at this point to mention that many people contend that certain abilities are inherent in chosen individuals. Mention is made of "born pilots," "born managers," "born mechanics." It is true that certain people naturally or innately have greater aptitude or ability in certain skills. Psychological and physiological research indicates that strong aptitudes and abilities can improve skill, also that those lacking natural ability can improve their performance and effectiveness with practice and training.

Example one, human skill development process. Due to a requirement to cut costs, the individual in charge of the flight department of a large corporation in Chicago was asked to present a budget outlining the cost of operating the three airplanes owned by the company together with plans to reduce expenditures while improving the utilization of the aircraft. Baffled and embarrassed by the request, he had the problem of not knowing what to do. He had never made a budget and did not know the cost of operating the airplanes. Fortunately he was able to ask for help in preparing a budget and a proposal for improving the flight operation from a person in finance whom he had flown several times.

The budget incident alerted the individual in charge that it would be prudent for him, if he wanted to keep his position, to equip himself with management knowledge. The first step was to enroll in a management course at the local community college. The management course whetted his appetite for further learning. The next step was to enroll in NBAA aviation management seminars formerly conducted by the Colgate Darden Graduate School of Business Administration. At the completion of seminars and management instruction he felt better equipped to handle his position as a corporate aviation manager and also be able to exercise control of his operation by knowing what was going on.

Example two, human and technical skill development process. A second officer after being employed for five years by a medium-size New York company could not see any future with the company. He liked the position and the people he worked with, but he could not see the possibility of the flight department expanding or any way in which he could become a captain and eventually the manager of the operation.

He found it difficult to get advice on the course to follow to obtain the necessary education and training to become eventually a corporate aviation manager with the necessary human and technical skills. By contacting the company personnel manager he was able to learn what guidelines the personnel manager used when the aviation department manager was hired. Using those guidelines, he set up a curriculum that he could handle between flight schedules including correspondence management courses given by a Florida university and attendance at various NBAA seminars for technical training. At the end of his studies he applied for and was awarded a position as chief pilot with a North Carolina corporation.

Example three, human and technical skill learning process. A young woman wanting a career with the aviation industry enrolled in a bachelor of science degree program in aviation management at the College of Technical Careers, Southern Illinois University at Carbondale. Her program included training at the university flight school. Her flight training included commercial certificate, instrument rating, and instructor's rating. After accumulating considerable time as flight instructor and charter pilot she obtained a position as first officer with a Chicago company where she is gaining experience for an eventual position as corporate aviation manager or chief pilot.

The three examples represent the human and technical training needed to obtain and keep a position as corporate aviation manager. The fact is that while aviation managers will accept managing as a primary responsibility, surprisingly few clearly understand what managing they should be doing and how to perform the work required. Today flight operations can be found whose manager or chief pilot does not participate in the managing of the flight operation because he or she lacks the technical and human skills that his or her contemporaries in other corporate departments possess. Most of those individuals are very defensive and fear anyone looking over their shoulders to see how their flight operations are doing, not realizing that control is lost when they are not cognizant of the ramifications of their flight operations. Many corporate aviation managers fail the test of competence but do not make self-examinations for fear that they may find themselves wanting.

BACKGROUND OF CORPORATE AVIATION MANAGERS

Regardless of the background and experience that an individual may possess he or she has to go through a learning period in a new position or job before becoming completely competent. For that reason it is important to assess and evaluate what the present position entails versus what the candidate for the position has accomplished in the past.

Corporate aviation managers can be recruited from other flight operations or from the Air Force, Army, Navy, or Marines: regional airline managers who have pilot ratings; retired military pilots that have management background and have been flying aircraft that are comparable to corporate airplanes; pilot-managers from government agencies such as the FAA and NASA; and individuals from state aviation departments. Some companies have hired persons with management or business degrees but no aviation technical skills. This system has worked well with some companies such as 3M, which hired an engineer as corporate aviation manager. His human skill allowed him to work well with the chief pilot, who had the aviation technical skill necessary to complement the engineer's human skill.

There are a number of colleges and universities that offer aviation management programs that can prepare an individual for a position in a flight operation where he or she can gain experience for an eventual position as a corporate aviation manager. Embry-Riddle Aeronautical University and Southern Illinois University offer such programs.

NOTES

1. Louis A. Allen, *Making Managerial Planning More Effective* (New York: McGraw-Hill, 1982).

2. Robert M. Fulmer, *The New Management* (New York: Macmillan, 1978).

3. Robert L. Katz, "Skills of an Effective Administrator," *Harvard Business Review* (Sept./Oct. 1984).

4

Principles to Follow in Corporate Aviation Management

The objective of this chapter is to show that in order to develop a standardized corporate aviation management concept or method, certain basic principles have to be established to produce an efficient corporate transportation service.

MANAGEMENT PRINCIPLES

Frederick W. Taylor was one of the earliest contributors to the study of scientific management and is usually referred to as the father of scientific management since his theories revolutionized the study of labor and management. The approach to scientific management is the belief that there is a one best way of doing a job. Both worker and supervisor must be committed to this basic principle for the Taylor approach to be effective. At the time that Taylor was making a name for himself in America, a French engineer, Henri Fayol, was making a contribution to the science of management in Europe. Fayol made many companies successful by the application of good management or *doctrine administrative* and the "Fayol Bridge."

Harold Koontz and Cyril O'Donnel wrote the largest-selling management textbook in the world, *Principles of Management*. These principles are reliable rules and laws used as guidelines in standardizing business activities.

Corporate aviation management principles are outlined and discussed below.

Accountability
Assured responsibility
Line of authority
Organizational structure
Lines of communication
Span of control
Flexibility

Accountability is defined as the obligation to carry out the duties and responsibilities of a position. Accountability must be shared with the idea that individuals in an operation are responsible, both for making plans and for carrying them out. Example: A new avionics device needs to be installed in an airplane. There are several types of units and various ways to install them. Although it is not necessary for the manager to supervise personally each function, a detailed plan must be decided upon to insure that proper unit selection and installation are achieved. Accountability is maintained by requiring the installation to follow the detailed plan.

Assured responsibility is defined as the obligation to perform work. Assured responsibility maintains that every individual performs his/her work correctly and on time, and that established schedules are met. Example: The detailed plan for the installation of the avionics device states that the installation will be completed at a certain date and time. Assured responsibility is maintained by making sure that completion of the work is on time.

Personnel in a corporate flight department must posses a high degree of reliability and moral obligation for passenger well-being and safety. However, timely completion of a flight and safe delivery of passengers to their destinations is only the end result of activities required to make the flight operation successful. Assured responsibility includes being held accountable for successful day-to-day departmental operations.

Line of authority includes the rights and powers vested in a position, which implies the right to command. Accountability, responsibility, and authority make a triad of principles required of each activity and job for the successful operation of a corporate aviation department. Example: A captain-pilot is listed on the schedule board for a four-day trip to transport a number of passengers to several destinations and return to home base on the fourth day. The captain picks up the flight release form with all the necessary information for the trip and is then on his or her own. The captain has the obligation and the power vested in him or her as a captain to complete the flight according to rules as prescribed in the operations manual. The captain has to make the flight plan; see that the airplane is properly fueled and taken out of the hangar at the proper time and that navigation charts are up-to-date; check weather to make sure that the flight can be completed safely and on-time and that all passenger requests are met according to the passenger request form, etc. *All personnel involved with the flight must have a well-defined and clear idea of the accountability, responsibility, and authority assigned to each job if a successful operation is to be achieved.*

A manager has to educate his/her superiors to accept the fact that: 1) he/she must be empowered with the necessary *authority* to lead his/her group to behave in the desired manner; and 2) he/she must be looked upon by his/her superiors as the company *aviation expert*, who advises them on the proper course to follow in the conduct of the aviation department.

Organizational structure is the manner in which a corporate flight operation manages its transport service. The organization of the department is depicted by the organization structure chart (see charts in chapter 5). An organization structure chart is important to a corporate aviation department because the chart shows the line of authority, chain of command, and the process of people working with each other toward common goals. Organization structure and organization charts will be presented in more detail in chapter five. *Note*: It may be proper at this time to mention line/staff organization relationships:

Line organization is characterized by the chain of command, direct lines of responsibility, authority, and communication. Staff organization makes available specialized advisory working personnel whose job is to advise the line on matters of decision but not command. The staff advises; the line commands. Most corporate aviation departments are too small to justify the need for separate line/staff organizations and, in many cases, one individual performs two or more functions in a specialized field. Therefore, the use of a functional organization or the division of work areas into specialized fields is more prevalent in corporate aviation. Example: A pilot in charge of training may make scheduled flights, give ground and flight instruction, perform check rides, and develop pilot and maintenance training programs.

Lines of communication are required in corporate aviation management due to the nature of its activities. There must be at least two contexts:

1. An effective communications network that will provide information to all levels of the work force affected when decisions are made. Communication must work from the top of the organization downward, and in reverse order.

2. Constant communication has to be maintained with top corporate management and persons using the aircraft. It would be an embarrassment if the passengers were taken to the wrong airport, or if the flight was canceled without notifying the passengers.

Span of control (Span of management supervision) deals with the number of persons a manager directly supervises,[1] as well as delegation of authority and assignment of responsibilities when the manager or chief pilot is away from home base. A manager who spends a significant percentage of his/her working time as a pilot on scheduled flights should set up the organization in such a manner as to have no more than six subordinates report directly to him/her. Also, when the manager is away from home base, the next in line should be delegated to make decisions up to a specified level.

Flexibility is imperative in a corporate aviation operation. Changes at a moment's notice should be feasible without sacrificing safety or good operational practices. Changes should be made to accommodate traveler convenience, or for the good of the company, but never for the sake of change.

Suppose a corporation decides to engage the ideal role-model of an aviation management company to operate its airplane. The corporation selects an organization that embraces standardized principles of managing all aircraft (i.e., accountability, assumed responsibility, line of authority, organizational structure, lines of communication, span of control, and flexibility). The employment of a management company to operate the corporation's airplane results in a uniform policy of administration, record keeping, training, and maintenance of the client corporation's airplane. Although there may be differences in amenities and other nonmanagement functions, all aircraft are ideally managed in basically the same way; this is what the aviation department manager or chief pilot should strive for.

TYPES OF MANAGERS

Pilots who are not versed in human relations and become managers run the risk of developing authoritarian or Machiavellian personalities[2] and becoming what the late Douglas McGregor, in his excellent book *The Human Side of Enterprise*, called "Theory X" managers, showing a tendency to be self-centered and self-serving, and favoring complete subjection to authority. McGregor contended that most organizations are structured and managed on the basis of assumptions about human nature, and he formulated these assumptions into two theories, X and Y.

The Machiavellian manager would not hesitate to communicate only those messages that serve his or her needs. The *Theory X Manager* assumes that people by nature lack integrity, are fundamentally lazy, desire to work as little as possible, avoid responsibility, are not interested in achievement, are incapable of directing their own behavior, are indifferent to organizational needs, prefer to be directed by others, avoid making decisions whenever possible, and are not very bright. Conversely, the *Theory Y Manager* assumes that people by nature have integrity, work hard toward objectives to which they are committed, assume responsibility within these commitments, desire to achieve, are capable of directing their own behavior, are not passive and submissive, want their organizations to succeed, will make decisions within their commitments, and have imagination and integrity. The truth is that if a manager believes in Theory X, he/she will manage accordingly. His/her people, in turn, will respond in kind, showing more and more of the Theory X traits. So, the manager gets tougher and tougher. It is the self-fulfilling prophecy in action. But the opposite is just as true. If a manager believes in Theory Y and he/she manages accordingly, the response will be a Theory Y response.[3]

The authority by which people are motivated is of paramount concern to an aviation manager. He or she needs the input and expertise of his/her people in order to develop a sound organization. Perceptive persons usually rebel against authoritarian management. This type of management is not generally detected by supervisors because the flight operation may be isolated from the rest of the company. The aviation manager must realize that, "as ye sow, so shall ye reap," and manage his/her operation somewhere between Theory X and Theory Y for optimum results.

COMMUNICATION

Normally, communication consumes 90 percent of a manager's workday. It is the method of getting meaningful work by coordinating the efforts of individuals in the organization.

Mark Twain once said that the difference between the right word and almost the right word can make a lot of difference—such as the meaning of

Figure 4.1. When communicating with
aviation department employees, more
detail is required for outlining tasks and
jobs minutely. *Source*: AIMS, Inc.,
Upland, CA

the word *lightning* and what happens to that meaning when you add a word
to it, as in *lightning bug*. Figures 4.1 and 4.2 indicate graphically the difference in communicating with subordinates and upper management. All employees have to understand and thoroughly accept management communication regarding policies, instructions, objectives, and goals.

Figure 4.3 shows the chain of command and how manager-employee
relations are established. Understanding is the magic of holding and controlling people. It would be very simple indeed if communication were a
one-way process, with messages received exactly as they were intended.
But, of course, that is not the case. When we communicate orally or by the
written word, formally or informally, the great misconception is to assume
that communication occurs perfectly, and with no breakdown.

There are seven basic modes of communication that are especially important in aviation.

    1.   Listening
    2.   Observation
    3.   Thinking
    4.   Reading
    5.   Speaking

Figure 4.2. When communicating with
upper management, be sure to use
language it can understand. Avoid
jargon and relay only matters with
which superiors need be concerned.
Source: AIMS, Inc., Upland, CA

6.   Writing
7.   Action

All these communication modes are dependent on how the person to
whom messages are being communicated *perceives* what has been transmitted. Freud suggested that people all tend to practice *selective perception*, seeing only those incidents or parts of incidents that they want to see or hear:
10 percent of what they read, 20 percent of what they learn, 30 percent of
what they see, and 50 percent of what they see and hear.

1. *Listening*. Of all the communication skills, listening is probably the
least understood, and the one that is never taught in elementary education.
The best way to arouse most individuals is to criticize their listening habits.
They will immediately tell you about the excellent report on their powers
of hearing they received from their eye, ear, nose, and throat physician.
They do not realize that hearing and listening are two very different things.

1.   The physiological process of *hearing* involves changing acoustical,
      mechanical, and electro-chemical energy into energy that the
      brain can act upon.

SAMPLE OF MANAGER–EMPLOYEE RELATIONS

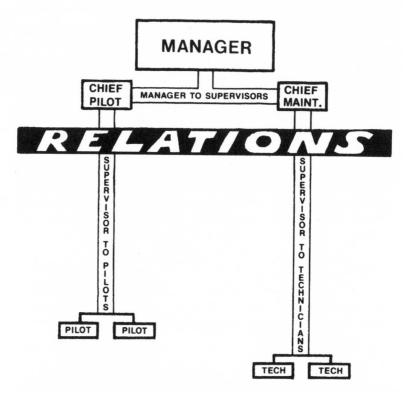

Figure 4.3. Manager-employee relations can best be facilitated by following the chain of command. *Source*: AIMS, Inc., Upland, CA

2.   The physiological process of *listening* permits us to attach sense to the patterns of energy we "hear."

We have to make a conscious effort to listen attentively to any conversation directed to us.

2. *Observation.* Observation plays a tremendous role in everyday aviation activities. Maintenance, scheduling, training, and flight planning are some of the activities that require close observation. Observation is a way of learning by doing; it is also a way of keeping tight control on what is happening around us

by intercepting or avoiding errors, and using care in performing the task at hand.

3. *Thinking*. All modes of communication involve thinking. As we listen or see, for example, we are also thinking to ourselves and forming ideas and reactions. However, thinking can be a mode of communication by itself. It can be identified as a receiving mode. Some of our time is spent communicating with ourselves, digesting thoughts, expanding ideas, organizing our work, *and preparing to communicate with others*. This is a mode of communication on which we should spend more time because it enhances our creative powers.

4. *Reading*. For an aviation manager, a good part of the business day is spent in reading reports, manuals, correspondence, and other official information. Regular reading is the only way to keep up and stay ahead. It is important not only to read rapidly but to be able to understand what you read.

5. *Speaking*. People speak to each other to develop relationships that serve certain needs. What specifically do you want to convey? What is your intent? The use of fewer words offers less opportunity to confuse the issue. In aviation, certain prescribed phrases are necessary to avoid confusion, e.g., on takeoff, "full power," rather than "takeoff power."

6. *Writing*. Writing is probably one of the most important modes of communication because it constitutes a permanent record and has the capability of conveying fairly complex data.[4] The person who understands his or her topic and his or her reader can write straight and to the point, without beating around the bush. As an example of overwriting, the Department of Defense specifications for holiday fruitcake for servicemen and women consume eighteen pages, as opposed to only two-thirds of a page for a standard fruitcake recipe in the established culinary bible, *The Joy of Cooking*. Two prime examples of economy in words are the Ten Commandments, which use only 279 words, and Lincoln's *Gettysburg Address* which contains only 266 words.

7. *Action*. In the aviation business, communication through action plays a very important role, because much of the ground and air activity is conducted by means of signals rather than by more traditional modes. These signals are precise and, when learned well, cannot be misinterpreted.

In using all of these methods of communication, we must not make the mistake of believing that all people are capable of understanding a subject at the same level of complexity. Communication is by nature a complicated matter. For instance, when communicating, six messages come to life (Douglas McGregor, *The Human Side of Enterprise*):

1. The message we intend to send
2. The message we actually send
3. The message the other person receives
4. The other person's interpretation of what was received
5. The other person's response
6. The difference between the response expected and the response received

All of this points up the need for careful communication practices and follow-up after communication has taken place. *Make sure the person receiving the communication understands the meaning of what was communicated.*

There is also the danger of not communicating at all. Too many managers have a tendency to treat information as private property, resulting in the belief that some information is not important enough to be shared, when it really is vital for employees to know about it. It should be remembered that every trade or profession has a jargon of its own. In the case of corporate aviation, when communicating with those outside of that environment, the jargon of the trade should not be used.

TIME MANAGEMENT

A corporate aviation manager must control his/her time to make sure that daily managerial activities are covered according to a planned distribution of time. One of the best ways to improve your managerial effectiveness is by improving your use of time. C. Northcote Parkinson, Raffles Professor of History at the University of Malaya, wrote a satire on organizations entitled *Parkinson's Law*. In this book, Parkinson's first principle is, "Work expands so as to fill the time available for its completion."

KINDS OF TIME

The following elements are present in practically all activities:

1. Creative time: Relates to planning, organizing, controlling, implementing, evaluating your own performance—in short, thinking about your job.
2. Preparation time: The setup phase of work, which includes arranging your work for a prompt start, having all facts or materials you

will need, reading reports beforehand, arming yourself for the "prime time" (e.g., an interview, presenting a report, holding a meeting, etc.).

3. Productive time: Premium time, which is the reason for your employment, the main core of your work, or regular activity (e.g., flying, daily tasks, delegating, overseeing, etc.).

4. Overhead time: Includes correspondence, reports, office work, personnel relations, and telephone contacts.

These activities relate to your position in the organization and your work as a whole in that organization.

Time perception is usually a personality trait that is hard to change. But a manager has to practice using his/her skills to avoid losing those minutes and hours. Lord Chesterfield recommended, "You take care of the minutes, for the hours will take care of themselves."

TIME-SAVING TIPS

1. The mail: Segregate mail according to importance. Answer important correspondence promptly. Save only what you need as reference.

2. The telephone: Have calls screened, if possible. Bunch return calls. Do not visit by phone.

3. Meetings: Develop and follow an agenda. Learn to direct for results within 45 minutes or less, no marathons. Develop ability to remember.

4. Reading: Select required reading; learn to skim. To inform your employees, assign reading; get written summaries.

5. Writing: Dictate; don't write letters longhand. In answering letters, have letter to be answered in hand. When writing letters or reports, plan to have no interruptions. Figure 4.4 shows the results of a time survey made of six flight operations comprised of one to six airplanes. A manager must make assessments of the important activities so he or she may distribute his or her time accordingly.

DELEGATING THE WORK TO MAKE TIME

Delegation and Time Control go hand in hand. There are managers

**NUMBER OF ACTIVITIES AND
DISTRIBUTION OF TIME**

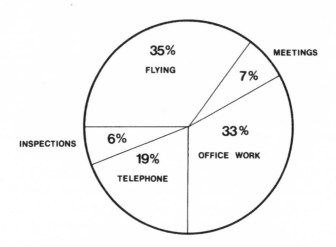

Figure 4.4. A manager must assess the relative
importance of activities in order to allocate his or her
time accordingly. *Source*: AIMS, Inc., Upland, CA

who prefer to make all managerial decisions personally. In so doing, they
are unable to spend their time on the broader duties of their positions. Despite risks and the time it takes, delegation works best when the following
rules are at work:

1. Accept delegation. Understand why delegation is necessary to a
    successful department. Look at the bottom line: employees may
    not do things the way you would do them; be prepared to accept
    their results.
2. Do not take back a delegated task. An employee may question
    your sincerity in work delegation. If the employee is not doing
    well, offer assistance.
3. Assess results. Appraise an employee's performance of a del-
    egated task. What training or motivation is needed to improve
    performance?
4. Set performance standards. Agree with subordinates on the stan-
    dards against which their performance will be measured.

How the aviation department goes about its work is dependent on the way the organization is structured.[5] The best way to prepare people for management is to acquaint them with the many available techniques, and encourage them to become what they can. The aforementioned corporate aviation management principles combined with the corporate aviation management functions (planning, organizing, controlling, and implementing, as discussed in chapter 3) are the foundation for the functions of a corporate aviation manager.

NOTES

1. In Robert M. Kane and Allan D. Vose, *Air Transportation* (Dubuque, IA: Kendall/Hunt, 1976).

2. "Machiavellian personalities": so named for Niccolò Machiavelli, an Italian statesman and writer on government, whose name has come to be associated with craftiness, deceitfulness, and manipulation of people of lesser status.

3. Douglas McGregor, *The Human Side of Enterprise* (New York: McGraw-Hill, 1960).

4. Paul R. Timm, *Managerial Communication* (Englewood Cliffs, NJ: Prentice-Hall, 1980).

5. Robert M. Fulmer, *The New Management* (New York: Macmillan 1978).

5

The Aviation
Department Structure
within the Corporation

After the delineation of specific management functions and principles there must be a chapter to present a general discussion of how the aviation manager fits into the overall corporate structure and how his or her functions differ from other managers within that structure.

Figure 5.1 shows where the aviation department should be positioned in relation to the corporate pyramid. Most people in corporate aviation, especially pilots, like their work and are interested in doing the best they can for their employer. However, in many cases, due to the differences in operating procedures in nonaviation industries, the manager of a corporate flight operation finds himself or herself in conflict with the corporation's management philosophy. This has been the source of many misunderstandings between the two groups: corporate management and flight operations management.

In most cases, the company airplane is used to save time, offer convenient schedules, have the proper working environment en route, and eliminate the hassle of airline travel. The busy executive usually has planned a trip for expected business results, and has the desire to get to where he/she

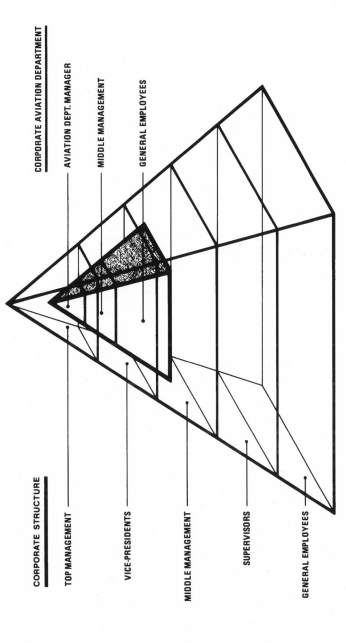

CORPORATE AVIATION DEPARTMENT

AVIATION DEPT. MANAGER

MIDDLE MANAGEMENT

GENERAL EMPLOYEES

CORPORATE STRUCTURE

TOP MANAGEMENT

VICE-PRESIDENTS

MIDDLE MANAGEMENT

SUPERVISORS

GENERAL EMPLOYEES

Figure 5.1. The aviation department provides service to top levels of management and therefore usually reports to the highest level in a corporation. *Source:* AIMS, Inc., Upland, CA

Figure 5.2. Caricature of table of
organization. *Source*: AIMS, Inc.,
Upland, CA

is going on time. A similarity exits in the goal that a pilot has to land his
airplane out of a precision instrument approach.

By using the company airplane, the executive believes that he/she has
chosen the most reliable and expedient form of transportation. An executive's nearness to the flight operation, and the fact that the operation is part
of the company, gives many executives the idea that the only thing they
have to do is command and the airplane has to go where they want to go,
regardless of circumstances beyond the control of the pilot that may prevent
the trip from being completed, such as weather, pilot fatigue, maintenance
problems, etc. Figure 5.2 caricatures the authoritarian executive who feels
compelled to run everything himself.

Many anecdotes have evolved from the tribulations corporate aviation
department chief pilots and/or managers suffer in their relations with top management. In the same vein, some chief pilots and/or managers have failed to
manage, communicate, or plan in such a manner as to give their superiors confidence in their ability to manage. As a result, the aviation department manager
or chief pilot loses control of his or her operation. Some of the problems are
self-inflicted by the chief pilots or aviation managers; others stem from executives who are unresponsive to the department's needs.

Actual Examples of Management Conflicts

A midwest operation had a large pilot turnover due to a very religious CEO who tried to force pilots to make approaches below minimums or to land at inadequate airports. His excuse was that the Good Lord would protect airplane and pilot. At Washington National, while in line waiting for takeoff, the CEO, being worried about making his appointment in Chicago, went to the cockpit and tried to force the pilot into going around the other airplanes in line for takeoff.

The vice-president of a large corporation was very disturbed because the pilots would not land at his home town, where the airport runway was too short for the equipment being flown.

An executive arrived at the airport with excessive baggage and one extra passenger, and asked the pilot to put the extra passenger in the unauthorized jump seat.

A Texas operator always landed at the Chicago lakefront airport. On a particular trip with weather below minimums, the pilot diverted to O'Hare. The chairman was livid and hired a consultant to tell him what was wrong with his operation. The consultant found that the pilot never told his boss that Meigs Lakefront Airport did not have a letdown procedure and that the runway was too short to land his jet on a wet runway.

An altitude-alerter ring was demonstrated to the manager of a Cincinnati flight operation at his request. He wanted to buy the rings, which were only $43.00 apiece, but could not buy them without asking his boss for the money. Who was in control? Who made the budget?

The suggestion was made to the manager of an eastern flight operation that he should have an operations manual. His remark was, "An operations manual is too restrictive, and nobody will pay attention to it anyway."

A consultant was called to solve the problem of a company that was not getting the proper utilization from its two aircraft. On studying the situation, it was discovered that the mechanic, who had worked for the company for 15 years, did not want to work overtime or adjust his hours to the aircraft schedule. Even if a small maintenance item, such as changing a light bulb, had to be done, the aircraft was grounded.

Top executives have too many things on their mind to worry about a $43.00 dollar item for the airplane, or whether the mechanic wants to work overtime or not. It should be the responsibility of the manager or chief pilot to set up his/her operation in a manner that keeps problems that he/

she can solve away from his/her boss. The manager's attitude toward his/her superior should be, "I will solve any problems I am qualified to handle, but I hope that I can come to you if I need help with other problems." That said, the chief pilot or manager should make sure that his/her operation has well-defined manuals with letters from the CEO stating the philosophy of the aviation department and the need to abide by the rules as contained in the manuals.

In most cases, managers of nonaviation company departments are allowed to develop and run their departments on sound management principles, using their expertise for the benefit of the department. Usually the manager presents a report to his/her superiors every quarter, or more frequently, if need be. The success of the department as a rule is evaluated by the profits it generates. This should also be the case with an aviation department manager. To maintain control of his/her aviation operation, the chief pilot or manager should be aware of what is going around him/her. Reports submitted should be comprised of cost analysis, utilization statistics, and future plans for the improvement of the operation.

ADAPTATION AND EDUCATION

Managing a corporate aviation department is a matter of *adaptation* and *education*. The manager must *adapt* to the management concepts of his/her particular corporation, and he/she must *educate* his/her superiors on how and why some of these concepts do or do not completely apply to his/her type of operation. In this regard, the aviation manager is faced with two heterogeneous elements in carrying out his/her responsibilities within the corporation. First, the vast majority of companies are simply not well versed in the various aspects of aircraft operations, and second, it is generally conceded in the industry that administrative skills are not usually the forte among those in the aviation community. Thus, the aviation manager, to overcome these two obstacles, must explain the function and responsibility of his/her divisional operation to corporate executives and demonstrate his/her ability to manage that operation. Adaptation and education require that the aviation manager develop a close working relationship with the administrators to whom he/she is responsible in order for him/her to maintain control of his/her operation.

EVALUATING THE OPERATION

Mitigating against the chief pilot or manager's rightful stature within the corporate structure is the fact that an aviation division or department is not a direct revenue-producing activity and cannot be evaluated by the usual bottom-line approach, showing profits generated. The flight operation is a non-revenue-producing service, which exists solely for the purpose of providing safe, efficient, convenient, and reliable transportation for corporate personnel. The flight operation provides an intangible product, which is a service. The product of this service is transportation. After the passenger has used the service, it is gone, and all he/she has to show for it is the fact that he/she is in a different city than before he/she used the service. The change of location was the reason to use the service. This is the relevant theory of time and place utility.

TRANSLATING THE SERVICE TO THE CORPORATION

It is the duty of the aviation manager to translate the importance and meaning of this service to the corporation. As a help in this direction, most corporate executives have come to realize that other nonprofit operations, such as research and development, and office support personnel and equipment are undeniably crucial to the successful operation of their enterprise. The executives should understand that the aviation division falls directly into this same and important category. This is not to say, however, that the aviation department, as a service, cannot be evaluated. It is important for its manager to develop an expertise in reporting its activities to his/her superiors in as clear a way as possible. The specifics of such methods, through written reports and graphics, are not new to the business world.

The aviation manager, then, has three main roles to perform within the corporate structure:

1. To create and nurture lines of communication with superiors for a close working relationship.
2. To demonstrate abilities as a manager by developing careful reporting methods for evaluating the operation.
3. To make it known with facts and due diplomacy that without the aircraft certain imminent transactions could not have been possible.

These roles when properly integrated can instill superiors with confidence in the corporate aviation manager. Through these roles, the manager can also demonstrate to them that the operation is continually pursuing new ways to utilize the corporate aircraft for the optimum benefit of the company.

ORGANIZATION STRUCTURE

In many instances, companies buy an airplane as if it were a lathe or another company production machine. An operator is hired to run that machine, without realizing that when an airplane is purchased, an operation or department has to be started to take care of the many adjunct functions entailed in the operation of an airplane as a transportation system. The complexity of an aviation department can best be detailed in aviation organization structure charts. It must be understood that regardless of the size of an aviation department, be it one airplane, one pilot, or a fleet of airplanes and the personnel to fly, schedule, and fix them, there is a need for organization. In addition:

1.   Organization also becomes necessary when the workload of an operation grows beyond what one person can do.
2.   Organization is a powerful tool of management; it fulfills specific needs. As needs change, new methods are necessary to cope with changing conditions.
3.   Organization charts have great value in providing the logical, basic framework of the organization. This logic can be of help in developing the organization structure.
4.   The organization structure provides a logical arrangement of the formal work functions, lines of authority, and the people necessary to achieve corporate objectives.
5.   The organization structure charts must be updated constantly and corrected to reflect the organizational needs of the future, and to make sure the right people are assigned to do the right work. Every employee should take some part in the continuing review and refinement of the flight operation structure.

The following charts are actual aviation department organization charts that show the various reporting levels and department reporting methods.

Figure 5.3 is a structure chart intended for a one- or two-airplane operation that contracts to other entities maintenance and pilot training. At the inception of the operation, the chief pilot writes the operations, train-

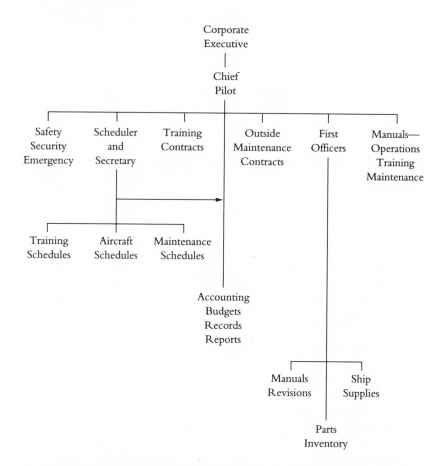

Figure 5.3.   Corporate aviation organization structure, one or two aircraft.
Source: AIMS, Inc., Upland, CA

ing, and maintenance manuals, sets up security and safety programs together with the pre-accident emergency plan, and also negotiates maintenance and training contracts with outside vendors. The scheduler/secretary
posts the flight schedules and arranges for training and maintenance schedules at the discretion of the chief pilot. A joint chief pilot–secretary effort
develops records and cost accounting and makes reports to upper management. First officers' ancillary duties are: revising manuals, parts inventory,
and stocking ship supplies.

Figure 5.4 structures a three or more airplane operation that has in-
house maintenance and training departments. Because the outside training

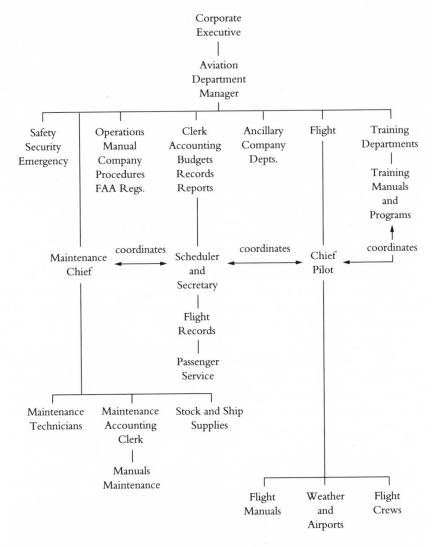

Figure 5.4.   Corporate aviation organization structure, three or more aircraft. *Source:* AIMS, Inc., Upland, CA

agency has flight simulators and training aids, pilot and mechanic training is contracted. However, personnel other than flight and maintenance are on-the-job trained. All training programs are written in-house to fit the operational requirements. The manager/pilot has arranged the span of control in that he has no more than six persons reporting directly to him/her. The chief pilot takes over when the manager is away from home base. The safety committee and training department are headed by a pilot as collateral duty. Ancillary company departments are departments within the company that, from time to time, may be of help to the aviation department, such as insurance, finance, purchasing, and law. Manuals, company procedures, and FAA regulations are the managers concern, together with the input from most of the department personnel.

Another interesting aspect is the coordination between the maintenance chief, chief pilot, and scheduler for the development of the flight schedules, as well as the coordination of chief pilot and training department manager for training schedules. A secretary and two clerks take care of budgets, accounting, activity records, reports, and flight records. All employees know whom they are reporting to, making for a smooth operation.

Figure 5.5 shows the functional manager working at the same level with the Euroflight (the European flight operations) manager, and the helicopter chief pilot/administrative manager. The functional manager, however, has both fixed-wing chief pilots, maintenance manager, and dual-assurance group report directly to him or her. Evidently this structure works well, as the company in question has been very successful with the operation of its aircraft.

In the structure shown in figure 5.6, the chief pilot and maintenance chief are at the same reporting level, sharing administrative duties. The scheduler coordinates with chief pilot and maintenance chief to develop the flight schedules.

The company represented in figure 5.7 shares the use of helicopters with another company and prefers to have an outside contractor operate their rotorcraft. The contractor, like the rest of the aviation department personnel, report to the aviation department vice president. The assistant chief pilots report to the director of flight rather than having all pilots report directly to him. This seems to be a roundabout system of reporting in view of the fact that there are only three crews for the fixed-wing aircraft. Figures 5.3 to 5.7 depict various corporate aviation department organization structures.

The charts show the line of authority, chain of command, and how a group of people can work effectively toward the goals that must be achieved.

In a one- or two-airplane operation with a maximum of three persons in the department reporting directly to the chief pilot, scheduler-secretary, and first officers, the chief pilot is also responsible for seeing that the other

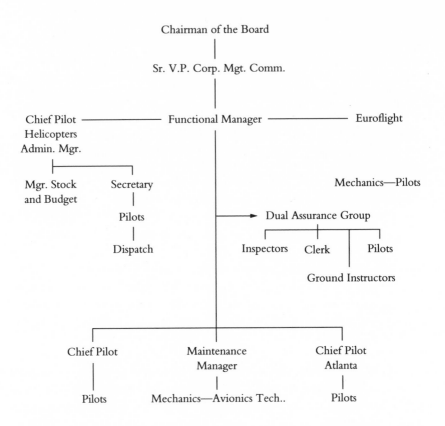

Figure 5.5.   Actual large international aviation department organization structure.

four sections in the department are in place and working under his or her administration. The chart depicted in figure 5.3 could not work for an operation with three or more airplanes because the chart in figure 5.4 with a minimum of three airplanes would require a flight section with a minimum of seven crew members, a maintenance section with a minimum of five technicians, a scheduler, two accounting clerks, and a secretary; the aviation department manager would have six people reporting directly to him. A corporate aviation department with three or more airplanes require a minimum of sixteen persons as depicted in figures 5.5 to 5.7. The success of the structure of a corporate aviation department is, in most instances, related to the acceptance of the department as an integral part of the company.

The members of the aviation department as a group see themselves as

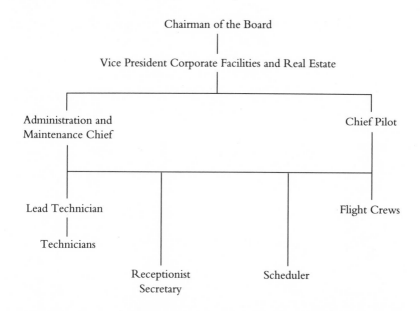

Figure 5.6.   Actual corporate aviation department organization structure.

professionals in every sense of the word. They must not feel that management, however, regards them as nothing more than an easily replaceable service. Leadership on the part of the company CEO consists to a large extent in the ability to work with a group of people for the success of the whole company. There can be no measure of success or failure of the aviation department without accountability. Therefore, the aviation department manager must be accountable for seeing that the service he or she provides is of value to the company.

The acceptability of the aviation department as an integral part of the company is susceptible to variable circumstances that force some flight operations to collapse while others survive. The survivors are not always the best-run operations, and the reason for that is that there are no standard guidelines or financial bottom line to evaluate a corporate aviation department by. The following case studies evidence the proof that there are no standard guidelines to evaluate the benefit derived from a corporate flight operation.

1. A Japanese billionaire bought an Akron, Ohio, tire company. His first executive edict was to get rid of a well-run aviation department that had been in the company since 1929. We don't have company airplanes in Japan so why should you? In this case, a study should have been made to

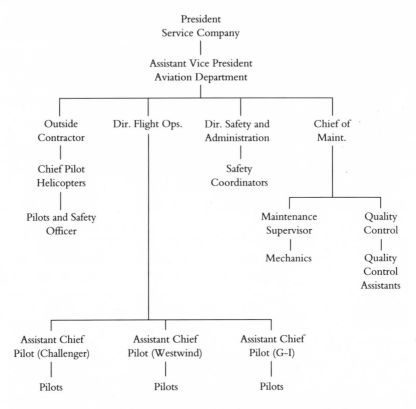

Figure 5.7.   Actual corporate aviation department organization structure.

ascertain what benefits were derived from the operation of the airplanes before closing the flight department.

2. A Canadian entrepreneur took over a Cincinnati, Ohio, retailer with a superbly run aviation department. The entrepreneur's financial difficulties prompted him to close the aviation department. As panic had set in, the byword was cut costs to the bone to try to keep the company going.

3. The new CEO of a New Jersey distiller closed the flight operation to impress his board with his abilities to cut costs. It is possible that several trips by the former CEO, such as a record around-the-world trip had something to do with the closing of the flight operation.

4. A Detroit car manufacturer closed the flight operation in order to get rid of the incompetent aviation department manager. The aviation operation was reopened nine months later with a new manager.

5. A California oil company operates their aircraft only 200 to 300

hours a year and provides very poor service to company personnel, and yet the operation keeps on flying. The company has not requested a proper audit of the operation as should be done from time to time.

Many operating parameters have to be considered in the evaluation of a corporate aviation department; cost of operation requires constant scrutiny because changes in operating costs usually indicate poor management control.

A New York oil company aviation department manager was heard to say, "Money is no object; we can spend any amount we want." A corporate flight operation should be operated in a business manner with quarterly reports and proper accounting. Hours flown can indicate utilization parameters, but care should be taken to make sure that hours flown are productive. A Minneapolis railroad company aviation department manager would fly empty to Seattle to pick up one passenger; a lot of hours were flown by this flight operation but very few were passenger productive hours. Passenger load factor is also important; many companies circulate the company aircraft schedule among top executives to improve load factor. The personnel requirement formulas in chapter 9 determine the number of mechanics and pilots required for an efficient flight operation. Overstaffing is wasteful; understaffing is inefficient.

Every corporate aviation department has its own aircraft utilization philosophy. If that utilization philosophy is documented, the process of evaluating the flight operation becomes a matter of proving the utilization philosophy correct.

6

Utilizing the Trade Associations in the Management Process

This chapter lists trade associations in order of importance to the aviation department. It outlines the benefits derived from joining the association and how to utilize the association services for the benefit of the aviation department.

HELP TO MANAGERS

Aviation trade associations can be of substantial help to an aviation manager in many ways:

1. For updating and exchanging industry information
2. For meeting others in the same profession
3. For furthering professional development—formal and informal
4. For exposure to new products and the exchange of ideas at conventions and seminars

Associations are worthwhile joining for the benefits they can supply. Most associations have their offices in Washington, DC, because their main effort is to try to influence the voting of legislators through lobbying for the benefit of the segment of industry they represent.

MEMBERSHIPS AND FEES

There are fees required for joining and retaining a membership, based in some cases on a sliding scale determined by the size of the aviation operation involved. Most memberships are in the name of the corporation, although some individual memberships are available.

LIST OF ASSOCIATIONS

Listed here[1] are the associations whose membership can be of benefit to a corporate aviation manager:

1.   National Business Aircraft Association, Inc. (NBAA)
1200 Eighteenth St. NW
Washington, DC 20036-2598
(202) 783-9000

NBAA is an association of companies and individuals who own and/or operate aircraft in the conduct of their business. The association was organized in 1947 for the purpose of furthering the cause of safety and economy of business aircraft operations. It continues to be the prime guardian of business aviation interests; it keeps a close watch on the problems facing business aviation today and in the future.

According to NBAA *1993 Business Aviation Fact Book*, NBAA consists of approximately 3,100 companies and another 3,700 subsidiaries and affiliates worldwide that own or operate over 5,000 aircraft for the purpose of providing transportation to advance their business objectives.

NBAA publications are:

Action Bulletins
Aviation Department Salary Survey
Business Aircraft Report
Business Aviation Management Guide
Business Flying
Business Flying Statistical Report
Customs Guide

For-Your-Information Reports
Guide to Congressional Standing Committees
Maintenance Bulletins
Management Aids
NBAA Reports (newsletter)
Noise Abatement Guide
Policy position papers
Public Relations for Business Aviation
RNAV and the Controller
Studies of Business Aviation Management Financial Analysis
A Study of Business Aviation in 1985

The main reason to join NBAA is that it actually keeps aircraft operators informed on all phases of the aviation industry and is the only lobby
group dedicated to representing corporate aviation. The NBAA annual
convention is probably the largest aviation show in the country where
members can meet, exchange ideas, and observe the marketplace.

2.   Flight Safety Foundation, Inc. (FSF)
     2200 Wilson Blvd., Suite 500
     Arlington, VA 22201-3306
     (703) 522-8300
     (FSF is not to be confused with Flight Safety Interna-
     tional, Inc., the training conglomerate.)

The Flight Safety Foundation is an independent, nonprofit organization, founded in 1945, with three basic tasks: 1) to anticipate flight safety
problems, 2) to study flight safety, and 3) to disseminate flight safety information.

The foundation is funded by the dues of its member organizations
(561 members in 73 countries, as of December 31, 1992) and is perhaps
best known for its annual safety seminars. It conducts three each year:

1.   The International Air Safety Seminar (IASS) meets annually in
     the fall in a world major city (e.g., 1988—Sydney, Australia;
     1989—Athens, Greece; 1990—Rome, Italy; 1991—Singapore;
     1992—Long Beach, CA; 1993—Kuala Lumpor, Malaysia). The
     seminar presents prominent world aviation safety experts in an
     informal, neutral environment that encourages sharing ideas for
     safety.
2.   The Corporate Aviation Safety Seminar (CASS) meets annually
     in North America (e.g., 1988—Williamsburg, VA; 1989—

Dearborn, MI; 1990—Montreal, Canada; 1991—White Plains, NY; 1992—Baltimore, MD; 1993—Dallas, TX). The seminar focuses on safety concerns of corporate aircraft operators.

3.   The European Corporate and Regional Aircraft Operators Safety Seminars (ECARAOSS) meets annually in Europe (e.g., 1992—Brussels, Belgium; 1993 and 1994—Amsterdam, The Netherlands).

Flight Safety Foundation also conducts aviation safety workshops on a need-to-do basis, which address specific aviation safety problems or issues that may be of concern to a particular group in the aviation community. The foundation encourages the use of safety audits and offers confidential aviation safety audits to its members and others who may desire such a service for their operation.

FSF publishes eight separate periodicals that are distributed free to its members, and are available on an individual subscription basis to others:

Accident Prevention Bulletin
Airport Operations Safety Bulletin
Aviation Mechanics Bulletin
Cabin Crew Safety Bulletin
Flight Safety Digest
Flight Safety Foundation Newsletter
Helicopter Safety Bulletin
Human Factors & Aviation Medicine Bulletin

In addition to a board of governors, which consists of well-known aviation luminaries, the Flight Safety Foundation uses the expertise within its members to help guide its affairs. It has two major standing committees, the International Advisory Committee and the Corporate Advisory Committee. Individual committee members serve by invitation. Any corporate flight operation or any person new to the aviation field interested in both air and ground safety needs to join FSF.

3.   Aircraft Owners & Pilots Association (AOPA)
     421 Aviation Way
     Frederick Airport
     Frederick, MD 21701
     (301) 695-2000

AOPA is an association charged with representation of general aviation in the United States. (AOPA has a comparable international federation,

IOPA, comprised of 29 organizations charged with worldwide representation of general aviation.)

AOPA member services are:

Accident Reports
Aircraft Purchasing
Aircraft Maintenance
AOPA Forum/CompuServe
FAA Rules and Regulations
Flight Planning Service
Air Traffic Control
Legal Information
Medical Certification
Pilot Training & Licensing
Government & Technical Affairs
Aviation Standards, Airports
Airspace Technology

AOPA publications are:

AOPA Pilot Magazine
Handbook for Pilots
Manual Listing Airports in the U.S.

AOPA is also involved in many educational programs. The main
reasons for joining AOPA are for its government affairs representation, various pilot assistance programs, the airport directory, and flight planning
service.

 4.   Professional Aviation Maintenance Association (PAMA)
                 500 Northwest Plaza, Suite 1016
                 St. Ann, MO 63074-2209
                 (314) 739-2580

PAMA is an association that promotes a high degree of professionalism
among aviation mechanics. It fosters the improvement of methods, skills,
and the learning process in the field of aviation maintenance; conducts national, state, and local meetings and seminars; recognizes and rewards
achievement in the field of aviation maintenance; publishes, distributes,
and disseminates technical bulletins, journals and other relevant publications; and collaborates with other aviation organizations in matters related
to governmental agencies' maintenance rules and regulations.

PAMA is a worthwhile organization to join because maintenance has a tremendous impact on safety and the budget. An organization that fosters good maintenance practices should be supported.

5. Helicopter Association International (HAI)
    1619 Duke Street
    Alexandria, VA 22314-3439
    (703) 683-4646

HAI is dedicated to the advancement and promotion of the commercial and civil helicopter industry worldwide. The membership includes helicopter owners and operators, users, manufacturers and suppliers, service organizations, and interested individuals.

HAI publications are:

Periodicals
> *Maintenance Update*
> *1994 Helicopter Annual*
> *Operations Update*
> *Preliminary Accident Reports*
> *Rotor Magazine*

Helicopter Career Information
> *Pilot/Mechanic Training Schools* (listing of schools)

Technical Manuals and Guides
> *Aeronautical Decision Making for Helicopter Pilots*
> *The Fly Neighborly Guide* and *The Fly Neighborly Pocket Guide*
> *Guide for the Presentation of Helicopter Operating Cost Estimates*
> *Helicopter User's Guide*
> *Heliport Development Guide*
> *Heliport Directory*
> *Holding onto Revenue*
> *Interim Guidance for Conducting In-Depth (Part 135) Inspections*
> *Safety Manual* (English or Spanish)
> *Visibility Unlimited*

Technical Reports and Papers
> *Community Rotorcraft Transportation Benefits & Opportunities*
> *FAA Helicopter Abstracts and Bibliography*
> *Helicopter Economics Factors Bibliography*

Anyone operating a helicopter or who has intentions of operating a helicopter should join and participate in HAI.

The following two organizations are specialized in their focus and in many cases may be of help with supplying information to the corporate aviation manager:

6.   General Aviation Manufacturers Association (GAMA)
Suite 801
1400 K St. NW
Washington, DC 20005-2485
(202) 393-1500

GAMA is what the name implies—a representative of aircraft manufacturers. It can be of help to the corporate aviation manager in that it can provide information on manufacturers and their products. Also the use of studies made for the industry such as *Business Aircraft Operations Financial Benefits and Intangible Advantages.*

7.   National Air Transportation Association (NATA)
4226 King St.
Alexandria, VA 22302
(703) 845-9000

The National Aviation Training Association was created in 1940 with 83 charter members to reflect the activity of its members before Congress and the various agencies of the federal government and to serve as a unifying front for general aviation. In 1975, because of the many changes in the aviation industry the name was changed to *National Air Transportation Association.*

NATA is close to 2,000 member companies strong and has a well-defined role representing and working to enhance the working interests of all general aviation service businesses. Through NATA, members have a united voice. They benefit from Washington representation, industry publications, business services, and educational efforts and campaigns, which are designed to keep member companies financially and operationally strong.

All corporate flight operations are dependent on FBO's for fueling and other services. This 54-year-old organization can be of help in solving corporate aviation service and flight charter problems. The association concentrates its efforts in the areas of legislation and industry affairs. The resources are also heavily used for other concerns, like better relations with airports and spending of the Aviation Trust Fund.

USING THE TRADE ASSOCIATIONS

It is important to know how to use the trade associations for the benefit of the member. Individuals and companies join associations to achieve together what they cannot achieve separately. The success of such affiliations depends largely on communication between those involved and the free flow of ideas and information.

A good example of what an association can accomplish is the work that NBAA is doing in regard to changing the "empty seat" policy imposed by IRS. At present, a tax can be collected for any "empty seats" on a corporate aircraft that may be filled at the last minute by guests of corporate executives. NBAA is fighting for the rescinding of that policy on the grounds that it impinges on the discretionary rights of a corporation. NBAA was successful on behalf of its members in having the FAA authorize the use of the minimum equipment list (MEL) by corporate airplanes.

It is not enough to join an association. There is a need for involvement and participation. Members should take advantage of meetings and conventions, know what the organization's services are, and how and when to use them.

The manager must develop procedures for distributing the materials that the association publishes. To that end, he/she may pass along the publications to his/her personnel for reading and initialing, signifying that the material has been read. A reference library system for bulletins, periodicals, and publications by category should be set up. Also, a list of services the associations provide should be posted for ready reference. This list should include telephone numbers and names of persons in the various trade association departments.

NOTE

1. Correspondence with NBAA, FSF, AOPA, PAMA, HAI, GAMA, NATA.

Part Two
Economics

7

Economics: Cost/Benefit Factors

This chapter analyzes the economics and financial determinants in acquisition of corporate aircraft. This chapter also examines the cost/benefit factors, tax implications, and methods to be used in the analysis for justifying company-operated air transportation.

CORPORATE AIRCRAFT BENEFITS

The value of a corporate aviation department is widely accepted and well established among successful companies. The recent airline concentration on hub and spoke patterns has enhanced the use of the company airplane, and companies are encouraging executives to save time by the use of the corporate airplane. Many small companies are finding that use of a corporate aircraft can increase management productivity, increase profit margins, and provide a competitive edge.

The cost/benefit derived from the operation of a corporate aircraft are in two categories: 1) tangible and 2) intangible. The tangible benefits are listed below and can be quantified by using the methods of calculation described in this chapter. The intangible benefits are difficult, if not impossible to quantify; however, they foster direct or indirect benefits of prime importance to the success of a company. When buying any type of equipment, there must be a need and a desire to own and operate that piece of equipment. When that desire and need is satisfied, the primary question should be what benefits are provided the company and its traveling employees in the correct operation of that equipment. The major intangible advantages of company-operated transportation can be usually divided into two areas: 1) advantages to traveling executives, and 2) advantages to general company business.

Advantages to Traveling Executives
1.   Time saved by reducing travel and airport waiting time
2.   Reliability of scheduling; increased flexibility
3.   Better utilization of time; more time at office
4.   Productive private conferences en route
5.   Removal of control by airline connections
6.   Retention of valuable executives
7.   Improved traveler security
8.   Maintenance of good employee morale by more time at home and less stressful travel
9.   Preservation of physical stamina and enhancement of mental alertness

Advantages to General Company Business
1.   Consumer relations, sales presentations to a captive audience, and competitive advantage
2.   Permits spreading of management talent over a large geographical area
3.   Allows decentralization of facilities
4.   Less personnel required because of increased mobility
5.   Eliminates overnight costs—hotel and subsistence
6.   Accessibility of locations not adequately served by commercial airlines
7.   Capability of quick response to unanticipated events
8.   More frequent visits to facilities in remote locations
9.   Increased revenues as indicated in studies by Aviation Data Service, Wichita, KS, of *Fortune* 500 companies that operate corporate aircraft

Evaluating and Justifying Company Aircraft

Aircraft ownership and operation often represents one of the largest single expenditures that a company makes. Company management is faced with the need to justify the airplane as a business tool to directors and stockholders. Increased management productivity is one of the most important justifications for operation of a company aircraft.

Many benefits of corporate aircraft ownership are difficult to quantify, despite being extensive. The corporate flight department manager must look for ways to quantify as many of these benefits as possible. He or she should set up management data collection on each factor. These data should be regularly supplied to the CEO and chief financial officer.

Many evaluation methods have been tried to establish a cost/benefit justification for owning and/or operating a company airplane. Because of the various company policies regarding utilization philosophies, it has been impossible to find a method that works in all cases. The methods that have been tried are as follows:

Placing a value on executives' time
En route productivity
Management accountability factor, that is, an attempt at a realistic time-
    value to a manager's responsibility to the company
A productivity factor that equates an individual's annual salary with
    contribution to the corporation

Fortune Magazine's measure of executive productivity is based on an overall picture of company performance: net income/sales, net income/equity, sales/employee, net income/employee. These four measures can reveal how effectively top management people spend their time.

The value of executive time varies not only with the level of decisions that have to be made but also with how those decisions affect the company's performance. To develop a "productivity factor," a numerical value has to be given to the "productivity performance" that certain decisions produce.

Figure 7.1 shows the numerical value given to the various duties of a top executive. It can be noticed that "office duty" rates below ten, while "merger meetings" rate forty-three. It has to be assumed that work on a friendly merger will enhance the performance of the corporation much more than routine office duty.

Figure 7.2 equates salary to productivity. The productivity factor

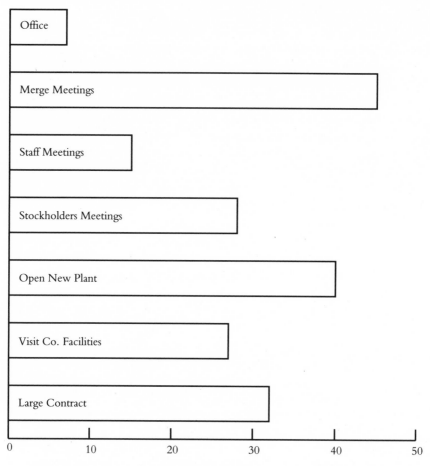

Figure 7.1.   Executive time numerical value.

assumes that greater executive productivity and broader responsibility merits higher salary, as indicated by the productivity factor line. However, two variables have to be considered: one, the time required and the number of people involved for certain duties; two, that normally one person can not be three times more efficient than another person by virtue of salary alone.

Figures 7.1 and 7.2 indicate that the span of numerical value becomes shorter as the numbers increase. It becomes evident that on the merger meetings a top executive requires the assistance of various specialists, thereby diluting his or her total decision process. The ultimate

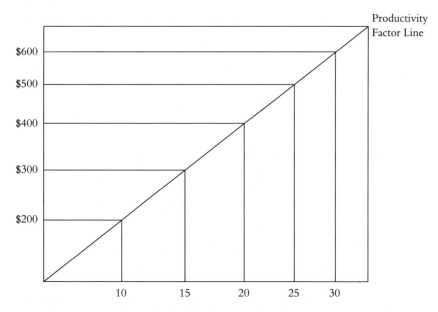

Figure 7.2.   Salary vs. productivity.

responsibility of the company performance remains solely that of the top executive.

An executive with a salary of $600,000 may have the responsibility of the whole company, while the executive with a salary of $200,000 may have the responsibility of a company department. Both persons may have the same productivity requirements, but with a different numerical productivity value by reason of responsibility. One can not do without the other.

The time numerical value number and the productivity factor number can be used as constants to develop the figure 7.3 formulas. The figure 7.1 time numerical value number is derived by averaging the duty bars for an approximate number of 26.75. The figure 7.2 productivity factor is derived by following the $600,000 line to the 30 productivity factor number. The preferred method can be used with the formula, with the numerical value of 26.75 (see figure 7.1) or the productivity factor 30 (see figure 7.2).

If the employee can spend an extra 260 hours of productive work a year at the office by using a company airplane, then 260 hours equates to $808,498.60 for the benefit of the company. Consideration has to be

Yearly salary	Hourly pay (2080 hrs)	Productivity Factor Hr. pay/ 26.75	Value per hour	Individual's annual $'s
$600,000	$288.46	10.78	$3,109.61	$808,498.60

Formula:

$$\frac{\text{Yr. Salary x Produc. Factor}}{\text{Hrs./Yr.}} = \frac{600,000 \text{ x } 10.78}{2080} = \$3,109.61$$

If this executive saves five hours a week using the company airplane:

$$5 \text{ x } 52 = 260 \text{ x } 3,109.61 = \$808,498.60$$

Figure 7.3. This presents a cost/benefit formula that may be applied as a basic starting point to generate ideas on how to measure the value of a company-operated aircraft. *Source:* AIMS, Inc., Upland, CA

given to the fact that, since as a rule top company personnel travel as a group, the CEO with his staff or a department manager with his assistants, time saving as a group must be considered.

Many American companies are dependent on corporate aviation as a means of transportation. As with any other company department, management is responsible for the selection of the proper equipment and its effective utilization. If the aviation department is well planned and managed intelligently, the aircraft will provide the desired results. On the other hand, poor management will drain the company finances without substantially benefiting the company.

AIRCRAFT JUSTIFICATION ANALYSIS

A cost/benefit analysis that justifies and defends the purchase and operation of a company airplane should be made following a phase one flow chart, figure 7.4. The flow chart can indicate a time limit placed on the completion of each segment of the study.

In-House Talent or Aviation Consultant

An aircraft cost/benefit analysis can be made with the in-house talent that most companies employ. Alternatively, it can be done by use of an aviation consultant. The disciplines required are: tax expertise, financial expertise, knowledge of aviation law–travel department or the ability to analyze

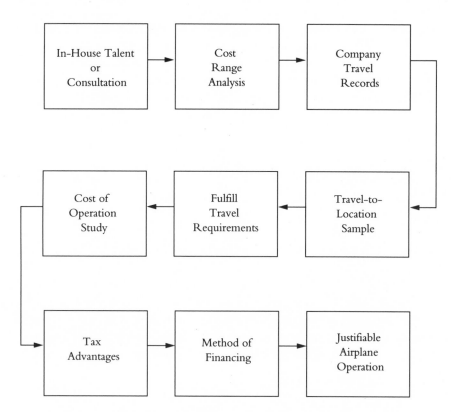

Figure 7.4. This phase one flow chart presents an aircraft cost/benefit justification analysis. *Source:* AIMS, Inc., Upland, CA

travel records. The team can be totally in-house, out-of-house, or a combination of the two.

COST RANGE ANALYSIS

The acquisition of an airplane must be evaluated in the same manner as any other capital investment. A budgetary cost range has to be determined that the company feels it can comfortably absorb.

The ownership estimated after-tax cash flow analysis (provided by the Cessna Aircraft Company) presents the total cash flow projection for a seven-year ownership. All costs are estimated for a typical operator, based on available data for the average aircraft. The estimated after-tax calculations shown in this study are based on the Tax Reform Act (TRA) of 1986. The figures calculated are based on the acquisition of the aircraft as of the first of the calendar and fiscal year. The cash flow reflects 84 months of ownership, spread over seven tax years. The corporate tax rate is 38 percent.

COMPUTATION CRITERIA

Purchase price is based on a typically equipped aircraft. The airplane's warranty is reflected in the total operating cost for five years. Decrease in resale value is forecast based on historical retail prices contained in McGowan's *Aircraft Price Digest*. Tables 7.1, 7.2, and 7.3 indicate airplane acquisition financing using the Tax Reform Act double declining balance method and estimated after-tax cash flow analysis.

Table 7.1 shows acquisition date, term of possession, aircraft acquisition price, resale value, basis for depreciation, and finance criteria. Trade-in Criteria is $0 as there is no trade-in involved. Table 7.2 presents purchase analysis for seven years. Table 7.3 presents finance analysis for seven years, loan amount, and after-tax effects. Table 7.4 is a summary of cash flow effects.

Company Travel Records

Company travel vouchers or travel expense account records provide the necessary figures for the annual mileage traveled by the segment of executives who use the airplane. The information should indicate destination, when, how often, and how many individuals traveled together to the same location.

Travel-to-Location Sample

To describe better the remaining segments of the cost/benefit analysis flow chart, figures for a hypothetical company, Amalgamated Widgets, Inc., are presented. The travel-to-location sample (table 7.5) uses a typical airplane operation. Amalgamated Widgets, Inc., is a $500 million annual sales manufacturing enterprise, located in a Chicago suburb, with offices and plants as listed in the travel-to-location sample. The company is ex-

TABLE 7.1. AMALGAMATED WIDGETS COMPANY ESTIMATED AFTER-TAX
CASH FLOW ANALYSIS, NEW CESSNA CITATION VII

The analysis that follows will provide estimates of the cash expenditures, both before and after taxes, of acquiring and operating a company aircraft. This analysis utilizes the following assumptions:

Acquisition date:	Jan/93
Term of possession (months)	84
Aircraft acquisition price:	$8,950,000
Annual usage (hours):	500
Aircraft resale value (% of acquisition price):	80%
Corporate tax rate:	38%
Sales tax:	5%
Basis for depreciation:	$9,397,500
Finance criteria:	
Down payment	10%
Aircraft loan amount (includes sales tax):	$8,457,750
Monthly payments (120 months @ 7.00%)	$98,202

Depreciation schedules are calculated using the double declining balance method prescribed by TRA 86. Sales tax is capitalized and factored into the depreciation base. Engine overhaul cost, when incurred, is capitalized and depreciated similar to the aircraft. Estimates of operating cost represent current national averages and may vary significantly with geographical location and types of operations.

As with any large acquisition, tax accountants and advisors should be consulted regarding the actual tax effects that would apply to a specific organization or individual.

Source: Cessna Aircraft Company, P.O. Box 1521, Wichita, KS 67201

panding the product line and its markets. The travel requirements have increased to the point where a choice has to be made, either to hire more marketing and sales personnel or select better transportation methods to improve personnel productivity.

From company travel records, a travel-to-location sample can be developed for the group of executives in the company who can use the company airplane to travel to company-owned locations or to other locations on company business. The average stage length (distance of each leg) for the sixteen round-trips is $26,336/32 = 823$ nm. The average number of travelers to locations is 5.56 passengers. The 212,268 nm. can be covered in 559 hours, at an average speed of 380 kts. per hour.

TABLE 7.2. AMALGAMATED WIDGETS ESTIMATED AFTER-TAX CASH FLOW ANALYSIS FOR A
NEW CESSNA CITATION VII, PURCHASE ANALYSIS

	1993	1994	1995	1996	1997	1998	1999	Total
—Cash Expenditures—								
Purchase price	$8,950,000							$ 8,950,000
Sales tax	$ 447,500							$ 447,500
Direct operating cost	$ 308,138	$ 349,339	$395,724	$395,724	$395,724	$399,600	$ 399,600	$ 2,643,000
Fixed operating cost	$ 178,800	$ 195,800	$195,800	$195,800	$195,800	$195,800	$ 195,800	$ 1,353,600
Engine maintenance overhaul	$ 103,800	$ 103,800	$103,800	$103,800	$103,800	$103,800	$ 103,800	$ 726,600
Total Cash Expenditures	$9,988,238	$ 648,939	$695,324	$695,324	$695,324	$699,200	$ 699,200	$14,121,549
—Cash Receipts—								
Sale of aircraft							($7,160,000)	($ 7,160,000)
Total Cash Receipts							($7,160,000)	($ 7,160,000)
Net Cash Flow	$9,988,238	$ 648,939	$695,324	$695,324	$695,324	$699,200	($6,460,800)	$ 6,961,549
—After-tax Cash Flow—								
Depreciation	$ 714,210	$1,142,736	$685,642	$411,385	$411,385	$205,692		$ 3,571,050
Direct operating cost	$ 117,092	$ 132,749	$150,375	$150,375	$150,375	$151,848	$ 151,848	$ 1,004,663
Fixed operating cost	$ 67,944	$ 74,404	$ 74,404	$ 74,404	$ 74,404	$ 74,404	$ 74,404	$ 514,368
Engine maintenance/overhaul	$ 39,444	$ 39,444	$ 39,444	$ 39,444	$ 39,444	$ 39,444	$ 39,444	$ 276,108
Sale of aircraft							($2,720,800)	($ 2,720,800)
Total Tax Effect	$ 938,690	$1,389,333	$949,865	$675,608	$675,608	$471,388	($2,455,104)	$ 2,645,389
Net After-tax Cash Flow	$9,049,547	($ 740,394)	($254,541)	$ 19,716	$ 19,716	$227,812	($4,005,696)	$ 4,316,160

Source: Cessna Aircraft Company, P.O. Box 1521, Wichita, KS 67201

TABLE 7.3. Amalgamated Widgets Estimated After-tax Cash Flow Analysis for a New Cessna Citation VII, Finance Analysis

	1993	1994	1995	1996	1997	1998	1999	Total
—Cash Expenditures—								
Purchase price less down payment	$ 8,055,000							$ 8,055,000
Sales tax financed	$ 402,750							$ 402,750
Down payment	$ 939,750							$ 939,750
Direct operating cost	$ 308,138	$ 349,339	$ 395,724	$ 395,724	$ 395,724	$ 399,600	$ 399,600	$ 2,643,849
Fixed operating cost	$ 178,800	$ 195,800	$ 195,800	$ 195,800	$ 195,800	$ 195,800	$ 195,800	$ 1,353,600
Engine maintenance overhaul	$ 103,800	$ 103,800	$ 103,800	$ 103,800	$ 103,800	$ 103,800	$ 103,800	$ 726,600
Principal payments	$ 605,561	$ 649,337	$ 696,278	$ 746,612	$ 800,584	$ 858,458	$ 920,516	$ 5,277,346
Interest payments	$ 572,859	$ 529,083	$ 482,142	$ 431,808	$ 377,836	$ 319,961	$ 257,903	$ 2,971,593
Loan payoff							$3,180,404	$ 3,180,404
Total Cash Expenditures	$11,166,658	$1,827,359	$1,873,744	$1,873,744	$1,873,744	$1,877,620	$5,058,024	$25,550,892
—Cash Receipts—								
Aircraft loan	($ 8,457,750)							($ 8,457,750)
Sale of aircraft							($7,160,000)	($ 7,160,000)
Total Cash Receipts	($ 8,457,750)						($7,160,000)	($15,617,750)
Net Cash Flow	$ 2,708,908	$1,827,359	$1,873,744	$1,873,744	$1,873,744	$1,877,620	($2,101,976)	$ 9,933,142
—After-tax Cash Flow—								
Depreciation	$ 714,210	$1,142,736	$ 685,642	$ 411,385	$ 411,385	$ 205,692		$ 3,571,050
Direct operating cost	$ 117,092	$ 132,749	$ 150,375	$ 150,375	$ 150,375	$ 151,848	$ 151,848	$ 1,004,663
Fixed operating cost	$ 67,944	$ 74,404	$ 74,404	$ 74,404	$ 74,404	$ 74,404	$ 74,404	$ 514,368
Interest payments	$ 217,686	$ 201,051	$ 183,214	$ 164,087	$ 143,578	$ 121,585	$ 98,003	$ 1,129,205
Engine maintenance overhaul	$ 39,444	$ 39,444	$ 39,444	$ 39,444	$ 39,444	$ 39,444	$ 39,444	$ 276,108
Sale of aircraft							($2,720,800)	($ 2,720,800)
Total Tax Effect	$ 1,156,377	$1,590,384	$1,133,079	$ 839,695	$ 819,186	$ 592,974	($2,357,101)	$ 3,774,594
Net After-tax Cash Flow	$ 1,552,531	$ 236,975	$ 740,665	$1,034,049	$1,054,558	$1,284,646	$ 255,125	$ 6,158,548

Source: Cessna Aircraft Company, P.O. Box 1521, Wichita, KS 67201

TABLE 7.4.   AMALGAMATED WIDGETS SUMMARY OF CASH FLOW EFFECTS
(1986 TAX REFORM ACT DOUBLE DECLINING BALANCE METHOD)

	Purchase	Finance
Year 1	$6,229,591	$1,292,317
Year 2	($ 443,983)	$ 253,414
Year 3	($ 50,238)	$ 662,314
Year 4	($ 39,255)	$ 690,041
Year 5	($3,137,023)	$1,106,845
60-month total	$2,559,091	$4,004,932
Average per tax year	$ 511,818	$ 800,986
Average per month	$ 42,652	$ 66,749

Source: Cessna Aircraft Company, P.O. Box 1521, Wichita, KS 67201

CORPORATE AIRPLANE VERSUS AIRLINE
COMPARISON STATISTICS

The travel-to-location sample can also be used to show additional data: locations visited most frequently, time spent at location, time to get to location, and whether commercial transportation provides flexible schedules that allow the required time at location. *Total hours of travel required should be less than hours spent at location.*

Figure 7.5 shows the percentage of company locations that can be reached by commercial airline and the percentage of locations for which one or more stops have to be made. All company locations can be reached directly by company airplane.

Figure 7.6 shows several examples of time-saving advantages of the corporate aircraft versus airline, as well as the fact that more time can be spent at company locations when traveling by corporate airplane.

Figures 7.7, 7.8, 7.9, and 7.10 show geographical comparisons of landing locations as used by company airplane. The time saved by utilizing other than commercial airline airports are also indicated.

Fulfill Travel Requirements

Business travelers using scheduled airlines are most often limited to one airport. Corporate aircraft travelers can choose from several airports in most large city areas. For example, Kansas City has three airports (MCI International, MKC Downtown, GVW Richard Gebaur) to choose from. The travel-to-location sample indicates that a company airplane can fulfill

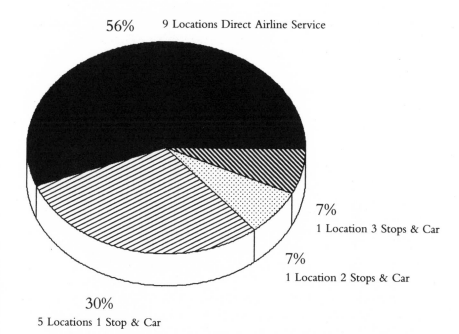

56%   9 Locations Direct Airline Service

7%
1 Location 3 Stops & Car

7%
1 Location 2 Stops & Car

30%
5 Locations 1 Stop & Car

Figure 7.5. Pie chart showing percentages of locations reached by airline and company plane. *Source*: AIMS, Inc., Upland, CA

the travel requirements of the twenty hypothetical executives allowed to request the airplane. Table 7.5 presents a summary table giving the number of locations visited, the distance between city pairs, number of trips, and number of passengers carried on each trip.

A preliminary survey using a year of travel records of a travel-to-location sample for twenty executives who would be permitted to request the airplane indicated that total round-trip mileage to the sixteen locations visited was 26,336 nautical miles. There was an average of 8.06 trips to each location, making the total mileage traveled 212,268 nm., for an average of 10,613 nm. for each of the twenty travelers.

When the survey of Amalgamated Widgets, Inc., was made, it was decided *not* to include the travel of executives from the regional offices, or the many cases in which stops were made en route to pick up passengers who might have been going to the same destination.

Ferry flights (flights with no passengers), training flights, and mainte-

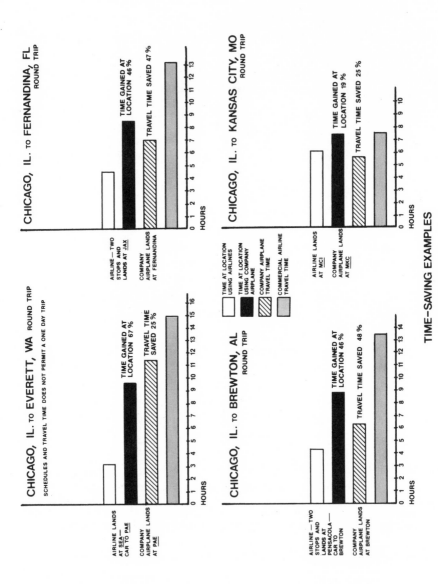

Figure 7.6. Time-saving examples. *Source:* AIMS, Inc., Upland, CA

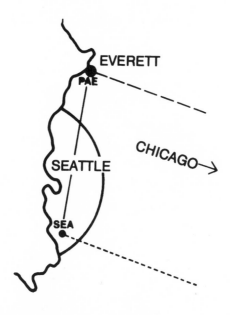

Company Airplane – 4.2 HRS.

Commercial Airline – 4.1 HRS.
By Car – 1 HR.

Commercial Airline - - - - - - - - - - - - - - - - -
Company Jet Aircraft   — — — — — — — — —
By Car _____

Airline Jet ORD Chicago to Seattle-Tacoma Airport, WA
Rent a car to Everett, WA
Company Jet Aircraft direct to Everett
Time saved over two hours
Cost of car rental saved

Figure 7.7. Time comparison, airline vs. company airplane, Chicago to Everett, WA. *Source*: AIMS, Inc., Upland, CA

Company Airplane – 2.2 HRS.

Commercial Airline – 4.6 HRS.
By Car – .6 HRS.

Commercial Airline - - - - - - - - - - - - - - - - -
Company Jet Aircraft —————————
By Car _____

Airline Jet ORD Chicago to Jacksonville International Airport, FL
One stop in Atlanta, GA
Rent a car in Fernandina, FL
Company Jet Aircraft direct to Fernandina Beach Airport
Time saved over three hours
Cost of car rental saved

Figure 7.8. Time comparison, airline vs. company airplane, Chicago to Fernandina, FL. *Source*: AIMS, Inc., Upland, CA

Company Airplane – 1.6 HRS.

Commercial Airline – 5.1 HRS.
By Car – 1 HR.

Commercial Airline - - - - - - - - - - - - - - - - - -
Company Jet Aircraft — — — — — — — — —
By Car _____

Airline Jet ORD Chicago to Pensacola Regional Airport, FL
One stop in Atlanta, GA
Possible Regional Turboprop Aircraft Atlanta to Pensacola
or Jacksonville to Pensacola
Rent a car Pensacola to Brewton, AL
Company Jet Aircraft direct to Brewton
Time saved over five hours in Company Jet Aircraft
Cost of car rental saved

Figure 7.9. Time comparison, airline vs. company airplane, Chicago to
Brewton, AL. *Source*: AIMS, Inc., Upland, CA

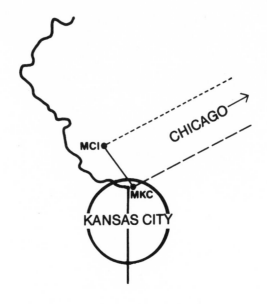

Company Airplane – 1 HR.

Commercial Airline – 1 HR.
By Car – .75 HR.

Commercial Airline - - - - - - - - - - - - - - - - -
Company Jet Aircraft   — — — — — — — —
By Car _____

Airline Jet ORD Chicago to Kansas City International Airport, MO
Company Jet Aircraft Direct to Kansas City, Downtown Airport, MO
Time saved over one hour
Cost of car rental saved

Figure 7.10. Time comparison, airline vs. company airplane, Chicago to
Kansas City, MO. *Source*: AIMS, Inc., Upland, CA

TABLE 7.5.   TRAVEL-TO-LOCATION SAMPLE

Number of Trips	Distance Nautical Miles	Number of Passengers	Chicago to:
7	170	8	Marion, IN
4	240	6	Mt. Vernon, IL
12	348	2	Kansas City, MO
5	574	6	Baltimore, MD .
7	583	5	Washington, DC
4	606	3	Ambler, PA
5	630	3	Ada, OK
8	670	7	New York, NY
8	676	5	Brewton, AL
5	773	6	Fernandina, FL
14	789	4	Denver, CO
12	898	7	Orlando, FL
10	1,526	8	Santa Ana, CA
8	1,538	5	Everett, WA
10	1,541	6	Oakland, CA
10	1,606	8	San Jose, CA
129/8.06 Av.	13,168	89/5.56 Av.	

The totals are: number of trips, mileage traveled, number of passengers, average number of trips, and average number of passengers carried.
Source: AIMS, Inc., Upland, CA

nance flight hours are included in the cost of operation analysis (hours flown by one airplane in the United States corporate fleet averages less than 559 hours annually). In addition, the positioning of an airplane away from base is required to pick up customers or other passengers for visits to company plants or demonstration sites. It is also important to understand that as the aviation manager educates the company executives on the many uses of the company airplane, utilization will increase.

COST OF OPERATION ANALYSIS

A cost of operation analysis can be made using the travel-to-location sample to determine the number of hours that the aircraft is flown per year. Cost-per-hour is the basis for calculating airplane cost of operation. In reality, per hour fixed costs become variable as the flying hours accumulate. The importance of keeping accurate aircraft operating costs records cannot be overemphasized. Recognizing and documenting the cost of operating an airplane and controlling the costs will enhance the success of the company's flight operation. A cost accounting system that will provide the following information is imperative and must show:

1. Utilization statistics, the basis for the budget
2. Cost per flight hour, cost per mile, cost per passenger mile
3. Measures (indicators) for evaluating the operation
4. Figures for preparation of the budget
5. Comparison with actual costs
6. Figures for allocating costs to various company subsidiaries or departments
7. Comparing costs with cost of similar aircraft
8. Comparing costs with costs of similar operations in the same area
9. Cost factors in aircraft design and quality

Company accounting procedures are not always entirely appropriate for the cost accounting methods required in airplane operation; however, the costs can be made to correlate with the overall company budget. *The budgets in this chapter are intended as a format for developing a cost accounting system based on the operating cost of the suggested airplane for Amalgamated Widgets, Inc. Maintenance budgets will be discussed at length in the maintenance chapter.* Cost-per-hour is the principal figure used when developing airplane cost of operation. The operating cost must include all possible costs, i.e., depreciation and/or loan payments, fuel, maintenance, training, insurance, miscellaneous fees, etc. To cover all possible costs, three budgets should be developed: operating budget, capital budget, and contingency budget.

OPERATING BUDGET

The operating budget is comprised of two costs: fixed, which includes factors of ownership, and variable, which includes factors of utilization. The fixed costs include payroll, rents, insurance, etc. The total fixed costs remain the same regardless of hours flown. However, fixed costs become variable when calculated on a cost-per-hour basis. Variable costs include fuel, travel expenses, maintenance, etc. Because of the many vari-

TABLE 7.6. BUDGET ESTIMATES UTILIZATION

Month _____ 19 ___ Aircraft _____	Base _____					
	Budget	Actual	Var. $	Var. %	Hr.	Mile
Hours flown	699					
Miles flown	265620					
Miles flown W/Pax	212420					
Miles flown WO/Pax	53200					
Pax carried	1548					
Pax seat factor %	.75					
Fuel consumed	169857				243	
Hours flown W/Pax	559					
Hours flown WO/Pax	140					
Passenger miles	1274520					
Average pax carried	6					
% hours flown WO/Pax	.25					
Locations visited	258					
Average speed	380					
Average stage length	823					
Cancel—weather						
Cancel—maintenance						

Source: AIMS, Inc., Upland, CA

ables in the cost of airplane operation, the operating budget should be a variable budget to accommodate changes in the number of hours flown every year. The budget should be reviewed and corrected every quarter. At the end of the third quarter, the actual operating cost figures are projected to year end for developing the budget for the following year with accuracy.[1]

See tables 7.6, 7.7, and 7.8.

CAPITAL BUDGET

The capital budget, as shown in table 7.9, is a statement of proposed expenditures, especially for engine overhauls, interior refurbishing, or other items that can be capitalized for tax purposes. (In this budget, money for engine overhauls is provided by the engine maintenance service plan [MSP]. If no MSP is available, money for engine overhaul should be set aside in the capital budget.)

TABLE 7.7.   BUDGET—UTILIZATION: SAMPLE FIGURES

A. Aircraft Dependent Constants	
1. Average speed of aircraft (nm/hr.)	380
2. Average fuel consumption (gal./hr. @ $2.10 gal)	243
3. Maximum passengers	8
B. Flight Operations Dependent Estimates	
10. Hours flown with passengers	559
11. Hours flown without passengers	140
12. Total hours flown per year	699
13. Ferry hours (%)	.25
14. Non-ferry hours (%) (100%—ferry hours)	.75
15. Passenger load factor (%)	.75
16. Average time/stage (decimal hrs.)	2.166
C. Calculations	
20. Hours flown W/Pax	559
21. Hours flown W/O Pax (10x13) 559x.25	140
22. Total hours flown/yr. (10+11) 559+140	699
23. Miles flown per year (1x12) 380x699	265,620
24. Miles flown W/Pax (1x10) 380x559	212,420
25. Miles flown W/O Pax (1x 11) 380x140	53,200
26. Average passenger flight (3x14) 8x.75	6
27. Pax miles per yr. (24x26) 212,420x6	1,274,520
28. Average stage length (nm) (1x16) 380x2.166	823
29. Locations visited per yr. (24/28) 212,420/823	258
30. Pax carried/per yr. (29x26) 258x6	1548

Source: AIMS, Inc., Upland, CA

CONTINGENCY FUND

The contingency fund is money set aside to cover unexpected expenses that have not been included in the operating budget. The contingency fund is usually from 8 to 12 percent of the operating budget.

FIXED AND VARIABLE COST ANALYSIS

Fixed costs are those that do not vary with the amount of service provided; i.e., aircraft depreciation, hangar rent, pilot's salary. Variable costs depend on the amount of service provided, i.e., costs of fuel, maintenance, and landing/parking fees. Cost per hour is the only practical method of calculating aircraft operating expense. As hours accumulate, the per-hour op-

TABLE 7.8. BUDGET ESTIMATES—COST 699 HOURS

Month _____ 19 __ Aircraft _____ Base _____

Fixed Costs	Budget	Actual	Var. %	Var. $	Hr.	Mile
Payroll + (benefits)	$ 115,000.00				$ 164.52	$0.43
Extra Crew	$ 6,400.00				$ 9.16	$0.02
Insurance	$ 38,200.00				$ 54.65	$0.14
Taxes	$ 14,200.00				$ 20.31	$0.05
Equipment Rental						
Depreciation	$ 510,150.00				$ 729.83	$1.92
Hangar Rent	$ 12,000.00				$ 17.17	$0.05
Ofice Rent	$ 6,000.00				$ 8.58	$0.02
Total Fixed Costs	$ 701,950.00				$1,004.22	$2.64
Var. Cost Maint.						
Total Maintenance	$ 287,379.00				$ 411.13	$1.08
Other Var. Costs						
Crew Travel	$ 24,660.00				$ 35.28	$0.09
Ship Supplies	$ 12,000.00				$ 17.17	$0.05
Stationery	$ 1,200.00				$ 1.72	$0.00
Telephone	$ 2,500.00				$ 3.58	$0.01
Fuel	$ 356,699.00				$ 510.30	$1.34
Oil	$ 196.00				$ 0.28	$0.00
Training	$ 17,000.00				$ 24.32	$0.06
Subscriptions/Dues	$ 680.00				$ 0.97	$0.00
Landing/Parking	$ 2,600.00				$ 3.72	$0.01
Other Misc.	$ 3,000.00				$ 4.29	$0.01
Other Var. Costs	$ 420,535.00				$ 601.62	$1.58
Gross Oper. Costs	$1,409,864.00				$2,016.97	$5.31
Less Depreciation	$ 510,150.00				$ 729.83	$1.92
Less Revenue						
Net Operating Cost	$ 899,714.00				$1,287.14	$3.39

Note: Ownership cost analysis calculations and information for tables 7.1, 7.2, 7.3, and 7.4 provided by Cessna Aircraft Company, P.O. Box 1521, Wichita, KS 67201. There are variations from Cessna's figures in the author's operating cost figures as shown in table 7.8 because Cessna calculated the cost of the Cessna Citation VII based on 500 hours per year while the author's computations were based on 699 hours per year.
Source: AIMS, Inc., Upland, CA

TABLE 7.9.   CAPITAL BUDGET 1993 (SAMPLE)

May 1993 overhaul APU	$ 35,000.00
July 1993 install Loran system	$ 40,000.00
October 1993 refurbish cabin interior	$ 65,000.00
Total 1993 Capital Budget	$140,000.00

Source: AIMS, Inc., Upland, CA

erating fixed costs are reduced because the amounts are extended over the range of hours flown. The variable dollar amount increases as hours accumulate. It is very important to understand which costs are fixed and which are variable. Utilization efficiency can be judged by the per-hour fixed cost versus the variable dollar amount cost. Any time the fixed per-hour costs exceed the variable dollar amount cost the airplane is not being utilized efficiently. When the airplane is not flown, the fixed costs continue but the owner is not benefiting from the use of the airplane.

Figure 7.11 depicts variable dollar amount costs versus fixed per-hour costs. For maximum efficiency, the airplane should be flown above the junction of the variable dollar amount cost line and the fixed cost per hour line. The per hour, per mile graphs, figures 7.12a and b and 7.13a and b, depict cost gradients as the number of hours flown varies. Figures 14a and b indicate the variance in passenger mile cost as the number of passenger and hours increases.

USER TAXES

The airport and other funding programs are financed in large part by a series of aviation user taxes deposited in the Airport and Airway Trust. The taxes that affect corporate aviation are: 5 percent tax on air freight, a tax on aircraft by weight and engine type, an excise tax on aircraft tubes and tires, a $.12 per gallon tax on aviation gasoline, and a $.14 per gallon tax on noncommercial jet fuel.[2]

TAX ADVANTAGES

The complexity of the current tax laws requires the employment of tax experts. Tax benefits offered by the federal government are important

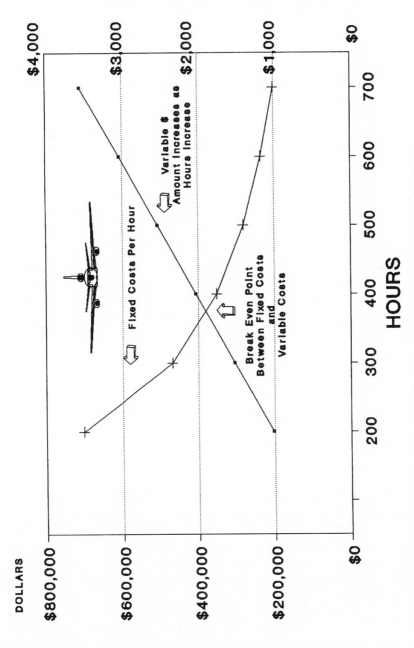

Figure 7.11. Operating variable and fixed cost graph. *Source*: AIMS, Inc., Upland, CA

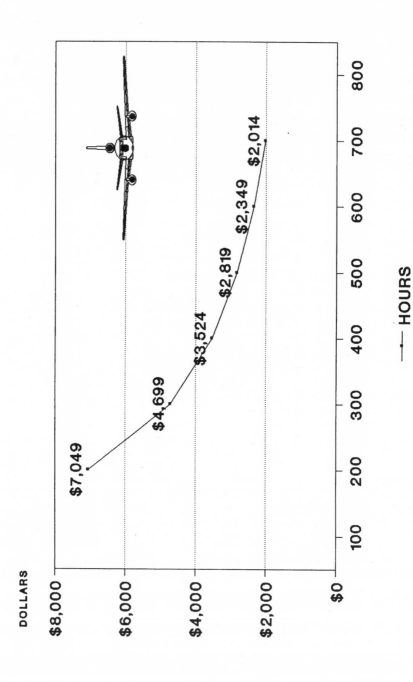

Figure 7.12a. Per hour cost graph (gross). *Source:* AIMS, Inc., Upland, CA

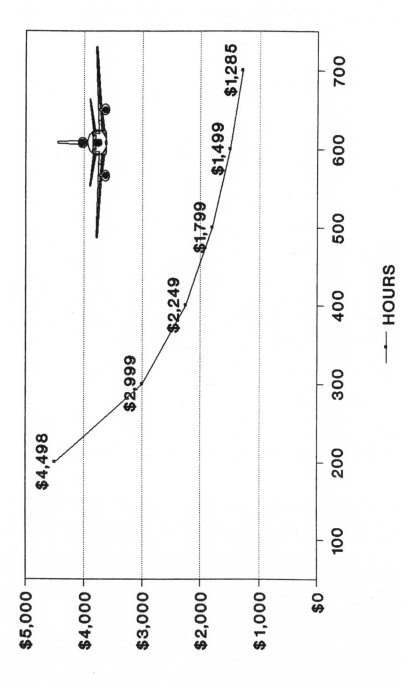

Figure 7.12b. Per hour cost graph (net). *Source*: AIMS, Inc., Upland, CA

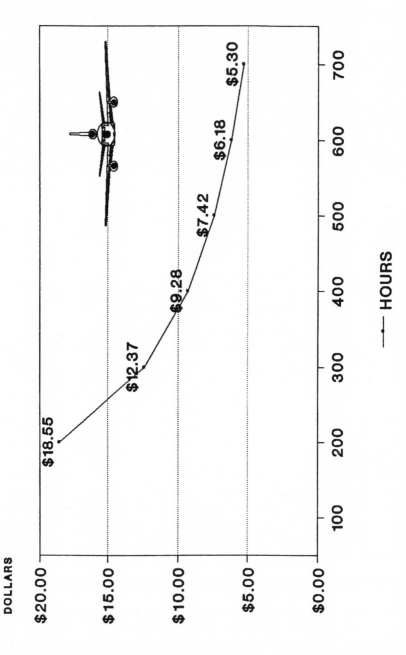

Figure 7.13a. Per mile cost graph (gross). *Source*: AIMS, Inc., Upland, CA

Dollars

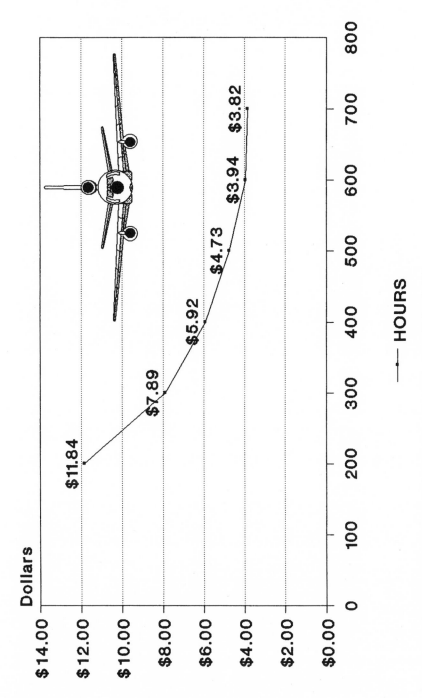

Figure 7.13b. Per mile cost graph (net). *Source:* AIMS, Inc., Upland, CA

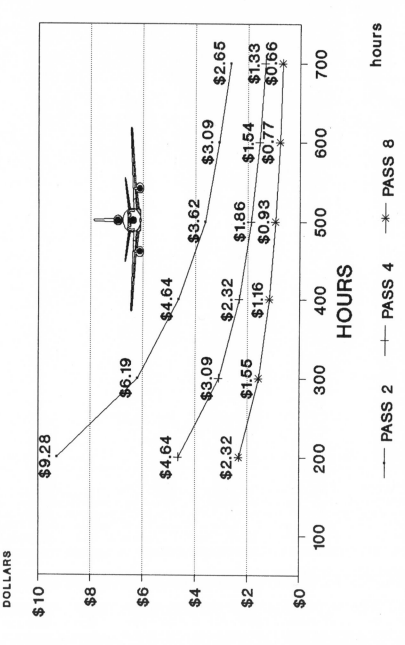

Figure 7.14a. Per passenger mile cost graph (gross). *Source*: AIMS, Inc., Upland, CA

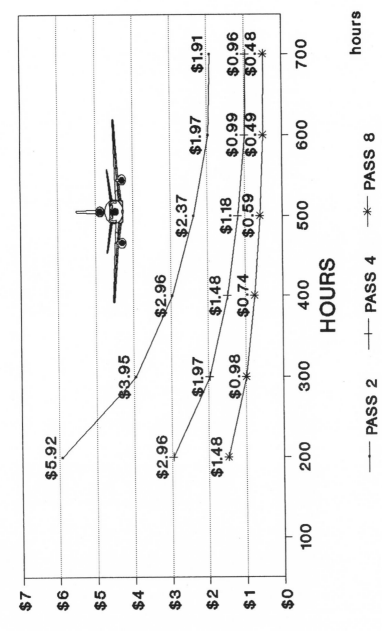

DOLLARS

$7

$6 — $5.92

$5

$4 — $3.95

$3 — $2.96 — $2.96 — $2.37

$2 — $1.48 — $1.97 — $1.97 — $1.91

$1 — $0.98 — $0.74 — $1.18 — $0.99 — $0.96
— $1.48 — $0.59 — $0.49 — $0.48

$0

100   200   300   400   500   600   700

HOURS

hours

—•— PASS 2   —+— PASS 4   —*— PASS 8

Figure 7.14b. Per passenger mile cost graph (net). *Source*: AIMS, Inc., Upland, CA

considerations in aircraft operation. Other items may be deductible, such as sales tax and operating expenses. The fuel tax is rebatable in some states.

TAX FORMS

Figures 7.15a and b are IRS Depreciation and Amortization form 4562 used for claiming deduction for depreciation and amortization. Tax forms change every year, so consult your tax expert.

ACCELERATED COST RECOVERY SYSTEM (ACRS)

Tax depreciation deductions allowed under Section 168(a) of the Internal Revenue Code, Equipment, fall into one of six classes: 3-year, 5-year, 7-year, 10-year, 15-year, or 20-year property. The owner of 5-year property may recover 15 percent of cost in the first year, 22 percent in the second year, and 21 percent in each of the next three years. All the ramifications of the current tax laws cannot be discussed here, as every situation and every company has its own tax peculiarities. Tax considerations of aircraft ownership are critical since taxes affect investment decisions. Tax implications should be reviewed to determine what current tax laws affect aircraft ownership. Consulting with the tax expert is imperative.

METHODS OF FINANCING

A determination as to what type of financing is best for the company must be made by personnel with knowledge of the company's financial condition and who are experienced in the intricacies of the new and used aircraft markets.

The most widely used methods of aircraft acquisition are:

1.   Cash purchase (mostly for used aircraft)
2.   Financing (down payment and monthly payments)
3.   Leasing (There are numerous types of leases to choose from that may fit the company requirements.) A lease arrangement can be quite complex. Companies that lease should employ the services of an expert before signing any lease.

Form **4562**

Depreciation and Amortization

(Including Information on Listed Property)

Department of the Treasury
Internal Revenue Service (0)

▶ **See separate Instructions.**   ▶ **Attach this form to your return.**

Name(s) shown on return

Identifying number

Business or activity to which this form relates

Part I Election To Expense Certain Tangible Property (Section 179) (Note: *If you have any "Listed Property,"* complete Part V before you complete Part I.)

1	Maximum dollar limitation (see instructions)	1	$10,000
2	Total cost of section 179 property placed in service during the tax year (see instructions) . .	2	
3	Threshold cost of section 179 property before reduction in limitation	3	$200,000
4	Reduction in limitation. Subtract line 3 from line 2, but do not enter less than -0-	4	
5	Dollar limitation for tax year. Subtract line 4 from line 1, but do not enter less than -0- . .	5	

	(a) Description of property	(b) Cost	(c) Elected cost	
6				

7	Listed property. Enter amount from line 26.	7	
8	Total elected cost of section 179 property. Add amounts in column (c), lines 6 and 7 . . .	8	
9	Tentative deduction. Enter the smaller of line 5 or line 8	9	
10	Carryover of disallowed deduction from 1991 (see instructions).	10	
11	Taxable income limitation. Enter the smaller of taxable income or line 5 (see instructions) . .	11	
12	Section 179 expense deduction. Add lines 9 and 10, but do not enter more than line 11 . .	12	
13	Carryover of disallowed deduction to 1993. Add lines 9 and 10, less line 12 ▶	13	

Note: *Do not use Part II or Part III below for automobiles, certain other vehicles, cellular telephones, computers, or property used for entertainment, recreation, or amusement (listed property). Instead, use Part V for listed property.*

Part II MACRS Depreciation For Assets Placed in Service ONLY During Your 1992 Tax Year (Do Not Include Listed Property)

(a) Classification of property	(b) Month and year placed in service	(c) Basis for depreciation (business/investment use only—see instructions)	(d) Recovery period	(e) Convention	(f) Method	(g) Depreciation deduction
14 General Depreciation System (GDS) (see instructions):						
a 3-year property						
b 5-year property						
c 7-year property						
d 10-year property						
e 15-year property						
f 20-year property						
g Residential rental property			27.5 yrs.	MM	S/L	
			27.5 yrs.	MM	S/L	
h Nonresidential real property			31.5 yrs.	MM	S/L	
			31.5 yrs.	MM	S/L	
15 Alternative Depreciation System (ADS) (see instructions):						
a Class life					S/L	
b 12-year			12 yrs.		S/L	
c 40-year			40 yrs.	MM	S/L	

Part III Other Depreciation (Do Not Include Listed Property)

16	GDS and ADS deductions for assets placed in service in tax years beginning before 1992 (see instructions)	16	
17	Property subject to section 168(f)(1) election (see instructions)	17	
18	ACRS and other depreciation (see instructions)	18	

Part IV Summary

19	Listed property. Enter amount from line 25.	19	
20	**Total.** Add deductions on line 12, lines 14 and 15 in column (g), and lines 16 through 19. Enter here and on the appropriate lines of your return. (Partnerships and S corporations—see instructions)	20	
21	For assets shown above and placed in service during the current year, enter the portion of the basis attributable to section 263A costs (see instructions)	21	

For Paperwork Reduction Act Notice, see page 1 of the separate Instructions.   Cat. No. 12906N   Form **4562** (1992)

Figure 7.15a. IRS Form 4562, front.

Form 4562 (1992)

Page **2**

Part V — Listed Property—Automobiles, Certain Other Vehicles, Cellular Telephones, Computers, and Property Used for Entertainment, Recreation, or Amusement

For any vehicle for which you are using the standard mileage rate or deducting lease expense, complete only 22a, 22b, columns (a) through (c) of Section A, all of Section B, and Section C if applicable.

Section A—Depreciation (Caution: See instructions for limitations for automobiles.)

22a Do you have evidence to support the business/investment use claimed? ☐ Yes ☐ No   22b If "Yes," is the evidence written? ☐ Yes ☐ No

(a) Type of property (list vehicles first)	(b) Date placed in service	(c) Business/ investment use percentage	(d) Cost or other basis	(e) Basis for depreciation (business/investment use only)	(f) Recovery period	(g) Method/ Convention	(h) Depreciation deduction	(i) Elected section 179 cost
23 Property used more than 50% in a qualified business use (see instructions):								
		%						
		%						
		%						
24 Property used 50% or less in a qualified business use (see instructions):								
		%				S/L –		
		%				S/L –		
		%				S/L –		

25 Add amounts in column (h). Enter the total here and on line 19, page 1 . . . . . . | 25 |
26 Add amounts in column (i). Enter the total here and on line 7, page 1 . . . . | 26 |

Section B—Information Regarding Use of Vehicles—If you deduct expenses for vehicles:
- Always complete this section for vehicles used by a sole proprietor, partner, or other "more than 5% owner," or related person.
- If you provided vehicles to your employees, first answer the questions in Section C to see if you meet an exception to completing this section for those vehicles.

	(a) Vehicle 1		(b) Vehicle 2		(c) Vehicle 3		(d) Vehicle 4		(e) Vehicle 5		(f) Vehicle 6	
27 Total business/investment miles driven during the year (DO NOT include commuting miles)												
28 Total commuting miles driven during the year												
29 Total other personal (noncommuting) miles driven												
30 Total miles driven during the year. Add lines 27 through 29.												
	Yes	No	Yes	No	Yes	No	Yes	No	Yes	No	Yes	No
31 Was the vehicle available for personal use during off-duty hours?												
32 Was the vehicle used primarily by a more than 5% owner or related person?												
33 Is another vehicle available for personal use?												

Section C—Questions for Employers Who Provide Vehicles for Use by Their Employees

Answer these questions to determine if you meet an exception to completing Section B. Note: Section B must always be completed for vehicles used by sole proprietors, partners, or other more than 5% owners or related persons.

	Yes	No
34 Do you maintain a written policy statement that prohibits all personal use of vehicles, including commuting, by your employees?		
35 Do you maintain a written policy statement that prohibits personal use of vehicles, except commuting, by your employees? (See instructions for vehicles used by corporate officers, directors, or 1% or more owners.)		
36 Do you treat all use of vehicles by employees as personal use?		
37 Do you provide more than five vehicles to your employees and retain the information received from your employees concerning the use of the vehicles?		
38 Do you meet the requirements concerning qualified automobile demonstration use (see instructions)? . .		

Note: If your answer to 34, 35, 36, 37, or 38 is "Yes," you need not complete Section B for the covered vehicles.

Part VI — Amortization

(a) Description of costs	(b) Date amortization begins	(c) Amortizable amount	(d) Code section	(e) Amortization period or percentage	(f) Amortization for this year
39 Amortization of costs that begins during your 1992 tax year:					

40 Amortization of costs that began before 1992 . . . . | 40 |
41 Total. Enter here and on "Other Deductions" or "Other Expenses" line of your return . . . | 41 |

☆U.S. GOVERNMENT PRINTING OFFICE: 1992-315-331

Figure 7.15b. IRS Form 4562, back.

4. Charter (If utilization is low, aircraft charter may be the most economical method of airplane operation.)

JUSTIFIABLE AIRPLANE OPERATION

Utilizing aircraft list and price data in table 8.2, it is deduced that the price range of the airplane that may fit the company requirements is between 8 to 9.5 million dollars. The prepared operating budget for 699 hours is $1,409,864.00 per year, $2,016.97 per hour, $5.31 per mile, and $.88 per passenger mile, based on a 75 percent load factor of 6 passengers. Having taken all cost/benefit factors into consideration, the company is now ready to choose the airplane that can fulfill its travel requirements as closely as possible.

NOTES

1. See three articles by Raoul Castro, all appearing in *Professional Pilot*: "Cost Effectiveness Points" (Aug. 1975); "Paperwork Systems" (Feb. 1969); and "How Castro's System Analysis Chose a Falcon and a Lear for Ward's" (Mar. 1968).

2. Harry P. Wolfe and David A. NewMyer, in *Aviation Industry Regulation* (Carbondale: Southern Illinois Univ. Press, 1985).

8

Selecting the Corporate Aircraft

Chapter 7 set forth a determination whether a corporate aircraft can be financially justified. The main objective of this chapter is to outline the various factors to be considered in the selection of the most appropriate aircraft to match the operational transportation needs of company personnel, once the decision to proceed has been made.

Complexity of aircraft selection. Most companies are far less familiar with the operation of an aviation department than of other departments of the corporation. Selecting the right aircraft and setting up a corporate flight operation can become a complex undertaking unless proper step-by-step analyses are conducted to determine what aircraft best meets the company travel requirements.[1]

Company policies vary depending on utilization philosophy. Some examples follow. A few companies take the "Royal Barge" approach, providing service only for the top executives or the Chief Executive Officer (CEO) alone. These departments are very vulnerable and fly fewer hours, making the operation inefficient and not in the best interest of the whole corporation.[2] A large retailer utilizes its airplanes for store visits and face-to-face contact with vendors that provide the goods it sells, as well as to fulfill the travel requirements of a wide range of management personnel. It would not be prudent for this retailer to fly customers, as the average customer spends an average of $2,500 on retail goods per year. A manufacturer of caskets and hospital furniture utilizes a substantial percentage of airplane time to bring prospective customers to its plants for product evaluation and rapport building. The rest of the airplane time is used for management travel from remote general office locations. Only two top echelons of management have access to the airplane belonging to a financial institution. The top echelon group travels all over the United States, Europe, and South America and, most of the time, a complete managers' staff is aboard. Yet another company essentially operates an employee mass-transit shuttle between its various plants. Such examples of company utilization policies point to the needs for an analysis to choose the most appropriate airplane out of many types on the market.

Selection study. Cost and affordability are only two of the many considerations when it comes to selecting the appropriate aircraft. Within the company's financial means there are likely to be several aircraft with widely divergent characteristics. The object of the phase two aircraft analysis is to determine which of these aircraft on balance best fits the company's needs. Now a selection study should be undertaken using a phase two flow chart (figure 8.1). The flow chart covers the necessary steps to be taken for aircraft selection.

Aircraft selection study rationale. It is good practice to do a selection study whether or not the company already owns aircraft. If the company operates aircraft, the experience and records exist to indicate the trends. Utilization parameters can be employed to advantage in the event that the company wants to upgrade or enlarge the fleet. When a new operation is being started, most of the information on employee travel habits can be obtained from company records, as was done for the discussion in chapter 7.

Consultant and/or manager-pilot. Two routes can be taken to produce an aircraft selection study: 1) the employment of a qualified consultant, or 2) the hiring of the manager-pilot at this time. It is advantageous to employ a consultant and hire a manager-pilot at the same time. The consultant can provide his/her varied aviation expertise, the manager-pilot during the process of the study will have the opportunity to learn how the company works. He/she will thus be in a better position to integrate into the company from the beginning. Also, the pilot's aviation knowledge can be helpful in the aircraft selection.

Travel-to-location patterns. These travel patterns are shown in figure 8.2, a map indicating the cities where Amalgamated Widgets, Inc., has locations

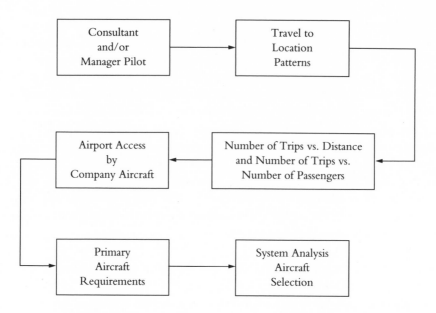

Figure 8.1. Phase two aircraft selection study flow chart. *Source*: AIMS, Inc., Upland, CA

that are visited by company personnel most frequently. The map projects approximate distances to locations. This information can be used to determine the required range of the aircraft and the location of the airport nearest to company facilities.

Number of trips versus distance. The first consideration in the aircraft range/performance is the fact that from previous calculations it was determined that the *average* stage length was 823 nautical miles Instrument Flight Rules (IFR); therefore, that is the *minimum* range required if the aircraft is to receive significant utilization. The second consideration is the *maximum* range required. The trips versus distance graph (figure 8.3) indicates that there were a number of trips of a distance beyond 1,600 nautical miles. Therefore, the maximum range must be an aircraft with a range/performance of better than a 1,600 nautical mile IFR range.

Number of trips versus number of passengers. The first consideration in the aircraft payload/performance is the fact that according to the travel-to-location sample the average number of passengers carried was 5.56 or 6 passengers. Therefore, the *minimum* desired passenger capacity is six passengers if the aircraft is to be utilized efficiently. The second consideration in the aircraft payload/performance is the *maximum* passenger capacity required.

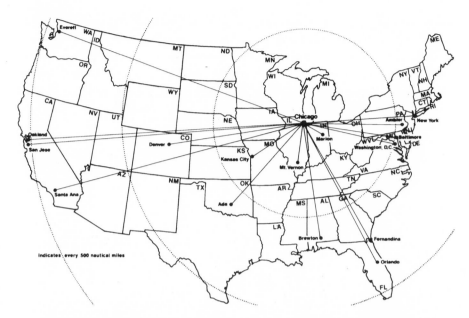

Figure 8.2. Travel-to-location patterns. *Source*: AIMS, Inc., Upland, CA

The trips versus number of passengers graph (figure 8.4) indicates that there were a number of trips where eight passengers were carried; therefore, an airplane with a maximum passenger capacity of eight passengers would be more appropriate.

Range/payload. Note: not all airplanes have the capability of carrying a full load of passengers and a full load of fuel. The next consideration is choosing an airplane that has a 1,600 nautical mile IFR reserve range with a 1,600 pound payload or eight passengers at 200 pounds each.

Airport access by company aircraft. Most airplanes are takeoff restricted by runway length. Runway length requirements are affected by payload, temperature, and field elevation; therefore, runway length versus range becomes an important consideration. Performance parameters have to be studied to ascertain whether the selected airplane will perform in and out of all the airports used or desired to be used by the company. In some cases fuel or passengers may have to be unloaded because of runway length, temperature, or field elevation.

The runway requirements of the various airplanes under review can be found in the manufacturers' airplane performance figures. These figures can be matched to the available runways at airports closest to the company locations. A field length versus range comparison can be made to deter-

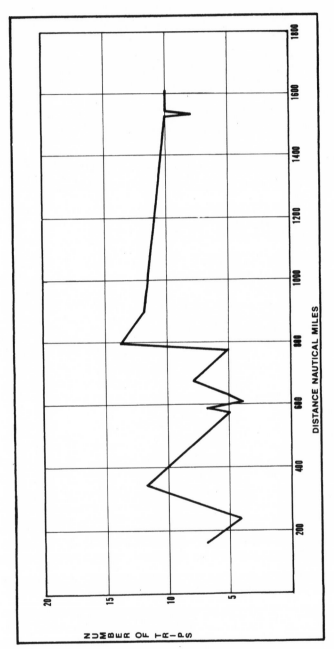

Figure 8.3. Number of trips *vs.* distance graph, which shows the number of trips taken and the distance of those trips. By showing ranges, this graph determines the types of aircraft required. *Source:* AIMS, Inc., Upland, CA

Passengers

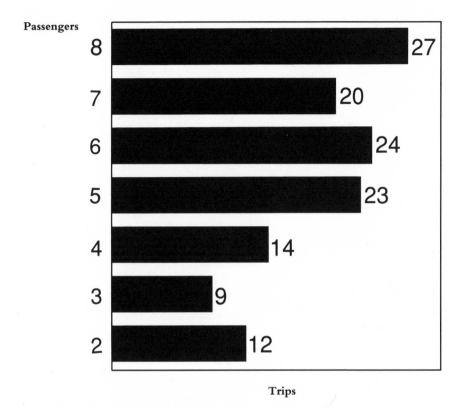

Trips

Figure 8.4. Number of trips vs. number of passengers graph. *Source*: AIMS, Inc., Upland, CA

mine at what gross weight the airplane can be operated from those runways taking into consideration airport temperatures. Airport runway lengths nationwide for the 15,000 public- and private-use fields may be found in the Aircraft Owners and Pilots Association directory (AOPA) or the Jeppesen Airport Charts.

PRIMARY AIRCRAFT REQUIREMENTS

Safety. The aircraft should contain all the safety features commensurate with the present state of the art.

Runway requirements. The airplane should be able to takeoff and land at most if not all airports near the location where the company does business. Moreover, the airplane should be able to takeoff and fly nonstop to the company home base from all company location airports with a full load of

$$\frac{\text{Pass. Cabin Cu. Area}}{\text{Number of seats}} = \frac{521 \text{ cu. feet}}{8} = 65 \text{ cu. ft. per passenger}$$

Figure 8.5. Comfort rating formula. *Source:* AIMS, Inc., Upland, CA

passengers and adequate fuel. There are five corporate jets that meet Amalgamated Widgets' price range of ten million new. There are only two corporate jets that meet Amalgamated Widgets runway requirement of 8,500 feet at an elevation of 5,000 feet, 25 degrees centigrade.

Range. The airplane should have adequate IFR reserve range to be able to proceed to company destinations nonstop with sufficient fuel reserves, or with no more than one stop for fuel. All five corporate jets within Amalgamated Widgets' price range meet the 1,600 IFR range.

Comfort rating. Cabin size equates to comfort, which in turn promotes personnel efficiency. There should be a specified number of cubic feet per passenger to allow passenger movement,[3] for a person 5'10" tall and weighing 175 to 190 lbs. For trips less than four hours, 32 to 43 cubic ft. per passenger, and for trips over four hours, 94 to 113 cubic ft. per passenger, should be provided. When flying for prolonged periods of time, over four hours, certain creature comforts become mandatory, such as livable space, private washroom facilities, and provisions for an adequate bill of fare. To arrive at a comfort rating, see figure 8.5.

Baggage space. Adequate baggage space is defined as not having to place baggage or briefcases in the aisle during takeoff and landing when carrying a full load of passengers. A place is needed to store hats, hang up suit bags, and to store briefcases accessible to passengers in flight.

Certification standards. FAR Part 23 prescribes airworthiness standards for normal, utility, and acrobatic category airplanes. These standards relate to flight, structure, design and construction, power plant, equipment, operating limitations, and information. All twin-engine piston and turboprop aircraft meet FAR Part 23 requirements. FAR Part 25 establishes airworthiness standards for transport category aircraft. Because of higher performance characteristics, as well as the fact that these aircraft transport the public for hire on a more frequent basis, these standards are more stringent then those included under Part 23. A corporate aircraft meeting only Part 23 standards may be adequate for some corporations, but serious consideration should be given to the desirability of meeting the more stringent transport category requirements of Part 25. All corporate jets meet FAR Part 25 performance requirements.

Initial cost. Initial cost is met through purchase of the best equipment for the money that the company is willing to pay to do the required missions.[4]

Cost of operation. The variables in operating cost are usually fuel and maintenance. These expenses must be determined for each airplane considered and should be carefully calculated in advance.

Cabin environment. The airplane should have an adequate environmental system to be able to maintain comfortable temperatures on the ground as well as in the air. Pressurization is mandatory for flight over 10,000 feet.

System Analysis. The following charts show how a system analysis can be used in the selection of a corporate aircraft best suited to the transportation needs of a company. Numbers one and two are small jets, and number three is a turboprop aircraft. To arrive at the system analysis aircraft selection numbers and compute a weight factor, the aircraft have to be compared in the following manner, as shown in figure 8.6.

Table 8.1 shows the numerical weighting and scoring system for determining how three different aircraft may be evaluated. The first column, on a scale of one to ten, shows the relative importance of the various factors under consideration. The second column lists the nine required factors. The other three columns indicate the score achieved by each aircraft for each factor. The totals line shows which aircraft on balance scores best. This is one of many available techniques for choosing among alternatives. Note that column one's relative weightings have substantial impact on the final outcome.

The figures indicate that number one aircraft has the highest numbers and is the one that meets the company requirements closely. It should be understood that the airplane selected is a compromise; there is never a perfect airplane for all missions. Another important point to be considered in system analysis is that a shift of primary factor emphasis impinges on the results obtained.

List of Available Aircraft

There are approximately one hundred different types of aircraft being manufactured, with new types being introduced almost every month. Table 8.2 lists a selection of aircraft and helicopters and gives prices and other pertinent information. Table 8.3 provides a list of aircraft operated by NBAA member companies.

Aircraft runway requirements $\{$Aircraft No. 1—4000′
Sea level—59 degree temp. $\{$Aircraft No. 2—6000′
                            $\{$Aircraft No. 3—3000′

No. 1 $= \dfrac{3000}{4000} = 75 \times 10 = 750$ No. 2 $= \dfrac{3000}{6000} = 50 \times 10 = 500$

Aircraft range $\{$Aircraft No. 1—1600 NM
8 passengers $\{$Aircraft No. 2—1400 NM
               $\{$Aircraft No. 3—1200 NM

No. 2 $= \dfrac{1400}{1600} = 88 \times 9 = 792$ No. 3 $= \dfrac{1200}{1600} = 75 \times 9 = 675$

Comfort rating—78 cubic feet per passenger preferred

No. 1 $= \dfrac{65}{78} = 83 \times 8 = 664$ No. 2 $= \dfrac{37}{78} = 47 \times 8 = 376$

No. 3 $= \dfrac{32}{78} = 41 \times 8 = 328$

Baggage space—70 cubic feet required

No. 1 $= \dfrac{66.5}{70} = 95 \times 8 = 760$ No. 2 $= \dfrac{56}{70} = 80 \times 8 = 640$

No. 3 $= \dfrac{50}{70} = 71 \times 8 = 568$

Initial cost $\{$Aircraft No. 1—\$6.7 million
Budget \$6.5 million $\{$Aircraft No. 2—\$5.8 million
                     $\{$Aircraft No. 3—\$4.7 million

No. 1 $= \dfrac{4.7}{6.7} = 70 \times 9 = 630$ No. 2 $= \dfrac{4.7}{5.8} = 81 \times 9 = 729$

                    $\{$Aircraft No. 1—\$1,219,558
Cost of operation $\{$Aircraft No. 2—\$1,089,620
                    $\{$Aircraft No. 3—\$ 950,240

No. 1 $= \dfrac{950,240}{1,219,558} = 78 \times 10 = 780$

No. 2 $= \dfrac{950,240}{1,089,620} = 87 \times 10 = 870$

Figure 8.6.   Comparison of aircraft.

TABLE 8.1.   AIRCRAFT SELECTION SYSTEM ANALYSIS

(1)	(2)	(3)		(4)		(5)	
	Numerical Rating	Number		──── Aircraft ──── Number		Number	
Weight 1–10	Consideration Base 100	1		2		3	
		★	★★	★	★★	★	★★
10	1. Safety	100	1000	100	1000	—0—	
10	2. Runway requirements	75	750	50	500	100	1000
9	3. Range	100	900	88	792	75	675
8	4. Comfort factor	83	664	47	376	41	328
8	5. Baggage Space	95	760	80	640	71	568
10	6. Certification standards	100	1000	100	1000	—0—	
9	7. Initial cost	70	630	81	729	100	900
10	8. Cost of operation	78	780	87	870	100	1000
10	9. Cabin environment	100	1000	100	1000	—0—	
	Totals	801	7484	733	6907	487	4471

★Score   ★★Score x weight

Source: Aims, Inc., Upland, CA

TABLE 8.2. AVAILABLE AIRCRAFT AND PRICES

Manufacturer	Designation	Number of Seats	True Air Speed	Loaded Range N. Miles	Equipped Price $
Single-Engine Piston Aircraft					
Mooney Aircraft	M-20J	1+3	156	550	146,500
Piper Aircraft	Saratoga	1+5	146	300	232,900
Beech Aircraft	A-36 Bonanza	1+4	168	700	342,000
Single-Engine Turboprop					
Cessna	Caravan I	1+9	181	1000	969,000
Multi-engine Piston					
Beech Aircraft	BE-58 Baron	1+4	189	789	605,000
Partenavia	P68C	1+5	155	600	570,000
Piper Aircraft	PA-34 Seneca	1+5	163	420	435,500
Multi-engine Turboprop					
Beech Aircraft	Be-200 KingAir	1+8	240	1,600	3,300,000
Beech Aircraft	Starship BE-2000	1+8	280	750	4,200,000
Canadair Aircraft	DHC-8-100 Dash 8	2+40	252	1,140	10,550,000
Piper Aircraft	400 Cheyenne	1+8	315	1,363	3,900,000
Piaggio	Avanti P-180	2+8	225	1,300	4,200,000
Dornier	DO-228	2+6	200	1,300	3,750,000
Fan-Turbojet					
Cessna Aircraft	Citation VII CE-550	2+8	415	1,800	8,950,000
Learjet	Lear LR-31	2+7	434	1,350	4,700,000
Learjet	Lear LR-60	2+8	410	2,291	8,300,000
Beech Aircraft	Beechjet BE-400A	2+6	410	1,400	5,200,000
Israel Aircraft	Astra 1A 1125	2+8	408	2,591	7,250,000
British Aero	Bae-125 1000	2+8	420	3,000	12,200,000
Dassault Falcon	Falcon 50	2+9	454	3,100	14,700,000
Dassault Falcon	Falcon 900	2+12	462	3,800	22,400,000
Gulfstream Aero	G-IV	2+14	460	3,800	24,500,000
Canadair	Challenger CL-601-3A	2+10	442	3,200	17,400,000
Boeing Airplane	BO-757-200	2+20	460	4,055	51,280,000
Helicopters–Single-Engine Piston					
Enstrom	F-28F	1+2	85	230	215,000
Robinson	R-22	1+1	90	165	110,000
Helicopters–Single-Engine Turbine					
Bell	206B Jet Ranger	1+3	115	360	610,000
Eurocopter	AS-350B	1+4	120	370	860,000

TABLE 8.2.   (CONT.)

Manufacturer	Designation	Number of Seats	True Air Speed	Loaded Range N. Miles	Equipped Price $
Helicopters–Multi-engine Turbine					
Eurocopter	AS-355F	1+4	120	375	1,650,000
Augusta	A-109C	1+6	149	435	2,700,000
Bell	212	2+8	110	250	4,000,000
Sikorsky	S-76B	2+6	140	360	4,400,000

TABLE 8.3.   LIST OF AIRCRAFT OPERATED BY NBAA MEMBER COMPANIES

Jet Aircraft 30,000 lbs. and over		Jet Aircraft Under 30,000 lbs.	
Boeing		Beechjet	
727	21	BE-400	17
737	5	MU-300	26
747	1	British Aerospace	
757	1	HS 125	34
767	1	HS 125-400	29
British Aerospace		HS 125-600	4
111	9	HS 125-700	114
111-200	1	HS 125-800	89
111-400	5	Cessna	
Canadair		500	53
CL 600	44	501	46
CL 601	75	550	220
Douglas		560	25
DC-9-14	1	650	104
DC-9-15	2	Falcon	
Falcon		10	85
200	14	20	92
50	113	100	7
900	35	Learjet	
Gulfstream		23	1
1159	119	24	36
1159A	95	25	76
1159B	24	28	3
IV	62	31	4
Lockheed JetStar		35	214
1329	13	36	12
1329-8	1	55	71
1329-11	3	Israel Aircraft	
1329-25	12	1121	10
1329-731	10	1124	120
		Sabreliner	
		265	22
		60	29
		65	46

TABLE 8.3.   (CONT.)

Turboprops
12,500 lbs. and over

Beechcraft
  200 338
  300 63
Fairchild
  27 10
Gulfstream
  159 38
Swearingen
  III to IV. 16

Turboprops
Under 12,500 lbs.

Beechcraft
  90 203
  100 44
Cessna
  441 53
Commander
  680 to 908. 41
Mitsubishi
  2, 2b, 2f, 2g, 2k, 2p 33

Helicopters
12,500 lbs. and over

Aerospatiale
  227,332 2
Bell
  214ST. 14
Sikorsky
  58 2

Helicopters
Under 12,500 lbs.

Aeospatiale
  350, 355, 365. .33
Bell
  206, b, l, ...107
Augusta
  109 13
Boelkow
  105 to 117. 12
Sikorsky
  76 52
McDonnell Douglas
  300 to 500 d,e .14

Multiengine Recip.
6,000 to 9,000 lbs.

Beechcraft
  58P, 50, 65, 18, ...34
Cessna
  401 to 412 101

Multiengine Recip.
Under 6,000 lbs.

Beechcraft
  50 to 78. 100
Cessna
  303 to 340. 93

NOTES

1. Raoul Castro, "Aircraft Selection" and "Castro Specs Out Marcor's New G-II," both in *Professional Pilot*, 1976 and 1978, respectively.

2. Charles E. Schneider, "Aircraft Utilization Stressed by Marcor," *Aviation Week & Space Technology*, (Nov. 27, 1972).

3. "Interior Superior," *The Gulfstreamer* (Spring 1975).

4. Aircraft performance information provided by Cessna Aircraft Company, P.O. Box 1521, Wichita, KS 67201.

Part Three
Operations—The Seven Key Factors

9

Corporate Flight Operations Management

This chapter delineates how the seven key factors of corporate aviation operations are managed and how management principles and management functions are used as management tools.

Corporate aviation operations can be divided into seven key factors that comprise three departments and four operational objectives. The departments are flight, maintenance, and schedule and passenger service. The operational objectives are safety, security, emergency and pre-accident plans, and training.

The flight department provides the crew, the maintenance department provides the airplane, and the schedule department combines airplane and crew with the primary objective of dispatching a flight to transport passengers according to requested schedules. The operational objectives encompass a safe flight operation, security for airplane and passengers, emergency and pre-accident plans, and training for the whole flight department for maximum safety and efficiency.

Table 9.1 outlines graphically the seven key factors, responsibility, and work function.

Each key factor encompasses functions that are designed to provide a safe, efficient, and economical corporate transportation system. Chapter 4

TABLE 9.1.   THE SEVEN KEY FACTORS OF OPERATIONS

Seven Key Factors	Responsibility to:	Work Function
Departments		
Flight......................	{ Provide crews	Qualified, proficient and legally ready to perform flight duties
Maintenance	{ Provide aircraft	Airworthy and legally maintained
Schedule..................	{ Develop schedule system	Dispatch aircraft and crew
and	and	
Passenger Service	{ Setup provisions for adequate passenger service	Supply amenities and other passenger requirements
Operational objectives		
Safety......................	{ Develop risk management programs	Implement risk management program
Security...................	{ Develop security programs	Implement security program
Emergency and Pre-Accident Plans..........	{ Develop emergency and pre-accident plans	Implement emergency and pre-accident plan
Training	{ Develop training programs for the entire aviation department	Implement training program for the entire aviation department

Source: AIMS, Inc., Upland, CA

alluded to management principles, four of which are: accountability, assured responsibility, line of authority, and organization. Management as used here refers also to the coordinative aspects of planning, organizing, controlling, and implementing as required of every corporate aviation manager. The philosophy of managing the key factors is one of personnel interaction and interdepartmental coordination using principles and functions of management for guidance. Under certain circumstances, the administrative method may vary as was seen in the organization structure charts, but the inescapable fact is that regardless of the number of airplanes that are operated, the management functions have to be implemented and documented in a practical manner as a means of controlling the operation and making administrative policies known to all employees.

The operations manual. The document used by most companies and supported by the Federal Aviation Administration, National Transportation Safety Board, and the NBAA is the company operations manual. The manuals are the most practical method for communicating common administrative and flight operations procedures to employees. Adherence to the spirit as well as the letter of the company operations manual and to the FARs, specially Parts 43, 61, 91, 135, and 121, are necessary to the safe conduct of all flights.[1]

The administrative functions can be divided into three areas.

1. Activities of the aviation manager: These are the activities required of the manager in the administrative process. The activities required may vary depending on the number of airplanes operated and the complexity of the operation.
2. Resources; human and physical facilities: Resources include the number of personnel and skills required. Job expectations and conduct expected of employees also fall under resources. Physical facilities required include hangar, offices, etc.
3. Interdepartmental coordination: The coordination of activities to achieve unity of purpose in the operating plans fits under interdepartmental coordination.

1. ACTIVITIES OF THE MANAGER

Managerial activities include the work that the manager is accountable for and has the responsibility for and the authority to carry out in the everyday operation of his or her organization.

Developing the Manuals

The first activity of the corporate aviation manager is to develop the necessary manuals to cover all aspects of the operation. Every corporate aviation department regardless of size should have four manuals:

1. Operations
2. Training
3. Maintenance
4. Employee handbook

At this point only the operations manual will be covered as this manual deals with administrative functions. The training manual will be covered under the chapter on training, and the maintenance manual will be discussed under the maintenance chapter. The employee handbook is usually provided by the company to all employees including the flight operation employees. Commercial operators operating under Federal Aviation Regulations Part 121 or under Part 135 are obligated to have an operations manual; corporate operators that operate under FAR Part 91 have no such obligation. Most well-managed aviation departments nevertheless have appropriate manuals.

The company aviation department operations manual provides personnel involved with flight operations a professional approach regarding general policies, procedures, and regulations of the company and concerned governmental agencies. Having and using the manual is regarded as the mark of a professionally managed aviation department. The National Transportation Safety Board (NTSB) after a fatal accident in 1977 at Lewisburg, WV, came out strongly for company operations manuals. As a result of the investigation, the NTSB believed that the accident could have been prevented if the company had specified procedures understood by the crew.

The NTSB has recommended through the National Business Aircraft Association that corporate aircraft operators adopt company operations manuals for the following reasons:

> In the present environment of sophisticated aircraft and complicated air traffic conditions, manuals protect the company and the pilot by dictating policies and procedures that are understood and adhered to by the pilots.
>
> An operations manual establishes common administrative and flight operations procedures that ensure that strong measures of standardization are conveyed to the pilots and company personnel utilizing the airplane. The operations phase has a direct bearing on the safety of the mission so every phase from flight preparation through parking at the ramp must be as detailed as possible.

Contents of an operations manual may vary in order to meet the needs of each operation; therefore, the manual should be tailored to the operational requirements to include coverage of the following subjects:

Signature file copy
Revision record
Revision control sheet

Manual distribution
Letter from upper management
Introduction and/or preface
Company management responsibilities
Operating philosophy
Structural format of the company aviation department
The seven key factors of corporate aviation operation

Writing an operations manual is usually difficult for the typical aviation manager or chief pilot. It is generally better to have an expert from one of the many consulting firms compile the manual in the proper language and proper format. Some suggestions that can be of help are:

Write the manual to the parties to be addressed.

Use the proper language.

The writing style must be consistent throughout the whole manual.

Get to the point of what has to be said in as plain a language as possible using a minimum of rhetoric; the manual is not a novel or biography.

Consider how other persons are going to interpret the text, especially a lawyer or FAA inspector.

Sectionalize the manual according to the seven key factors or to company needs.

Avoid being redundant; do not repeat material from one section to another.

Do not stray from the format of the Federal Aviation Regulations; adapt as much as possible to the style and text of FAR Part 121 or Part 135 of the FAA manuals as well as the airman's information manual.

The aviation department organization structure should be well presented to let employees know to whom they report and what are their responsibilities.

The text is intended for professionals; do not use basic instructions.

The manual cover letter should be signed by the CEO, president, or executive vice president of the company.

Budgets

Budget preparation is the next activity that the manager or chief pilot has to develop in the process of developing the organization.

Operating budget. This is all costs dealing with the everyday expenditures to keep facilities and airplanes operating. The key to cost con-

trol is knowing accurately what the costs are. For that reason, it is imperative that budget preparation be initiated by the manager and undertaken
with information from all aviation department heads. Every department
should make its own budget. The budget should clearly reflect fixed and
variable costs and also in-house and contract expenditures. Utilization statistics are essential to budget preparation as cost variance is dependent on
number of hours flown. Statistics are also necessary for the evaluation of
productivity.

Capital budget. This is all expenditures in connection with facilities
such as hangars; any improvements on aircraft that can be capitalized such as
engine overhaul, rotables, and aircraft modifications; and depreciation of
aircraft and facilities.

Contingency fund. This is the money set aside to cover unexpected expenses that have not been included in the operating budget, and amounts to
about 8 to 12 percent of the operating budget.

Projections. At budget time, a report of major expenditures such as
engine overhauls and airplane improvements should be made for the coming year.

Reports. Reports to upper management should be concise and
give meaningful and useful information. Means should be used to present
information that is easy to read and analyze. A quarterly activity and financial report presented on the appropriate forms for each aircraft and
combined fleet should include utilization statistics such as hours flown,
ferry time, number of passengers carried, fuel consumed, etc. The annual
report submitted at the end of the fiscal year can be a summation of the
quarterly reports plus other pertinent information of interest to upper management.

Purchasing

There are three types of purchasing:

1.   Budgeted purchasing
2.   Out-of-pocket purchasing
3.   Nonbudget purchasing

Each type has to be treated according to procedures established in the purchasing process to make sure that expenditures will not get out of hand and
that the goods and services are received as ordered.

Budgeted purchasing. This is controlled by the budget. Any expenditures in this category are approved when the annual budget is approved. However, the manager has to make sure that any expenditure will not cause the operation to be over budget. A purchase order form should be executed for all purchases above a certain dollar minimum as it would be inefficient to write P.O.'s for anything less than $50.00.

Out-of-pocket purchasing. For expenditures of a small dollar figure, a kitty is usually set up with a system for keeping track of those out-of-pocket expenditures. The manager's secretary usually disburses and controls the kitty.

Nonbudget purchasing. This relates to expenditures that for some reason were not included in any of the budgets or for some items that were impossible to plan for. It is usually necessary to make an appropriation request so the money can be appropriated from one of the company's funds reserved for this type of situation. An appropriation in most instances limits the money to a percent above the money requested and for that reason the person making the request must be sure that the expenditure is not going to exceed the requested amount plus the percent allowed. When making a nonbudget request for money, two forms must be executed—the purchase order form and the appropriation request form.

Figure 9.1 shows a simple purchase/work order form that can be used when purchasing material or having outside work performed. Figure 9.2 is an appropriation request form to be used when requesting money for nonbudget expenditures.

Travel Regulations

Practically all corporations have policies and procedures for business travel and expenses. Control, administration, and documentation of travel expenses is mandatory due to the increasing requirements of the Internal Revenue Service and other regulatory agencies. As a rule, employees of the aviation department are guided by a set of common expense guidelines issued by the corporation. In most cases, flight crews are given a permanent travel advance to take care of expenses that cannot be charged directly to the company or to a credit card. The aviation department should develop its own travel expense statement form following the lines of the standard company expense form but including space for the airplane number for ease of charging crew travel expenses to each airplane. Figure 9.3 is a sample travel expense statement form that includes all possible charges.

COMPANY NAME

Purchase Order No. 93-125   Date: 08-10-93

Work Order No._____Vendor's Contact__John King_____

Confirmation P.O. 93-125_____Original P.O._____

Vendor: Amalgamated Widgets, Inc._____

       Midway Airport, Chicago, Illinois_____

Via: Federal Express_____

BILLING ADDRESS: P.O. Box 1784 Clearing Industrial Center_____

Chicago, IL 60287

AIRCRAFT NO: 710 MR   MODEL: Falcon 50_____

ITEM QTY.	DESCRIPTION	PART No.	TYPE TRANS.	A/C NO.	COST
1	Starter Gen.	GE65268	P.O.	710MR	$5,200
2	Reverse Current	GE12523	P.O.	710MR	$2.200

IMPORTANT: Our purchase order No. must appear on all invoices, packing slips & correspondence. Billing address is listed above unless otherwise specified.

SIGNED:_____
TITLE: Chief of Maint.

Figure 9.1. Purchase order form. *Source*: AIMS, Inc., Upland, CA

Credit Cards

Most companies provide each flight crew member a set of credit cards that include American Express or Visa, telephone credit cards, and auto rental credit cards. These cards are to be used in addition to the travel ad–

TO: ☐ PAY IN CURRENCY ☐ ISSUE CHECK	COMPANY NAME **REQUISITION FOR DISBURSEMENT** (TRAN. CODE 0111) DATE_____19_____

PAY TO THE ORDER OF (NAME AND ADDRESS)_____

_____

_____ $_____

ON ACCOUNT OF _____

	ISSUING LOC.	JOURNAL TICKET NO.

MEMO ONLY	ACCT. NUMBER	LOCATION CHARGED	AMOUNT	MDSE. DEPT.	DETAIL	ADD'L. DATA	DESCRIPTION

REQUESTED BY_____   SIGNED_____

DEPT. _____   SIGNED_____

                                    APPROVED BY_____

COMMENTS: _____

ENDORSEMENT FOR CASH RECEIVED

34504-1

Figure 9.2. Appropriation request form.

vance. As a rule, all charges are to be listed on the expense report. A set of the frequently used oil company credit cards is provided by the oil companies at the request of the manager or chief pilot. The cards are usually carried on board each aircraft to facilitate the purchase of fuel and other associated items. Fuel and oil charges are in most cases entered in the flight report together with the amounts of fuel and oil taken on board. This information is important for recording the cost and amount of fuel and oil used. Credit card charge slips obtained after the purchases and checked by one of the pilots prior to signing are turned in to the operations office with the flight log.

Record keeping

Records and the information that records provide are invaluable in maintaining control of the operation and an adjunct to making decisions. A

COMPANY
TRAVEL EXPENSE STATEMENT

		LOCATION CHARGED		LOCATION CODE NO.	
NAME (Last) (First) (Middle)		PHONE		ACCOUNT NO.	

											TOTALS
DATE											
DAY OF THE WEEK											
AIRPLANE #											
FROM CITY											
TO CITY											
MILEAGE Personal vehicle											
1. Auto or Truck Allow.											
*2. Garage and parking fee (Except Co. vehicles)											
*3. Plane											
*4. Rail or bus fare											
5. Taxi, Carfare, Airport(E) Limousine & Helicopter											
*6. Room											
7. Breakfast											
8. Lunch (Including Tax & Tip)											
9. Dinner											
10. Tips (except meals and taxi)											
*11. Tel, Telegraph (E)											
*12. Valet and Laundry											
*13. Other expenses (E)											
*14. Entertainment (F)											
15. TOTAL FOR PERIOD											

REASON FOR TRIP

	CASH ADVANCED
	DUE TRAVELER
	DUE COMPANY

DETAIL OF OTHER EXPENSES KEYED (E)

DATE	AMOUNT	EXPLANATION

MEMO EXPENSE SUMMARY

16. TOTAL FOR PERIOD (From Line 15) $ _____

EXPENSES PAID DIRECTLY BY COMPANY

17. Air Scrip   _____

18. Auto Rental   _____

19. Other (Explain) _____   _____

20. TOTAL EXPENSE (Sum Lines 16 thru 19) $ _____

ACCOUNTING DISTRIBUTION
(Please Leave Blank)

DETAIL OF ENTERTAINMENT EXPENSE KEYED (F)
ITEMIZE EXPENDITURES—ATTACH RECEIPT FOR EACH PAYMENT

DATE	AMOUNT	PERSON ENTERTAINED Name, Title, or Position, Firm	EXPLANATION (Place and Type of Entertainment, Purpose)

SIGNED (TRAVELER)	DATE	APPROVED

M5365-1   (SEE INSTRUCTIONS ON BACK)

Figure 9.3. Expense account form.

good record system is imperative whether done by hand or automated. The record system should include all the information that can be of value in improving or expanding the operation and also in providing upper management with information on the advantages of aircraft operation.

Accounting

Corporate aviation accounting is simply a method of keeping track of expenditures and comparing these expenditures with the budget in per cent and dollar amount. Chapter 7, on economics, presented operating budgets that might be used in the accounting process. As cost of purchasing and operating may vary with different types of airplanes and in some cases with the same type of airplane, it is important to develop an accounting system for each airplane.

Corporate Aviation Insurance

An insurance policy is a contract—a guarantee of performance between two parties—in this instance between the insurance company (the insurer) and the corporation (the insured). It has the two necessary requisites of a valid contract—an offer and an acceptance. The insurer offers to provide protection against monetary loss to the insured, and the insured, by payment of the premium, agrees to accept the offer and to operate the aircraft in accordance with the terms of the policy.

Legal Matters

All companies in the business world today need advice and help in legal matters. A corporate flight operation has to deal with a multiplicity of federal, state, and local laws and regulations, in addition to contracts of various types that require legal assistance. The legal department in many cases can work through NBAA regarding legal actions and legal advice.

Language on Agreements and Contracts

Any time a transaction or agreement is undertaken, the language on the paper to be signed should be approved for proper content by an attorney. A sample list of agreements or contracts follows:

Language required on purchase orders

Airplane purchase and sale contracts
   New Airplanes
   Used airplanes
Agreements with
   Hangar owners

Brokers
Consultants
Maintenance contractors
Aircraft outfitters
Aircraft charter operators
A company in the business of operating airplanes for other companies.

How to Prepare for a Meeting with Your Attorney

Make sure you have all the facts at hand. Enumerate items that need to be brought to the attention of the lawyer. If possible have all the information in writing to make sure you do not forget important items that may be of vital use to the lawyer. Preparation saves time all around.

Library

A library or reading file is essential in operations of any size because of the requirement to keep personnel abreast of industry activities, regulations, and developments in the state of the art. The library should be well organized and cataloged according to subject. The library should contain pertinent information on policies, company periodicals, safety bulletins, Flight Safety Foundation and National Business Aircraft Association information, flight manuals for each aircraft type, texts on weather, texts on aircraft performance, FAA regulations, company manuals on operations, training, and maintenance, and any other information of interest to departmental employees.[2]

Future Planning, Feasibility Studies, Audits

A corporate aviation manager or chief pilot must make constant review of his/her operation to determine how his/her operation can be improved and what is necessary to provide better passenger service and better equipment utilization. From time to time an analysis should be made of the efficiency and performance of the equipment being operated to determine if it is feasible to improve the service with different equipment, or different operating procedures. A periodic management audit by an outside auditor or consultant can be of value for improving the operation. A self-audit can be valuable if performed regularly and impartially to improve management. Obviously there are several management characteristics that are hard to control. People never seem to testify against themselves; also few managers relish finding out their own shortcomings and those of their employees.

Communication

The aviation department manager or chief pilot must interrelate with his/her employees to stay abreast of all the developments of the operation. A high percentage of the misconceptions, frustrations, and inefficiencies in the working relationship of the aviation manager and his/her employees is attributable to poor communication. This is especially true in the aviation industry by virtue of the operational and technical complexities. In almost every instance of inefficient performance it is found that somewhere along the line there was a breakdown in communication. To avoid misunderstandings and misinterpretations, it is important to stress the reliance on clear and concise information.

2. RESOURCES (ADMINISTRATIVE)

Human Resources

Many managers mention that staffing is the most critical activity that they are responsible for. As in any business the success of the aviation department is determined by the strength of its people. Managers who abjure the opportunity to hire strong employees deserve all the deadbeats they hire. The sophistication and complexity of the equipment and the operation of that equipment require that the aviation department be composed of individuals who have extensive background and experience in the various facets of aviation.

Studies conducted in recent years indicate that there is a shortage of experienced personnel to fulfill the personnel needs of corporate aviation. This situation has created a problem for corporate operators. Whereas in the past there was an ample number of qualified persons to choose from in the labor market, now the corporation has to entice with better pay or better working conditions personnel from other corporate operators or other segments of industry.

In the past, turnover of personnel was relatively low, which resulted in a stable situation for the manager. The unexpected turnover was mostly in co-pilots or mechanics who wanted to upgrade to captain or chief mechanic. The

consequences of turnover are both financial and operational. Training, indoc-
trination, and the fact that a new employee may have to be brought in at a
higher salary not only affects the budget but also the morale of all employees.

People needed for a corporate flight operation can be categorized as
follows:

1.   Managerial
2.   Secretarial
3.   Accounting
4.   Scheduling
5.   Flight crews
6.   Technical

Of interest is the fact that there are very few real corporate aviation
managers out there. The following qualifications from an advertisement in
the *Wall Street Journal* brought fifty-four replies, but only two applicants
outlined their management background and abilities, while the rest ex-
pounded on their flying experience and flying background.

Opening for Corporate Aviation Department Manager
Must Have Management Background
Management Degree Desirable
Must Have ATP but Flight Experience not First Consideration
Salary Commensurate with Experience and Background

Of the two applicants with management background and experience, the
one hired had a management degree and considerable flying experience.

Some corporations are placing managers who have no aviation experience in charge of their flight operations. This system seems to work well
when the manager and chief pilot work together toward the common goal
of an efficient operation.

Secretarial personnel in a corporate flight operation can be classified as
any person with several skills such as handling correspondence, record
keeping, accounting, report writing, and scheduling. Usually a person for
this position is a competent secretary within the company who is tired of
routine, likes diversity, and is willing to train for the position.

Flight crews are classified as captains and first officers. It is assumed
that captains are only hired at the inception of the operation with the idea
that first officers will be hired with sufficient experience to be able to upgrade to captain when the opportunity arises. The fact is that any well-
managed operation will upgrade from within to prevent turnover and

maintain high morale. Captains have to be brought in from the military, the commuter airlines, or other corporate flight operations; first officers are recruited from commuter airlines, the military, flight schools, and air-charter operations.

Well-qualified maintenance technicians are probably the hardest personnel to find. Any sound, well-qualified technician is employed and is not available unless he or she is unhappy with his or her present salary or working conditions. Sources of most of the technical personnel are the military or schools such as the College of Technical Careers, Southern Illinois University at Carbondale, Parks College, and Embry-Riddle Aeronautical University.

One of the most critical actions of a manager is the selection and development of personnel with the proper talent and ability to perform the tasks related to the organization structure. Identifying personnel requirements for a corporate aviation department begins with the development of the organization structure. The corporate aviation organization structure chart together with the job descriptions identifies the number of employees needed and the skills required.

Job Descriptions

Job descriptions play an important role in identifying the tasks to be performed and can be used as a guide in recruiting, interviewing, reviewing, and promoting. Appendix A contains job descriptions outlining the position basic function, duties and responsibilities, and also the training and background expected.

Staffing Formulas

As previously mentioned, identifying personnel needs takes place during the development of the organization structure. However, the number of employees does not become definitive until the type of equipment and the number of hours that the equipment is to be flown is determined. Figure 9.4 points out the various factors affecting aircraft utilization for a specific operation. It shows why it is difficult to schedule a corporate airplane more than 750 hours a year.

Because of the number of hours that a corporate crew spends waiting for passengers, it is difficult to schedule a crew more than 750 hours a year without violating duty-time limitations. Nonflying days such as vacation,

A. Number of hours per year that airplane is not utilized.★

    1. Hours that airplane is not requested.
      a. Hours after regular working day.
      b. Holidays, weekends, etc.

    2. Hours required for maintenance.

    3. Waiting time on ground during trips.

B. The speed of the airplane is a factor in determining its ability to handle other assignments while passengers are conducting their business.

C. The longer the stage lengths, the more flying time accumulated, thus more utilization of the airplane in a given period of time.

D. Pilot time is a factor if only one crew is used for each airplane since a crew should not fly more than 750 hours per year.

> Actual available hours per year 8760
> ★Hours airplane not requested . . . .−6400
>   2360
> Maintenance (man hours) . . . .−350
>   2010
> Waiting time (65%) . . . .−1306
> Maximum hours aircraft utilization 704
> (for specific operation)

Figure 9.4. Factors affecting corporate aircraft utilization. *Source:* AIMS, Inc., Upland, CA

training, and holidays also have a bearing on the number of hours that a pilot can be scheduled. The number of mechanics required is determined by the burden (human efficiency) and the number of airplane maintenance hours per flight hour. Figure 9.5 present pilot and mechanic staffing formulas that are helpful in accurately staffing a flight operation.

Personnel Performance Appraisal

Performance appraisal systems have been used to justify salary increases, promotions, terminations, and as a vehicle for developing and motivating workers. But how often is the performance appraisal a true link between compensation and performance? Subordinates fear appraisals because the supervisor holds the future of employees in the palm of his/her hand. A supervisor has to develop trust among his/her employees and remember that he or she is trying to help people to develop themselves, so that they can give the company the best that they have to offer. The same appraisal criteria should not be used to evaluate different jobs or job clas-

Formula for Determining Number of Pilots Required for a three-airplane operation

$$\frac{\text{CREW SEATS x 365}}{\text{365—DAYS OFF/YEAR}} = \text{PILOTS}$$

CREW SEATS = Total crew seats of three airplanes.
DAYS OFF/YEAR = Total nonworking days one pilot.
(Below variables are determined by specific operation.)

Compute nonworking days:

Average vacation days off....................................... 15
Days off per week (2 x 52) 104
Training... 10
Sick leave... 10
Holidays.. 8
Standby 5
DAYS OFF/YEAR 152

To apply formula:

$$\frac{6 \times 365}{365-152} = \frac{2190}{213} = 10.3 \text{ PILOTS REQUIRED}$$

Formula for Number of Mechanics Required for three different type airplanes

Preliminaries:

EFFICIENCY = 1.0 BURDEN (in decimal form).
EFFICIENCY x HRS./MAN = EFFECTIVE HRS./MAN
(Including efficiency adjustments to the formula to compensate for less than optimal work output.)

$$\frac{(\text{FLT. HRS./YR.}) \times (\text{MAINT. HRS./FLT. HR.})}{(\text{EFFICIENCY}) \times (\text{HRS./MAN/YR.})}$$

Variables:

Hours flown per year:

Type A (turboprop)   600 hrs.
Type B (turbojet)   750 hrs.
Type C (turbojet)   1000 hrs.
Burden   25%

HRS. OF MAINTENANCE PER FLT. HR.

Type A   5
Type B   3
Type C   2.5

PER YEAR HRS. OF WORK ....2080 (standard hours of work per year)

To apply formula:

$$\text{Type A} = \frac{600 \times 5}{.75 \times 2080} = \frac{3000}{1560} = 1.9 \text{ Mechanics}$$

$$\text{Type B} = \frac{750 \times 3}{.75 \times 2080} = \frac{2250}{1560} = 1.4 \text{ Mechanics}$$

$$\text{Type C} = \frac{1000 \times 2.5}{.75 \times 2080} = \frac{2500}{1560} = 1.6 \text{ Mechanics}$$

Total Mechanics Required 4.9

Figure 9.5. Staffing formulas.

sifications. Anything less than specific criteria for specific jobs may be unsatisfactory. A manager with a reasonable amount of sensitivity for the feelings of others and a genuine desire to help employees develop can conduct an effective appraisal by following a few simple principles:

1. Before you discuss the person, discuss the job. There may be different ideas about the exact nature of the responsibilities. Review the job description together to see if revision is required.
2. Ask before you tell employees. Ask them to tell you what they think they have done well and what they would like to do better.
3. When you must criticize, criticize the person's performance, not the person. The person may be able to change his or her performance. It is doubtful whether the individual can do much about changing his/her personality.

Figure 9.6 is a sample form that may be used for personnel performance appraisal.

Probationary Period

Most corporations have a probationary period when new employees are hired. This probationary period is usually six months. This probationary period can be adopted for all new office and maintenance personnel. A three-month probationary period usually applies for flight crew members.

Personnel Records

The following list identifies the file used by corporate aviation for personnel records.

A. Application for employment
B. Airman certificates (copies)
C. Radio licenses (copies)
D. Receipt for manuals and company materials issued
E. Correspondence—should include duplicates of all letters of commendation, criticism, and discipline, and review reports
F. FAA medical certificate (copy) and company physical examination record
G. Record of company forms filled out by employee
H. Pilot proficiency check reports
I. Pilots and mechanics training records
J. Reports of accidents or incidents

Personnel Performance Appraisal Form

NAME _____ AGE _____ DATE _____

REPORTING PERIOD: ANNUAL ____ SEMIANNUAL ____ SPECIAL ____

POSITION _____

QUALIFICATION:
(Background, Training, Ratings, Licenses, Etc.)

_____

_____

| PERFORMANCE FACTORS: | AVERAGE | ABOVE AVERAGE |

A. Job Knowledge
   (Depth, Currency) _____

B. Judgment & Decisions
   (Consistent, Accurate & Effective) _____

C. Professional Qualities
   (Attitude, Cooperation) _____

D. Appearance
   (General) _____

   (Uniform on Job) _____

E. Adaptability to Stress
   (Stable, Flexible & Dependable) _____

F. Plan, Organize and Manage Work
   (Timely, Personnel, Material) _____

G. Oral and Written Communications
   (Clear, Concise, Organized) _____

H. Crew Member/Passenger Relations
   (Sensitivity, Treatment) _____

J. Remarks:
   (Counseling, Etc.)

_____

SCHEDULE FOR FUTURE TRAINING:

_____

_____

REVIEWER _____ TITLE _____

EMPLOYEE _____ TITLE _____ DATE _____

Figure 9.6. Personnel performance appraisal form. *Source*: AIMS, Inc., Upland, CA

Personnel may be permitted to review their files, as established by Freedom of Information Act.

Facilities

Although most corporate flight operations rent their hangar and office facilities from fixed base operators (FBOs), there are some operators that rent a whole hangar bay from the FBO or a whole hangar from the airport. A good number of the larger operators have built their own hangars together with fueling facilities planned to take care of all the activities of the operation. Usually a fixed base operator at the airport provides some services such as hangar space, office space, passenger lounge, fueling, some maintenance, airplane cleaning, and sale of some parts not provided by the manufacturer. Corporate aviation facilities can be divided into three categories: 1) office facilities, 2) hangar facilities, and 3) storage space.

Office facilities can range from a one-room office for the one-airplane operation to the multioffice complex to house the passenger lounge, manager's office, chief pilot's office, scheduling department, accounting department, training department, library, and flight planning room.

Hangar facilities requirements are determined by the number of airplanes to be stored and the amount of maintenance work to be done inhouse. The one- or two-airplane operator does not need more than the hangar space for the airplanes plus storage space for commissary and spare parts. Larger fleet operators may require a whole hangar bay to store airplanes plus an office for the chief of maintenance, a shop for mechanics, a stockroom for parts, and a commissary room for ship supplies. Full service fixed base operators usually restrict the airplane tenant from doing maintenance that the FBO can perform. In this case, as a rule, when the arrangement is made for hangar space, the lessor spells out the amount and type of work that the lessee can do on the company airplane.

Storage space is usually space for storing parts or equipment that is infrequently used. When contemplating building or modifying a hangar, the following should be taken into consideration:

1. *Function.* The hangar must be designed for maximum efficiency and minimum loss of time when going to and from the various departments.

2. *Required Space.* Adequate space should be provided for present and future activities of the operation.

3. *Working environment.* The requirements for lighting, color of office

walls, and ventilation should be anticipated; also, employee and equipment considerations should be included in the planning.

4. Safety, security, and cleanliness. For the maintenance of a proper safe environment and pleasant working conditions, the building should be functional and devoid of unsafe construction and easy to keep clean. The architecture should provide no security problems.

Up to this point the activities of the manager or chief pilot have been covered; those are the responsibilities that he or she alone can be accountable for. Following are the activities that require the interaction and coordination of the staff to implement the operating plans.

3. Interdepartmental Coordination

The scheduling, flight, and maintenance departments are the three operating groups that have direct responsibility in the performance of flight schedules. The activities of each group must constantly be coordinated in the progressive development and function of organizational operating plans. Coordination commences with the scheduling department, which coordinates with the flight and maintenance departments. The flight department provides the crews, the maintenance department provides the airplanes, and the scheduling department puts it all together with the primary objective and unity of purpose in transporting passengers throughout the country as safely and efficiently and with as little distress or disturbance as possible. Regardless of the size and the number of airplanes that are being operated, interdepartmental coordination is necessary. By setting a one-airplane scenario, it can be seen that all the activities of a large operation are there but in a more compressed concept; the one- or two-airplane organizational structure in figure 5.3 attests to that.

The airplane and crew have to be scheduled not only for flights but also for maintenance and training. This may be done by a part-time scheduler (in a one- or two-airplane operation) whose main job is being a secretary. All maintenance can be farmed out, but the manager or chief pilot has to select and arrange the maintenance contracts with a maintenance provider that can do the work on the type of airplane that is being operated. The maintenance has to be done in accordance with the flight schedules; therefore it is imperative that the maintenance work be done on an exact time schedule. The maintenance provider has to advise the scheduler as to when the airplane will be ready for flight. The crew, which is the flight department in a one- or two-airplane operation, coordinates with and provides inputs to the scheduler as to maintenance and training required. The scheduler then arranges for the dates and time for maintenance and training.

Communication Policy

The scope and complexity of a business aviation operation conducted over large geographical areas requires definite lines of communication to enable constant coordination of activities to be effective. The schedule is the master plan; however, elements such as weather, mechanical difficulties, air traffic control delays, and airport facilities can upset the schedule so that action is required to overcome these variables. Accordingly, through the lines of communication available, established coordination procedures must take place between all levels of the operating departments.

Coordination Policies for each level of operation are established as follows:

Operations level. The aviation department manager and/or the chief pilot are charged with the responsibility of proper planning of flight-schedule activity. This responsibility requires that they maintain an active liaison with each department concerning their capabilities and problems in order to determine if schedules can be maintained. When situations occur that will cause irregular operations, the aviation department manager and/or the chief pilot must immediately be advised and a plan for counteraction must be developed. When such a plan has been formed, further coordination must occur between department heads and the involved line pilots. All affected personnel must be properly notified.

Maintenance department level. It shall be considered the responsibility of the maintenance chief or maintenance contractor to advise the aviation department manager or chief pilot of any abnormalities or problems concerning the maintenance of aircraft or of mechanical functions that will impair or disrupt the scheduling of aircraft or of any given flight. It is imperative that the maintenance chief or maintenance contractor advise the aviation department manager or chief pilot well in advance of any pending aircraft inspection or foreseen down time of a maintenance function. The phrase "well in advance" is defined as two (2) weeks before the maintenance function or twenty-four (24) hours before the pending inspection. This notification must be in writing with a copy routed to maintenance files. This responsibility may not be delegated to a maintenance subordinate other than to a secretary for the purpose of typing and distribution. In the event that a pilot should call from the field with a maintenance problem, the maintenance chief or maintenance contractor shall advise the pilot on a course of action and then notify the chief pilot.

Line pilot level. The captain is in command of his or her operating flight and is responsible for carrying out the planned operation of the flight insofar as flight operations and the mechanical condition of the airplane are concerned. The captain, in exercising the responsibility as commander of the flight shall make such operating decisions logically as deemed necessary for the safe conduct and operation of the flight.

The captain must notify the aviation department manager or chief pilot of a deviation in the schedule of the flight via the most expeditious method. Should a maintenance problem occur, the captain shall notify the maintenance chief or maintenance contractor immediately for instructions as to how to proceed.

Should a command decision that involves deviation from the schedule in any manner become necessary in the field and the department heads cannot be contacted, the captain is duly authorized to make said decision and will report to the chief pilot as to the situation that occurred, the decision that was made and its basis, the action that was carried out, the result of this action, and the effect on the flight. The captain may not delegate this responsibility to any other crew member. When anticipating excessive delays or unforeseen late arrivals at home base, a call should be made so that a crew change for the following day can be planned if necessary.

The following administrative functions as outlined in previous pages is the work that a manager is accountable for and has the responsibility and authority to carry out in the everyday operation of the organization.

1. Activities of the manager
2. Resources (human and facilities)
3. Interdepartmental coordination

These functions and further regulations should be covered in the operations manual. Appendix B is an example of company and FAA regulations that should be used to develop the operations manual.

FAA REGULATIONS

The FAA regulations that cover the flight section follow.[3] Aviation regulations have been in existence for many years. As early as 1920, the

United States Army Air Service issued regulations for the operation of aircraft. The flight operations manager or chief pilot has to know how existing regulations affect his or her operation. As regulations become more complex and harder to comply with, flight operations personnel have to be alert to prevent infractions.

Aviation regulations as they apply to corporate aviation embrace four areas: safety, environment consumer protection, and industry promotion. Safety of the public—both flying and on the ground—is governed by regulations that also encompass airspace utilization, aircraft operations, and airport development. Environmental regulation seeks to protect the quality of the human and natural environment. It is geared toward reducing aircraft noise levels and engine emission pollution. Consumer protection benefits inherently from safety regulation. The aviation industry is promoted through a number of funding programs. For example, the Federal Aviation Administration finances airport development, planning, and aeronautical research.

The major sources of aviation industry regulation are the government, the industry itself, and the marketplace. The aviation industry is regulated at all levels of government. The federal government's specific role in aviation industry regulation is carried out by the Federal Aviation Administration and the aviation branch of the National Transportation Safety Board (NTSB). State and local governments supplement the federal regulators.

Examples of self-regulation include industry associations' development of programs, standards, or guidelines for their members. The National Business Aircraft Association (NBAA) and the Flight Safety Foundation (FSF) have established a number of formats on training, maintenance, manuals, and safety. Finally, the marketplace plays a regulatory role in the performance of the aviation industry. If a product or service does not sell, whether it is an aircraft or an FBO service, the marketplace governs through the response that lack of sales receives. In this book, regulations will be introduced in the respective chapter: maintenance regulations under the maintenance chapter, flying regulations under the flight section administrative chapter, and so on.

Procedural Rules

FAR Part 11 deals with "General Rule Making Procedures," and is divided into two categories—rules other than airspace assignment and use, and rules and procedures for airspace assignment and use. The FAA Administrator initiates the rule-making process but may be encouraged to do so by petitions from interested parties. FAR Part 13 is entitled "Investigation and Enforcement Procedures." This regulation explains how to file a complaint against any person who violates a regulation, prescribes civil penalties for violating aviation regulations, explains circumstances under which an aircraft may be seized by the federal government, identifies how to request a hearing, and explains how an investigation is to be carried out by order of the Administrator.

Aircraft

Airworthiness standards are established for different categories of aircraft and aircraft components. A description of some of the specific FARs in this category is presented below.

FAR Part 21 covers procedures for the FAA certification of aircraft and related appliances, in particular, type, production, and airworthiness. Type certificates are required for new aircraft, engines, and propellers, and signify that they meet applicable airworthiness and noise standards. An airworthiness certificate signifies that an aircraft meets all prescribed FAA standards.

FAR Part 23 prescribes airworthiness standards for normal, utility, and acrobatic category airplanes. These standards relate to flight, structure, design and construction, powerplant, equipment, and operating limitations, and information.

FAR Part 25 establishes airworthiness standards for transport category aircraft. Because of higher performance characteristics, as well as the fact that these aircraft transport the public for hire on a more frequent basis, these standards are more stringent than those included under Part 23.

FAR Part 36 establishes maximum permissible noise levels for most aircraft types. Different thresholds are established for each model of aircraft and included in that model's type certificate. Turbojet and large transport category aircraft must have their noise levels reported in units of Effective Perceived Noise Level (EPNdB) in decibels.

Airmen

FARs designated by Parts 61, 63, 65, and 67 deal with the certification of airmen. Airmen include both pilots and nonpilots whose work is closely associated with commanding an aircraft or other object of flight.

Part 61 describes the requirements for pilots and flight instructors.

Part 63 identifies the standards for flight crew members other than pilots such as "flight engineers and navigators."

Part 65 prescribes certification requirements for nonpilot airmen including air traffic control operators, aircraft dispatchers, mechanics, repairmen, and parachute riggers. Part 67 establishes medical standards for the different classes of pilot. The first-, second-, and third-class medicals have progressively lower physical requirements. A medical certificate may be issued with operating limitations or waiver for those who do not meet medical standards.

Airspace

FARs in the 70s category deal with airspace designation and usage. FAR Part 71 designates federal airways, area low routes, controlled airspace, and reporting points, while FAR 73 defines special-use airspace. Special-use airspace is airspace of defined dimensions identified by an area on the surface of the earth where limitations are imposed on aircraft operations. Typical examples include military operations areas, military restricted areas, and the airspace over the White House.

FAR Part 75 covers jet routes and area high routes, which means routes generally between 18,000 feet and 45,000 feet.

FAR Part 77 sets standards for determining obstructions in navigable airspace; it sets requirements for notifying the Administrator of the FAA of construction that might pose a hazard to flight. Five types of geometrical planes are defined known as civil imaginary surfaces in three-dimensional space around an airport and its runways. If an object penetrates the geometrical plane, it is considered an obstruction.

Air Traffic and General Operating Rules

Corporate aircraft operators like any other aircraft operator have to abide by air traffic and general operating rules as specified in FAR Part 91. Corporate aircraft operators that want to operate for hire must obtain a certificate under FAR Part 121 or FAR Part 135.

FAR Part 91 specifies general operating and flight rules and is a particularly important regulation for pilots and corporate aviation personnel to be thoroughly familiar with. General operating rules relate to pilot-in-command responsibility, preflight actions, the position of flight crew members during takeoff and landing, fuel requirements, limitations on alcohol consumption, dropping objects from aircraft, VHF omnidirectional radio range, VOR equipment check, and so forth. Flight rules relate to altimeter settings, operations at airports with control towers, VFR minimums, and so forth.

FAR Parts 93, 95, 97, and 99 are highly specialized and relate to special procedures to be followed for takeoffs and landings, especially under instrument flight conditions.

FAR Part 93 details special air traffic control rules and airport traffic patterns. These special procedures are arranged by airport or airway. For example, Subpart D prescribes traffic patterns for Anchorage, Alaska. Part 93 also contains rules for high-density airports.

FAR Part 95 prescribes the altitudes governing the operation of aircraft under IFR conditions on federal airways, jet routes, and so forth. It has one section dealing with mountainous areas.

FAR Part 97 specifies "Standard Instrument Approach Procedures," while Part 99 sets rules for the operation of aircraft in the Air Defense Identification Zone (ADIZ). FAR Part 101 prescribes rules governing the operation of moored balloons, kites, unmanned rockets, and free balloons.

FAR Part 103 prescribes operating rules for ultralights. This regulation stops short of certifying operators or the vehicles they use but does impose operating rules on ultralights to ensure their safe usage.

Air Passenger Carriers, Certification, and Operation

This category of regulation prescribes rules and standards that may be adapted in part for the development of the corporate aviation operations manual. The types of air carriers governed by these rules include major domestic and flag carriers, charter carriers, air travel clubs, helicopter carriers, foreign air carriers, rotorcraft external-load operators, and agricultural aircraft operations. One of the regulations in this category also prescribes standards for airports that are served by air carriers.

FAR Part 121 governs the certification and operations of major air carriers using large aircraft. This lengthy regulation contains twenty-three subparts. Topics covered in the subparts that can be of importance to corporate aircraft operators are:

1. Certification rules and operating specifications.
2. Description of the procedures for preparing and maintaining a manual for the use and guidance of flight and ground operations.
3. Airplane performance defines operating limits for one engine-out and takeoff and landing limitations.

4. Special airworthiness requirements. These pertain to ventilation, the location of fuel tanks, fire extinguishing systems, and so forth.
5. Flight operations. These requirements prescribe standards including but not limited to crew-member responsibilities, emergency procedures, takeoff and landing procedures under normal and engine inoperative conditions, passenger briefings, and airplane security.
6. Training programs. This identifies the training requirements for crew members and other personnel.

FAR Part 135 applies to air taxi operators and commercial operators of small aircraft. These are aircraft that have a maximum capacity of thirty seats or less or a maximum payload capacity of 7,500 pounds or less. There is also a special provision, however, that covers air taxi operations with large aircraft.

Airports

FAR Part 150 series deals with airports. This regulation establishes a single airport noise measuring technique and single system for determining human response to airport noise. It also prescribes a standardized airport noise compatibility program.

Hazardous Materials

FAR Part 175, "Hazardous Materials Regulation: Carriage by Aircraft," sets forth requirements for aircraft operators transporting hazardous materials. Among its general rules are those concerning notifying passengers about hazardous materials restrictions, notifying the pilot in command of the presence of hazardous materials, marking hazardous materials and assuring that they are accompanied with the appropriate paper work, and reporting hazardous materials incidents. More specific rules govern the loading, unloading, and handling of hazardous materials, and the classification of hazardous materials so that the conditions under which they may be carried can be clearly defined.

NOTES

1. Information gleaned from NBAA *Business Aviation Management Guide*.

2. Excerpts from Aims, Inc., Flight operations manuals, Aims, Inc., Upland, CA.

3. Harry P. Wolfe and David A. NewMyer, *Aviation Industry Regulation* (Carbondale: Southern Illinois Univ. Press, 1985).

10

Corporate Aviation Maintenance

This chapter reviews corporate aviation maintenance management activities that are essential to a well-run maintenance department: safety, organization, planning, economics, dependability, and utilization.

MAINTENANCE MANAGEMENT

The chapter does not cover maintenance programs or requirements as covered by FAA Part 43. Most aircraft manufacturers offer maintenance programs approved by the FAA for the particular type and model of airplane. There are also several private companies such as CAMP Systems that offer computerized maintenance programs for practically all corporate aircraft tailored to the operators' requirements. The importance of aircraft maintenance management has been underestimated since the airplane was invented. Once the airplane took to the air, flying became the focal point of aviation, with the tremendous impact of maintenance on safety and the budget minimized.

COORDINATION OF MAINTENANCE WITH FLIGHT AND SCHEDULE

An efficient scheduling system requires that the maintenance department coordinate with the flight and scheduling departments to make sure that the three organizations are in accord with each other on when the airplane or airplanes are needed to cover planned trips. The scheduler must know at all times the aircraft maintenance status and have the maintenance due list posted in the scheduling system in order to know when the maintenance department can provide the aircraft.

MAINTENANCE SAFETY INVOLVEMENT

Safety through effective maintenance is an extremely important responsibility. The policies that are established have a direct effect on the safety of the passengers, crew, and equipment. Maintenance is an adjunct to safety. Good maintenance provides safer airplanes, dependable schedules, and therefore better aircraft utilization.

Maintenance plays a vital safety role in operational reliability. Safety through operational reliability encompasses: 1) the safety that is engineered into the aircraft, 2) the inherent ease of that aircraft to be maintained, and 3) the workmanship by mechanics who are restricted by the airplane's basic design.

Mechanical safety engineered into the aircraft includes the fail-safe design concept—the maintain safe and install correctly provision. There are many design deficiencies that inhibit maintenance safety. It is proper to assume that an airplane designed for ease of maintenance will present fewer difficulties to the mechanic, hence minimizing safety risks incurred during maintenance.

Workmanship by mechanics who are restricted by the airplane's basic design raises the question, What is the end result of a mechanic's best efforts when a part can be installed incorrectly with the added frustration of working by feel in a remote compartment? Many component failures are attributed to improper installation. The goal of a maintenance enterprise has to be the development of good practices and procedures together with the added ability to overcome the aircraft design deficiencies for error-free maintenance that will provide maintenance-induced safety. The goal should be to find the proper procedures and the amount of maintenance necessary. Machines are made to run, not to be taken apart and put together again and again. Too much maintenance is as bad as too little maintenance. In the former case, components may become worn from excessive handling and the law of averages regarding human error has more opportunity to manifest itself. With too little maintenance, deterioration of the aircraft will result. A happy medium between the two is the secret of good maintenance.

ORGANIZATION

Through organization, a maintenance structure is developed that provides a means of controlling the maintenance of company-owned aircraft. The owner company is directly responsible for maintaining the aircraft in an airworthy condition. The FAA conditions are: 1) the aircraft must at all times conform with its type certificate, 2) the aircraft must be in a safe operating condition. As the company representative, the manager or chief pilot assumes the responsibility of organizing and selecting the maintenance programs that meet not only the FAA conditions but also the company flight schedule requirements.

Regardless of the number of airplanes that a corporation operates, some maintenance has to be farmed out to specialized maintenance contract agencies. It would be inefficient and uneconomical to purchase specialized equipment, maintain limited-use inventory, and hire personnel to do all the maintenance in-house for a small number of airplanes. As an example, some large airlines do contract work for smaller airlines, with both parties benefiting—one from being able to utilize more efficiently their large facilities and personnel and the other in saving on personnel, equipment, and inventory.

The methods for accomplishing corporate aircraft maintenance vary depending on:

1. Number of airplanes, type of trips (days away from home base), and the number of hours the airplane or airplanes are utilized per year. These factors have a definite bearing on the amount of maintenance that can efficiently and economically be done in-house. If the airplane is not in the hangar at home base, it cannot be worked on. So what do the maintenance people do when the airplanes are away from home base?

2. Percentage of maintenance to be performed in-house and percentage to be contracted out depends on the number of hours or days the airplanes are available for maintenance. A substantial amount of maintenance can be performed in-house if the airplanes are available for maintenance evenings and on weekends. It is usually nec-

essary to take the airplane out of the schedule for contracted scheduled inspections or unscheduled maintenance work.

3. Availability of contract maintenance facilities at home base
    airport or within a reasonable distance. Excessive ferry time
    (nonproductive flying) and costly long crew layovers for contract
    maintenance away from base should be prevented if possible.
    With a readily accessible maintenance facility, unscheduled
    maintenance problems can be corrected without canceling flight
    schedules. In this case the ideal situation is to hangar with
    an FBO that has the trained personnel and equipment to per-
    form most of the scheduled and unscheduled maintenance.

4. Inadequate physical facilities and work restrictions can become
    a deterrent to the performance of scheduled maintenance. Many
    corporate aviation departments depend on the local fixed
    base operator (FBO) for hangar space and some maintenance.
    If the hangar facilities are not adequate or if the fixed base
    operator (FBO) restricts the amount of maintenance the tenant
    can perform in his or her hangar, the tenant will have to do most
    of the maintenance away from home base.

5. Number of mechanics required, their expertise to perform
    the predicated level of in-house maintenance, and the number
    of hours the airplane or airplanes are available to be worked
    on while at home base are considerations that have to be estab-
    lished before forming an in-house maintenance department.

If the operation consists of one or two airplanes with all the maintenance being contracted, the person in charge of the operation is responsible
for coordinating maintenance schedules.

In a large operation with three or more airplanes and a maintenance
department, the maintenance manager or chief of maintenance can be delegated the maintenance responsibility. In any case, before entering into any
agreement with a maintenance facility the operator should consider the following:

1. The maintenance facility should be an FAA Approved Repair
    Station for the rating and class of aircraft to be maintained. The
    facility should have well-trained maintenance personnel to cover
    all maintenance requirements, i.e., airframe, engines, electronics,
    and avionics.

2. Only a well-organized, qualified, and reputable maintenance
    contract agency should be considered. The organization and its

management and its bank and insurance company references should be checked.

3. The contract agency should have the necessary insurance to cover the aircraft while at the facility and while doing any operational tests.

4. A primary agreement should be signed by both parties covering labor rates, flat-rate prices, parts discounts offered, and overtime charges. The contractor will abide by the maintenance program selected by the operator. To prevent the disruption of flight schedules, an agreement as to time and date the aircraft is to be delivered to the maintenance facility and returned to the customer should be agreed upon by both parties at the beginning of any maintenance work. A penalty may be imposed if the aircraft is delivered late.

5. A work order supplied by the operator for the work performed. If additional work is required after the initial inspection, another work order should be agreed upon and signed.

6. On completion of work, certification is made by entry in the log book or on proper forms for all work performed. Any deferred items should be entered on the deferred-item form.

7. Maintenance record keeping is the basis for efficient maintenance. Records should not only be kept to abide by FAA requirements but also to have control of all maintenance functions including cost control and the planning of future work.

Record keeping starts with a well-arranged log form followed by the necessary forms that provide the necessary information to the chief of maintenance and to the flight crews. Figure 10.1 is a sample form that can be used as a work order. Figure 10.2 is a deferred discrepancy log that provides information as to what items have been deferred due to unavailable parts or waiting for the proper occasion to install the part. Figure 10.3 is a mechanical irregularities and defects report form that lists the aircraft malfunctions, correction of malfunctions, and who performed the work.

STAFFING THE MAINTENANCE DEPARTMENT

Competent maintenance personnel are the key to keeping corporate aircraft in airworthy condition. The manager or chief pilot should be aware of the qualifications and certification required of maintenance personnel whether in-house or contract maintenance is used. Samples of job descriptions are provided in Appendix A.

COMPANY NAME

Purchase Order No._____   Date: _08-09-93_

Work Order No. _93-81_____Vendor's Contact_ Ralph Krieger _

Confirmation P.O._93-81_____Original P.O._____

Vendor:_ K & D Aviation, Appleton, WI _____

_____

Via:_____

BILLING ADDRESS: _P.O. Box 1784 Clearing Industrial Center_____

Chicago, IL 60287

AIRCRAFT NO:_710 MR_____MODEL:_Falcon 50_____

ITEM QTY.	DESCRIPTION	PART No.	TYPE TRANS.	A/C NO.	COST
	Right Engine Change			710MR	
	Loaner being shipped to				
	Appleton, WI				
	Work to be Completed By:	08-12-93			

IMPORTANT: Our purchase order No. must appear on all invoices, packing slips & correspondence. Billing address is listed above unless otherwise specified.

SIGNED:_____
TITLE: Chief of Maint.

Figure 10.1. Work order form.

PLANNING

Planning means identifying short-range and long-range objectives of the maintenance activity and determining what means will be used to achieve them.

COMPANY NAME DEFERRED DISCREPANCY LOG					
Entry Date	No. of Items	Discrepancy	Corrective Action	Mech. Date	Insp. Date
8/12/93	1	Rotating Beacon	Parts Ordered	8/14	8/12/93
8/14/93	2	Rt. EPR Gauge	Gauge Ordered	8/14	8/14/93

Figure 10.2. Deferred discrepancy log. *Source*: AIMS, Inc., Upland, CA

The first determination in managing corporate aviation maintenance is to decide whether to set up or not set up an in-house maintenance department. It is important to realize that some maintenance has to be contracted out.

The second determination in planning is what level of maintenance (how much maintenance) can be done in-house.

COMPANY NAME MECHANICAL IRREGULARITIES & DEFECTS REPORT				
Airworthiness Release BY:_____	Refer Log Dated 8/12	Plane No. 710MR	Capt. P. Warren	T.T. 3225
ITEM	MALFUNCTION	WORK PERFORMED, DATE MECH. MAKING CORRECTION		
1	Top rotating beacon does not rotate	Deferred awaiting parts J.D.		
2	Rt. EPR gauge inop.	Deferred awaiting parts		
3	Brakes weak	Replaced brake pads		

Figure 10.3. Mechanical irregularities and defects report. *Source*: AIMS, Inc., Upland, CA

The third determination in planning is what FAR 91.217 maintenance program option best fits the flight operation to allow flexible flight schedules.

The first determination is controlled by the number of airplanes being operated, and the number of in-house hours available for maintenance. If less than three airplanes are being operated, the practicability of an in-house maintenance department should be thoroughly evaluated.

Six hundred ninety-nine (699) hours of flight time (from the example in chapter 7) for one airplane usually takes between 1,748 to 2,796 maintenance labor hours depending on the type of airplane, or 2.5 to 4 hours of maintenance for 1 hour of flight, respectively. Flying 699 hours per year and being away from home base for long periods of time would not permit enough time for one or two mechanics to perform all the maintenance required, also the four basic maintenance work disciplines—airframe, engine, electronics, and avionics—cannot be covered by one or two mechanics. It normally takes between five to eight mechanics with the various maintenance work disciplines to cover 1,748 to 2,796 hours of labor.

The second determination for in-house maintenance relates to the level of maintenance such as airframe and engine inspections, airframe and engine overhaul, avionics test and repair, and unscheduled maintenance. The percentage level that can efficiently and economically be performed in-house must also be considered. To justify an in-house maintenance department, a minimum of 50 percent of the maintenance should be done in-house. If the resources such as adequate hangar facilities, experienced mechanics, equipment and tools, parts and material inventory are not available or cannot economically be justified, other maintenance means should be considered.

The third determination is the selection of an inspection program, as outlined in Part 91, Subpart D, FAR 91.217, that is best suited to the flight schedule requirements of the operation to allow the maximum utilization of the aircraft. Maintenance should be performed in relation to the flight schedules rather than canceling flights to do maintenance.

FAR Part 91.217(a) states that no person may operate a large airplane, or a turbojet, or turbopropeller-powered multiengine airplane, unless the airplane is inspected in accordance with an inspection program selected from one of the five options listed below.

1.   A continuous airworthiness inspection program currently in use by Part 121 operator
2.   An approved aircraft inspection program currently in use by a Part 135 operator
3,   An approved continuous inspection program currently in use by a Part 123 operator
4.   A current inspection program recommended by the manufacturer

5.   Any other inspection program established by the registered
      owner or operator of that airplane and approved by the admin-
      istrator

If an airline-type airplane is being operated under conditions one,
two, or three, a maintenance program can be obtained from an airline that
operates that type equipment. The airline may also be interested in performing some or all of the maintenance. Airline aircraft maintenance programs are developed to permit high equipment utilization. As corporate
airplanes fly about one-fourth of the hours of the airline counterpart, this
type of program works well for corporate operations. Most corporate-type
airplanes are maintained in accordance with options four or five. It has to
be understood that when a flight operation obtains an unfamiliar airplane a
maintenance learning curve has to be developed. For that reason the best
program at the inception is the manufacturer's suggested program. When
the maintenance and the schedules are well established, consideration
should be given to implementing an option five maintenance program that
provides maximum utilization and is cost effective.

Guidance and control for the operation of a corporate maintenance
department is provided by the Federal Aviation Regulations in Part 43—
Maintenance, Preventive Maintenance, Rebuilding and Alteration. "Maintenance" means inspection, overhaul, repair, preservation, and replacement
of parts, but excludes preventive maintenance. "Preventive maintenance"
means simple or minor preservation operations and the replacement of
small standard parts, not involving complex assembly operations. "Major
repair" means repair: 1) that, if improperly done, might appreciably affect
weight, balance, structural strength, performance, power plan operation,
flight characteristics, or other qualities affecting airworthiness; or 2) that is
not done according to accepted practices or cannot be done by elementary
operations. "Major alteration" means an alteration not listed in the aircraft,
aircraft engine, or propeller specifications: 1) that might appreciably affect
weight, balance, structural strength, performance, power plant operation,
flight characteristics, or other qualities affecting airworthiness; or 2) that is
not done according to accepted practices or cannot be done by elementary
operations.

ECONOMICS OF MAINTENANCE MANAGEMENT

Economics is the science dealing with the production and consump-

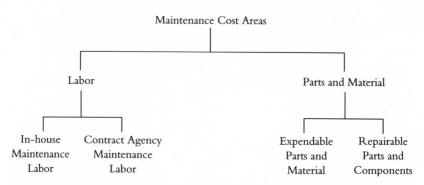

Figure 10.4. Maintenance cost areas. *Source*: AIMS, Inc., Upland, CA

tion of goods and services. From the definition it can be asked what finances are required for the economics of providing the required maintenance services—in this case, corporate aircraft maintenance. With respect to corporate aviation maintenance, economics means management and control of costs. Cost-control discipline should permeate all maintenance activities with the added advantage of providing safe, efficient, and dependable aircraft.

Four major maintenance cost areas that have to be considered are described in Figure 10.4

In-house maintenance labor costs are the salaries plus benefits paid maintenance personnel. Budget figure for one mechanic—2,080 hrs. per yr. × \$15.00 = \$31,200 × 35 percent benefits = \$10,920 + 31,200 = \$42,120.

Contract agency maintenance labor is the hourly charge for work performed on an airplane. The contract agency has to make a profit on maintenance personnel and equipment used. For that reason the contract agency charges have to be above what a mechanic can be hired for.

Parts and material that have to be replaced are classed as expendable items, i.e., tires, O-rings, gaskets, fluids, etc.

Rotable items, i.e., starters, generators, hydraulic pumps, also components such as instruments, APU, etc., are classed as repairable.

Airplanes of different types have variations in labor, parts, time, and costs that are required for maintenance. Some airplanes require fewer man-hours to maintain than others. Some engines require less attention than others. In order to measure maintenance efficiency and costs, quantitative statistics are necessary:

TABLE 10.1. MAINTENANCE HOURS / FLIGHT HOURS

Labor	Man Hours/Flight Hours	% Hours
Airframe Inspection and repair labor	1.2	48%
Instrumentation Avionics Inspection, repair labor, calibration	0.5	20%
Engine Routine maintenance	0.8	32%
Total	2.5	100%

Source: AIMS, Inc., Upland, CA

Maintenance man-hours per flight hour—to gauge aircraft maintainability and know the number of mechanics required

Maintenance cost distribution—to compare the cost of various maintenance segments

Mean time to repair—to gauge component life and obtain approval for
time extensions from the appropriate regulatory agency

Maintenance cost control begins with knowing the quantitative statistics together with effective use of available resources and effective maintenance programs, which are in turn dependent on aircraft maintainability.

Table 10.1 demonstrates maintenance hours per flight hour for each
segment of maintenance on a specific airplane. It also shows the percent of
hours required for each segment. Maintenance hours per flight hour vary
depending on maintenance efficiency, work environment, pilot technique,
and operating conditions. Numbers can be obtained from the aircraft
manufacturer, other aircraft operators, or from experience in operating the
type aircraft in question.

Table 10.2 demonstrates costs of components, parts, and materials for
each segment of maintenance on a specific airplane. Table 10.2 also shows the
dollar percent for each segment. Maintenance per hour costs vary depending
on maintenance efficiency and operating conditions. (See tables 10.3 and
10.4.) Numbers can be obtained from the aircraft manufacturer, other aircraft
operators, or from experience in operating the type aircraft in question.

With all the numbers assembled, the maintenance budget can now be
prepared. (See table 10.5.) In this case, the assumption is that all maintenance for one airplane is to be contracted.

TABLE 10.2.   CONTRACT MAINTENANCE LABOR BUDGET ESTIMATES

Components	Per Hour Cost	% $
Repairable (Overhaul) Rotable, i.e., Starter Generator Pumps Servos APU	$42.00	47%
Expendable Items i.e., Tires Brakes O rings Gaskets Hardware Fluids	$32.00	36%
Instrumentation Avionics Parts	$15.00	17%
Totals	$89.00	100%

Source: AIMS, Inc., Upland, CA

Different types of maintenance budgets have been developed for corporate flight operations. The variable maintenance budget has been successful in a number of organizations in identifying the values and costs of each activity and in evaluating the benefits of performance. In order for the variable maintenance budget to work, careful review and modifications have to be made quarterly or even monthly if necessary.

Budgeting is often confused with planning. Many managers or chief pilots, when talking of planning are really speaking about the annual budget. One reason is that planning was derived from the budgeting process. The role that budgeting plays in control has to be recognized. Unfortunately most organizations define budgeting as "telling money where to go" rather than asking "where it went."

Maintenance expenditures are the most difficult expenses to control in a flight operation and also the easiest to get out of hand. For that reason, methods of cost control are essential in a well-run maintenance operation. Cost

TABLE 10.3.   ESTIMATES

1. Hrs. Maintenance/Flight hrs.	2.5
2. Average Maint. cost/hr.	$41.00
3. % airframe labor time	48
4. % avionics, instruments labor time....................................... (should total 100%)	20
5. % engine labor time...............................	32
6. Hours flown	699
7. Maintenance crew size (all disciplines)	

Source: AIMS, Inc., Upland, CA

TABLE 10.4.   BUDGET CALCULATIONS

21.	Labor hours required/year	(6x1)	699x2.5=1748
22.	Labor costs/year	(21x2)	1,748x$41=$71,668
23.	Labor man hours	(21/7)	1,748/5=350
24.	Labor man days (8 hrs./day)	(23/7)	350/5=70
25.	Airframe labor time (hrs.)	(21x3)	1,748x.48=839
26.	Avionics labor time (hrs.)	(21x4)	1,748x.20=350
27.	Engine labor time (hrs.)	(21x5)	1,748x.32=559
28.	Airframe labor cost	(25x2)	839x$41=$34,399
29.	Avionics, instrumentation labor cost	(26x2)	350x$41=$14,350
30.	Engine labor cost	(27x2)	559x$41=$22,919
31.	Repairable items cost		699x$42=$29,358
32.	Expendable items cost		699x$32=$22,368
33.	Instrumentation, avionics parts cost		699x$15=$10,485

Source: AIMS, Inc., Upland, CA

control, or "where did the money go" starts with the budget. It was asked in another chapter, "How can you cost control if you don't know what the costs are?" The actual versus budget cost variance needs to be expressed in dollars and percents and used as a management tool to obtain a true picture and to effect overexpenditure corrections whenever necessary. If the actual expenditures greatly exceed the budget, problems can be identified as poor control, lack of proper paperwork, poor input of operating costs, lack of value analysis, poor vendor selection, and poor inventory control.

MAINTENANCE INVENTORY MANAGEMENT

Inventory management has come a long way from the day when in-

Part Three: Seven Key Factors

TABLE 10.5.   MAINTENANCE BUDGET ESTIMATES

Month _____ 19 __ Aircraft _____ Base _____

Var. Costs Maint.	Budget	Actual	Var. $	Var. %	Flight Hour	Mile
Airframe labor	34,399				49.21	.13
Avionics inst. labor	14,350				20.53	.05
Engine labor	22,919				32.79	.09
Repairable items	29,358				42.00	.11
Expendable items	22,368				32.00	.08
Inst. avionics parts	10,485				15.00	.04
Engine MSP★	145,112				207.60	.55
Misc. maint.	8,388				12.00	.03
Total Maintenance	287,379				411.13	1.08

★Engine maintenance service plan
Source: AIMS, Inc., Upland, CA

ventory levels were maintained at the discretion of the users and when full accounting of the inventory was taken only once a year. Today with the high price of parts and components large amounts of money can be tied-up in inventory that may run out of shelf life or that may not be used for long periods of time.

A corporate aviation inventory system, computerized or by hand, is a system in which the following details are subject to control:

1. What items to stock
2. How many to stock
3. When to stock them
4. When and what items are best obtained from vendors on short notice

Inventory control is concerned with making decisions that minimize the total cost of inventory yet provide parts and components when needed.

A basic inventory system can be implemented by using the following forms: Figure 10.5, stockroom aircraft parts inventory form, lists all the pertinent information related to each inventoried item. Figure 10.6, inventory record form, records the necessary information when a component or part is

```
                                    COMPANY NAME
Item_____AIRCRAFT PARTS INVENTORY FORM
```

Date	Order#	Part#	Serial#	Location	Condition	Value	Qty Recd	Qty Used

Figure 10.5. Aircraft parts inventory form. *Source*: AIMS, Inc., Upland,

removed from the airplane. Figure 10.7 is an aircraft data form that is carried in the airplane to provide information on each particular aircraft. Figure 10.8 provides an inventory of the equipment to be carried in the airplane.

Dependability and Utilization

Good maintenance provides dependable aircraft; well-planned maintenance enhances utilization. To provide guidance for standard procedures and policies in performing the various tasks in the course of maintaining corporate airplanes, a maintenance manual should be provided.

Contents of Maintenance Manual

Maintenance policy and procedures
Organization and duties
Flight handling reports
FAA/NTSB required reports and records
Maintenance forms and records
Maintenance planning and control procedures
Material control procedures

COMPANY NAME

Inventory Record
A/C Maint.

Total Airplane Time _____

Total Accessory Time _____

Date _____

Part Name _____

Part No. _____ Serial No. Off _____

Plane No. _____ Serial No. On _____

Reason for Removal _____

Disposition — For Repair _____ For Exchange _____

For Overhaul _____ Non-Repairable _____

Defective Part sent to _____ Date _____ P.O. _____

Date Returned _____ Put in stock _____ Put in Plane No. _____

Signed _____

M3168-1

Figure 10.6. Inventory record form. *Source*: AIMS, Inc., Upland, CA

Inspection procedures and required inspections
Quality control
Aircraft ground handling and safety
Airworthiness directives and service bulletin control
Safety/Health and miscellaneous
Aircraft weight and balance control
Minimum equipment list (MEL) manual
Shop procedures
Maintenance personnel training
Facility maintenance

Appendix C outlines the maintenance manual.

FAA REGULATIONS

Maintenance and Registration

FAR Part 43 describes "Maintenance, Preventive Maintenance, Rebuilding and Alteration" standards. FAR Part 43 describes who is authorized to perform maintenance and repair work, how to return an

COMPANY NAME
AIRCRAFT DATA FORM

Aircraft Registration No._____

Manufacturer_____Model No._____Serial No._____

Engine Manufacturer_____Model No._____

Left Engine S/N_____

Center Engine S/N_____

Right Engine S/N_____

Engine Oil Type Used_____

Hydraulic Fluid Used Type Used_____

A P U Oil Type Used_____

Service Landing Gear Oleos with Type_____

Aircraft Paint Specs.

Basic Fuselage Color_____Paint No._____

Stripes Color_____Paint No._____

Color_____Paint No._____

Color_____Paint No._____

Current Empty Weight_____C G_____

Figure 10.7. Aircraft data form. *Source*: AIMS, Inc., Upland, CA

aircraft to service after maintenance, how to keep maintenance records, and the work-performance rules that must be adhered to in working on aircraft.

FAR Part 45 explains the standards for the identification and registration marking of aircraft. Each aircraft and many of its components must be marked in a prescribed fashion, and the markings must be visible. The markings must contain certain information related to the builder's name, model designation, builder's serial number, type certificate number, production certificate number, and so forth. All United States registered aircraft must have nationality and registration marks of prescribed specifica-

AIRCRAFT EQUIPMENT INVENTORY FORM

_____ Company Checklist & Performance
_____ Aircraft Equipment Operating
_____ Airinc Book   _____ Preflight Form
_____ Log Books   _____ Maint. Forms
_____ Airworthiness Certificate   _____ Flight Report Form
_____ FAA Registration   _____ Flight Report Form
_____ State Registration   _____ Passenger List Form
_____ FCC Radio License   _____ Latest #337 Form
_____ Flash Lights   _____ Weight & Balance
_____ Oxygen Bottle with Mask
_____ Pencils   MANUALS
_____ Note Pads   _____ Flight
_____ Calculator   _____ Company Operations
_____ Plotter
_____ Credit Cards
_____ Telephone Inst. Cards
_____ Head Sets (2)
_____ Smoke Goggles (2)

BAGGAGE-GALLEY AREA:
_____ Tool Kit
_____ Spare Light Bulbs
_____ Jack Pads & T/R Locks
_____ Umbrellas (2)
_____ Trash Bags
_____ Baggage Straps
_____ Drinking Cups

Figure 10.8. Aircraft equipment inventory form. _Source_: AIMS, Inc., Upland, CA

tions. There are rules for how markings are to be displayed, where they are to be located, and what size they should be.

FAR Part 47 explains when aircraft registration is required and how to register the aircraft. The purpose of registration is to provide evidence of ownership or interest, control transfer from one individual to another, help establish the location of the owner in the event of problems, and help to identify the number of civil aircraft in the United States.

FAR Part 49 deals with the "Recording of Aircraft Titles and Security Documents." It explains procedures to be followed and fees charged, and defines encumbrances against aircraft or aircraft parts.

FAR Part 91 also covers maintenance requirements and large- and turbine-powered multiengine requirements. Subpart 91.217 specifies inspection programs:

(a) No person may operate a large airplane, or a turbojet, or turbopropeller powered multiengine airplane, unless the replacement times for life-limited parts specified in the aircraft data sheets or other documents approved by the administrator are complied with, and the airplane, including the airframe, engines, propellers, appliances, survival equipment, and emergency equipment is inspected in accordance with an inspection program selected under the provisions of this section.

(b) The registered owner or operator of each airplane governed by this subpart must select and must use one of the following programs for the inspection of that airplane:

1. A continuous airworthiness inspection program that is part of a continuous airworthiness maintenance program currently in use by a person holding an air carrier or commercial operator certificate under Part 121 of this chapter.

2. An approved aircraft inspection program currently in use by a person holding an ATCO certificate under Part 135 of this chapter.

3. An approved continuous inspection program currently in use by a person certificated as an Air Travel Club under Part 123 of this chapter.

4. A current inspection program recommended by the manufacturer.

5. Any other inspection program established by the registered owner or operator of that airplane and approved by the Administrator under paragraph (c) of this section.

(c) Notice of the inspection program selected shall be sent to the local FAA District Office having jurisdiction over the area in which the airplane is based. The notice must be in writing and include: 1) make, model, and serial number of the airplane; 2) registration number of the airplane; 3) the inspection program selected under paragraph (b) of this section; and 4) the name and address of the person responsible for scheduling the inspections required under the selected inspection program.

(d) The registered owner or operator may not change the inspection program for an airplane unless he has given notice thereof as provided in paragraph (c) of this section and the new program has been approved by the FAA, where appropriate.

(e) Each registered owner or operator of an airplane desiring to establish an approved inspection program under paragraph (b) (5) of this section must submit the program for approval to the local FAA District Office having jurisdiction over the area in which the airplane is based. The program must include the following information:

(1) Instructions and procedures for the conduct of inspections for the particular make and model airplane, including necessary tests and checks. The instructions and procedures must set forth in detail the parts and areas of the airplane, engines, propellers, and appliances, including emergency equipment required to be inspected.

(2) A schedule for the performance of the inspections that must be performed under the program expressed in terms of the time in service, calendar time, number of system operations, or any combination of these.

91.219 Availability of Inspection Program

Each owner or operator of an airplane shall make a copy of the inspection program selected under 91.217 available to: (a) The person responsible for the scheduling of the inspections; (b) Any person performing inspections on the airplane; and (c) Upon request, to the administrator.

FAR Parts 121 and 135 have sections that should be of interest to corporate aircraft operators dealing with maintenance, preventive maintenance and alterations, dispatch and flight release rules, and records and reports. This specifies standards governing responsibility for airworthiness, inspection programs, maintenance procedures, manual requirements, authority to perform maintenance, personnel, and so forth.

Airmen Maintenance, Schools, and Other Certified Agencies

FAR Part 65 describes the requirements for flight engineers, aircraft mechanics, and repairmen.

FAR Part 145 covers the requirements for issuing repair-station certificates. Specific ratings issued include airframes, engines, propellers, radios, instruments, and other accessories. The holder of the repair-station certificate must demonstrate that the facility has adequate space for storing equipment and materials, adequate work and assembly space, and proper ventilation, lighting, and temperature to assure that the quality of work is not impaired. Individuals working in the station must have adequate training and proper supervision.

FAR Part 147 establishes the requirements for issuing aviation maintenance technician school certificates and associated ratings and the rules governing the holders of those certificates. The three types of rating issued under this part are airframe, powerplant, and airframe and powerplant. The requirements in this regulation cover facilities, equipment and materials, instructional equipment, tools and shop equipment, and general curriculum and instructors.

Airworthiness Directives

The FAA may issue an Airworthiness Directive with respect to aircraft, aircraft engines, propellers, or appliances when unsafe conditions exist in a product and those conditions are likely to exist or develop in other products of the same type of design. The directive is designed to correct the unsafe condition. Airworthiness Directives are actually considered amendments to FAR Part 39.

Advisory Circulars

Advisory Circulars are prepared by the FAA and provide information and guidance on complying with FAA regulations. The Advisory Circular numbering system corresponds to the numerical arrangement of the FARs. Thus, for example, while FARs in the 150 category pertain to airports, related Advisory Circulars are denoted AC-150. When an Advisory Circular is referenced in a regulation, it becomes a part of the regulation and is legally binding. Advisory Circulars that are not cited in a regulation provide guidance, but their use is not mandatory. Nevertheless, the FAA often expects the aviation community to use these circulars for needed direction.

While the subjects covered in the Advisory Circulars are too numerous to elaborate on, the FAA publishes an Index (AC 00-2TT), which is updated annually. This index lists all the circulars and provides a brief summary of the contents of each.

11

Scheduling and Passenger Service

This chapter discusses the objectives as they relate to scheduling and passenger service.

PRIMARY OBJECTIVE OF A
CORPORATE FLIGHT OPERATION

The primary objective of a corporate flight operation is to provide safe, efficient, reliable, and comfortable transportation flexible enough to let corporate personnel plan their itineraries within a convenient schedule not offered by any other mode of transportation. In an earlier chapter the advantage and benefits to passengers provided by corporate airplane operation were discussed. Flexibility in scheduling permits company personnel that use the corporate aircraft to set their own schedules rather than having to abide by those of airlines. Flexibility increases employee productivity and increases access to geographically dispersed locations not served by commercial airlines.

Scheduling is part of passenger service; the schedule must fit the passenger requirements and needs. E. Tilson Peabody, former flight operations

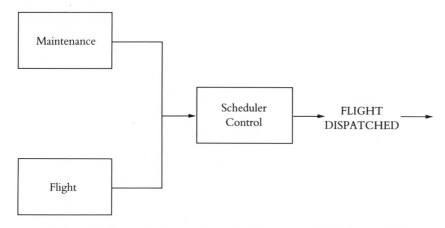

Figure 11.1. Schedule coordinating diagram. *Source*: AIMS, Inc., Upland, CA

director of General Motors, once remarked, "We fly people; we don't fly airplanes." In saying that, Peabody was expressing the thought that passengers are the first consideration in aircraft operating schedules.

In order to have an efficient, workable passenger scheduling system, coordination of schedule with flight and maintenance must take place. Figure 11.1 shows graphically how the coordination between maintenance, flight, and schedule takes place. Maintenance provides the airplanes, flight provides the crews, and the scheduler puts them together and coordinates the schedules.

SCHEDULE INPUTS

Normally four inputs are necessary to develop the passenger schedule. The inputs are:

1.   Request for the use of the company airplane
2.   In-flight services
3.   Passenger trip requirements
4.   Passenger limitations and restrictions

1. Request for the Use of the Company Airplane

This starts with the need by company personnel to travel to various destinations in the conduct of business. The request should be made through a trained scheduler or a person familiar with the activities and requirements of planning a flight, i.e., someone with knowledge of aircraft seating capacity, range of aircraft, aircraft runway requirements, aircraft speed, etc. All persons involved in requesting the airplanes must be briefed on procedures of how to provide the necessary information to the scheduler. See the list of information needed, which follows:

Date of trip
Departure time
Departure city
Destination city/cities
Number of stops
Number of passengers and their names for each leg
Passenger services required (catering, ground transport, etc.)
Name of person authorizing the trip
Date of request
Person making request
Telephone contact of person making request

The scheduler will in turn fill out the aircraft request form and after coordinating with flight and maintenance, the scheduler will provide the requester the following information:

Airplane available on requested date
Airport information
Fixed base operator to be used by crew (location, phone number etc.)
Time en route
Other pertinent information

The aircraft request form figure 11.2 can be used to give the scheduler ready sequential information relating to the trip. The person requesting the aircraft should provide the pertinent information as listed in the same type form.

Schedule and management systems. The efficient management of a corporate flight operation requires a schedule and management system that provides all the necessary tools to assist management in running an efficient and cost-effective operation. The schedule management system can be a by-hand method or a computerized program such as Aviation Analysis ADMS III Scheduling or AIMS, Inc., CAMP Systems. As the flight schedule is the heart of any flight operation, the management system must start

REQUEST FOR USE OF COMPANY AIRCRAFT   AIRCRAFT #   PASSENGERS

				PASSENGERS
DATE: 8-17-93 DEPART: ORD 07+00	TIME: 09+30 ARRIVE: ATL	DATE: DEPART:	TIME: ARRIVE:	P. Hern, A. Donnel, A. Jones, J. Peters
DATE: 8-17-93 DEPART: ATL 10+15	TIME: 11+40 ARRIVE: FLL	DATE: DEPART:	TIME: ARRIVE:	Pick up ATL United Beech J. Romeo, H. Starzek
DATE: 8-17-93 DEPART: FLL 12+30	TIME: 12+40 ARRIVE: MSY	DATE: 8-18-93 DEPART: MSY 13+00	TIME: 15+05 ARRIVE: FLL	M. McGinnes, A. Crane, R Hauser
DATE: 8-18-93 DEPART: FLL 17+00	TIME: 18+30 ARRIVE: ATL	DATE: DEPART:	TIME: ARRIVE:	P. Hern, A. Donnel, A. Jones J. Romeo, H. Starzek, McGinnes A. Crane, R. Hauser
DATE: 8-18-93 DEPART: ATL 19+15	TIME: 19+45 ARRIVE: ORD	DATE: DEPART:	TIME: ARRIVE:	P. Hern, A. Donnel, A. Jones J. Peters
DATE: DEPART: ATL	TIME: ARRIVE:	DATE: DEPART:	TIME: ARRIVE:	
DATE: DEPART: ATL	TIME: ARRIVE: FLL	DATE: DEPART:	TIME: ARRIVE:	

CATERING NEEDED According to flight release

PURPOSE OF FLIGHT Visit customer FLL Plant MSY

OK'D By: McKnight

DATE OF REQUEST: 8-15-93

REQUEST MADE BY: P. Hern

TELEPHONE CONTACT: 708-562-3500

Figure 11.2. Aircraft request form. Source: AIMS, Inc., Upland, CA

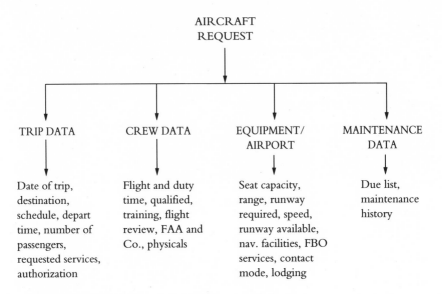

Figure 11.3. Aircraft request diagram.

with an Airplane Request—"If you don't have schedules you don't need airplanes." Figures 11.3, 11.5, 11.6, and 11.8 present a sequential format for the development of a comprehensive schedule and management system.

The information in figure 11.3 lists the essential information necessary for developing the schedule from an airplane request. The scheduling system must project for at least a month all that can be scheduled, i.e., aircraft, crews, training, physicals, vacations, line checks, proficiency checks, maintenance, etc. The schedule must provide information as depicted on a schedule board or computer printout. The schedule board or printout should at a glance provide the scheduler or anyone interested with a complete picture of all items related to availability of aircraft and crews. Requests for airplanes beyond the present month can be carried on a separate form or calendar. Figure 11.4 depicts a sample schedule board format. The availability of a crew is dependent on factors as listed in figure 11.3—duty time limitations, biennial or six month review, required FAA and company physical, and required recurrent training. The availability of the airplane is dependent on mechanical condition and major or minor maintenance requirements. Maintenance information is provided by the maintenance due list. (Figures 11.5 and 11.6 diagram flight planning and utilization statistics.)

After the scheduler has ascertained that aircraft and crew are available, the scheduler firms the flight and processes the flight release form. Figure

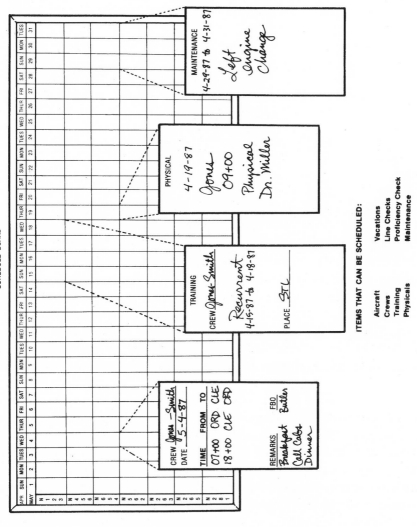

Figure 11.4. Schedule board format. *Source:* AIMS, Inc., Upland, CA

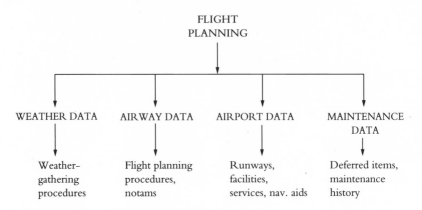

Figure 11.5.   Flight planning diagram.

11.7, the flight release form, provides the crews with all the information required to develop the flight plan.

The aircraft log book should provide all the data necessary to develop the statistical report. For work projection purposes, aircraft and engine times must be averaged.

The inputs for the cost analysis shown in figure 11.8, are the bills as they are processed for payment. The statistics information provides a means for arriving at a per-hour cost of operation. Actual cost of operation should be presented quarterly. There are a number of by-hand methods for pilot record keeping, and in the last few years a number of scheduling and management computer programs have appeared on the market. Practically all new aircraft offer computerized maintenance programs that can project all maintenance information.

Passenger service. Passenger service can be listed as one of the many advantages in the use of corporate aircraft, beginning with a planned, convenient schedule that eliminates changing airplanes at airline hubs, standing in line at ticket counters, waiting for baggage, and other hassles encountered in public air transportation modes. Corporate aviation also offers portal-to-portal transportation, which means that the passenger or passengers are assured transportation from home or office to final-destination office or hotel. The ability to depart, arrive, or change schedule as dictated by business-appointment demands is important in order to save time and cover several facilities in one day.

Below are the objectives as they relate to passenger service.

Safety as related to schedule and passenger service may be depicted by

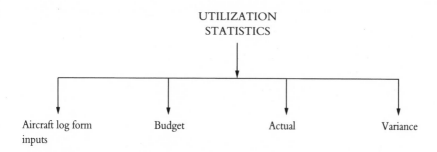

Figure 11.6.   Utilization statistics diagram.

the word *anticipation*. Every act and procedure should be coordinated and planned in such a manner as to anticipate all possible contingencies. If the possibility exists that the flight cannot be completed safely, an alternative should be provided.

Efficient utilization can be accomplished by proper scheduling and routing of the aircraft and by selecting the proper aircraft for the mission. It also means the efficient operation from the standpoint of cost. Cost control and maintenance planned to fit the schedules can contribute to a dependable and economical operation.

Reliable and predictable transport service can be accomplished by proper coordination and planning.

The passenger comfort factor was discussed in chapter 8, "Selecting the Corporate Aircraft." However, passenger comfort can be enhanced by providing the amenities that can increase the habitability of the airplane cabin. Cabin area in some of the smaller airplanes may affect comfort to a small degree, but the ability to move around the airplane and the services provided in corporate aircraft compensate for the large cabin in airline first-class service.

2. In-flight services

These are predicated on the length of the flight and the capability of the airplane cabin to accommodate all the equipment necessary for full-cabin service. Toilet and galley facilities can be limited on flights of two hours or less. But when stage hours average up to five hours, a private toilet and food-service galley are necessary. Work services provided include flight phone, dictaphone, video presentations, etc.

Entertainment services include video movies, music, playing cards,

FLIGHT RELEASE FORM

PLANE # _____   CREW: _____   DATE: _____

STATION	DATE	TIME	TERMINAL	HOTEL	FOOD	PASS. INFO. SPEC. INSTRUCTIONS
ORD to ATL	8/17	07+00	Signature Flight		Hot Breakfast	Mr. Hern 708-562-3500
ATL to FLL	8-17	10+15	United Beech		Sandwich Lunch	Request Limo FLL
FLL to MSY	8-17	12+30	AMR Combs	Holiday Inn Airport		Call Cab MSY
MSY to FLL	8-18	13+00	General Aviation		Snack	
FLL to ATL	8-18	17+00				
ATL to ORD	8-18	19+15			Hot Dinner	

It is imperative that the manager or chief pilot know the whereabouts of the crew at all times. If there are any changes in the schedule, it is mandatory that the Flight Office be contacted.
DISPATCH RELEASE _____

Figure 11.7. Flight release form. *Source:* AIMS, Inc., Upland, CA

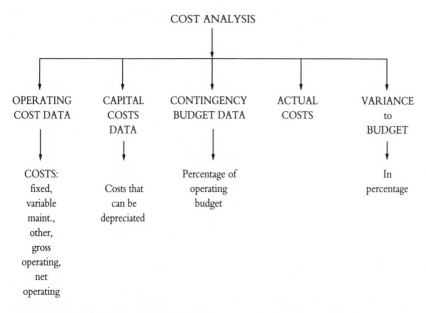

Figure 11.8.   Cost analysis diagram.

games, reading material such as newspapers and magazines. Food service should include refreshment bar, snacks, and the capability for hot meals.

Before each takeoff, passengers should be briefed through the equipment available in the airplane (be it audiotape or videotape on the safety aspects of the airplane and should be advised to study the briefing card carried in a location adjacent to the passenger seat. Figure 11.9 is a sample passenger briefing card (located near each seat).

3. Passenger Trip Requirements

These are the items that can make the passengers' itinerary go according to plan and make the trip a success. These items include portal-to-portal ground transportation to and from the airport (which should be planned), advance information to persons meeting the flight, food service planned to save time, advance information on the airport of intended landing, including expected weather. Also, in the event of a delay due to weather, air traffic control, or any other circumstance, passengers should be notified and given a revised estimated time of arrival. A form with the names of crew members, name and phone number of fixed base operator to

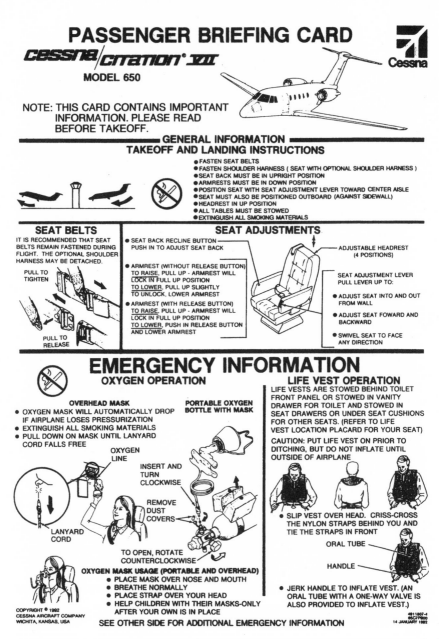

Figure 11.9. Passenger briefing card, front and back. *Source*: Cessna Aircraft Company

EMERGENCY INFORMATION
EMERGENCY EXITS
(WHEN EXITING, DO NOT TAKE ANY LUGGAGE WITH YOU)

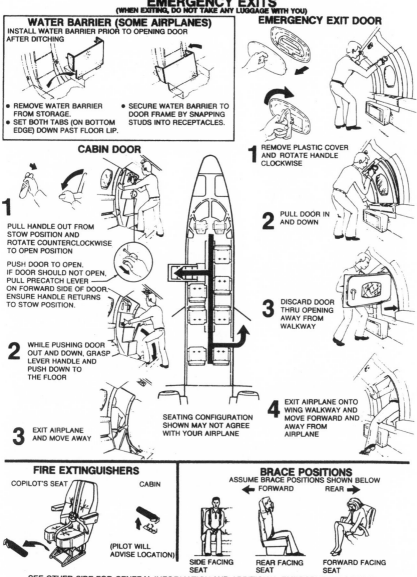

WATER BARRIER (SOME AIRPLANES)

INSTALL WATER BARRIER PRIOR TO OPENING DOOR AFTER DITCHING

- REMOVE WATER BARRIER FROM STORAGE.
- SET BOTH TABS (ON BOTTOM EDGE) DOWN PAST FLOOR LIP.
- SECURE WATER BARRIER TO DOOR FRAME BY SNAPPING STUDS INTO RECEPTACLES.

EMERGENCY EXIT DOOR

1 REMOVE PLASTIC COVER AND ROTATE HANDLE CLOCKWISE

2 PULL DOOR IN AND DOWN

3 DISCARD DOOR THRU OPENING AWAY FROM WALKWAY

4 EXIT AIRPLANE ONTO WING WALKWAY AND MOVE FORWARD AND AWAY FROM AIRPLANE

CABIN DOOR

1 PULL HANDLE OUT FROM STOW POSITION AND ROTATE COUNTERCLOCKWISE TO OPEN POSITION

PUSH DOOR TO OPEN. IF DOOR SHOULD NOT OPEN, PULL PRECATCH LEVER ON FORWARD SIDE OF DOOR. ENSURE HANDLE RETURNS TO STOW POSITION.

2 WHILE PUSHING DOOR OUT AND DOWN, GRASP LEVER HANDLE AND PUSH DOWN TO THE FLOOR

3 EXIT AIRPLANE AND MOVE AWAY

SEATING CONFIGURATION SHOWN MAY NOT AGREE WITH YOUR AIRPLANE

FIRE EXTINGUISHERS

COPILOT'S SEAT

CABIN

(PILOT WILL ADVISE LOCATION)

BRACE POSITIONS

ASSUME BRACE POSITIONS SHOWN BELOW

← FORWARD   REAR →

SIDE FACING SEAT

REAR FACING SEAT

FORWARD FACING SEAT

SEE OTHER SIDE FOR GENERAL INFORMATION AND ADDITIONAL EMERGENCY PROCEDURES

Crew Contact Form

| Captain _____ |
| First/Officer _____ |
| Hotel _____ |
| Phone # _____ |
| Pager # _____ |
| Other Info. _____ |
| FBO name & phone _____ |
| _____ |

Figure 11.10. Crew contact form.

be used, and crew contacts should be given to the passenger in charge of the flight. Figure 11.10 is a crew contact form.

4. Passenger Limitations and Restrictions

These encompass situations or conditions that may affect the safety of the airplane and its passengers or that may involve the company in legal liability.

The transportation of ill or injured passengers can be a case in point because it may require the approval of a physician for this type of passenger to travel aboard the company aircraft and the need to comply with his/her instructions as to what medical services will be required. The airplane's passenger capacity is restricted by the number of seat belts available for passengers. It would be an infraction of federal regulations if passengers were carried beyond the number of seat belts available.

Most companies restrict the number of the corporation's top managerial personnel that can travel together in the company airplane or on the airlines. This restriction is usually in the form of an "air travel restriction policy."

FAA regulations state that, except in an emergency, no pilot of a civil aircraft may allow a person who is obviously under the influence of intoxicating liquors or drugs (except a medical patient under proper care) to be carried in an aircraft.

Passenger and baggage weights should not be such that the takeoff weight and center of gravity is exceeded beyond the permissible limits as specified by the airplane flight manuals.

COMPANY NAME
PASSENGER MANIFEST

Trip No.   Date   From ORD, ATL, FLL, MSY, FLL, ATL, ORD

PROPOSED PAX LIST		( ) Check	
		Boarded	Deleted
1	P. Hern ORD–FLL–ORD		
2	A. Donnel ORD–FLL–ORD		
3	A. Jones ORD–FLL–ORD		
4	J. Peters ORD–FLL–ORD		
5	J. Romeo ATL–FLL–ATL		
6	H. Starzek ATL–FLL–ATL		
7	M. McGinnes FLL–MSY–FLL		
8	A. Crane FLL–MSY–FLL		
9	R. Hauser FLL–MSY–FLL		
10			
Substitutions			

Figure 11.11. Passenger manifest form. *Source*: AIMS, Inc., Upland, CA

As a rule, most operations permit a passenger to observe cockpit procedures from the companionway but restrict anyone other than authorized persons from occupying a pilot seat while the aircraft is in flight.

Unauthorized materials that are classified as hazardous or dangerous by the Department of Transportation and in the Code of Federal Regulations (CFR-49) should not be carried aboard a company airplane as the materials may pose a risk to the safety and health of passengers.

Smuggled and contraband articles are prohibited by federal law from being transported into the United States. Persons knowingly involved in such violation are subject to penalties and aircraft confiscation.

Passenger manifest. The importance of knowing what passengers are in the airplane is obvious. The passenger manifest form should be attached to the flight release form listing the number and name of all passengers that are to be boarded. It is the responsibility of the captain to check to see if the names and number of passengers boarding coincide with the scheduler's list. Any changes in passenger boarding at base or away from base must be made known to the schedule department.

A method of calling schedule or leaving a passenger manifest form with the FBO or other reliable agency is imperative information in knowing who is on board every flight. Figure 11.11 is a sample passenger manifest form that provides a proposed passenger list. Substitutions can be entered at the bottom of the page.

12

Corporate Aviation Safety

This chapter discusses why a flight department manager or chief pilot must be aware of the consequences of an accident, and how management must recognize the contributing elements that can cause accidents and find the means for the successful implementation of accident prevention.

Much attention is given to aviation safety in one way or another, yet accidents continue to occur. Are we guilty of trying to eliminate the disease without first treating the symptoms? Safety has to be the primary objective of every employee in a flight operation, because every activity and function has a direct relationship to safety. Likewise, it is essential that management integrate a holistic* approach to safety in the air, as well as on the ground. The goal is the complete elimination of accidents.

Accidents don't just happen; they manifest themselves from a sequence of minor incidents. The causes of accidents are many. Accidents have resulted from such varied situations as poor operational actions, switching on the wrong fuel tank, tuning to the wrong frequency, fueling the aircraft with the wrong fuel, a bolt left unsafetied, improper part installation, poor pilot-copilot coordination, lack of altitude awareness, etc.

*Holistic: The theory that whole entities of reality have an existence greater than the mere sum of their parts.

The National Transportation Safety Board (NTSB) statistics for the last ten years have indicated that general aviation flying has become safer. The 1,956 accidents that were classified as general aviation (not operated under Parts 121 or 135) in 1992 represented the lowest number recorded since NTSB began compiling aviation accident records in 1967.

Although the number of accidents resulting in deaths decreased, the actual number of fatalities increased. A total of 814 persons lost their lives in 408 fatal general aviation accidents in 1992, compared with 746 deaths in 414 fatal crashes in 1991. Two of the deaths occurred on the ground in 1992, compared with 6 in 1991. All told, there were 2,143 general aviation accidents in 1991.

The NTSB used the revised FAA estimate of 27,190,000 general aviation hours flown to reach its figures of 7.19 accidents per 100,000 aircraft hours flown, and 1.5 fatal accidents per 100,000 hours for 1992. The 1991 figures were 7.87 and 1.52, respectively, but the number of hours flown was higher at 27,226,000.

The 1992 statistics released by the NTSB show fewer people killed in commuter aviation accidents, and the number of persons who died in accidents involving Part 121 carriers dropped to its lowest level since 1986. Overall, 951 people lost their lives in 2,105 aviation accidents either in the United States or in accidents involving United States–registered civil aircraft. There were 7 fatal commuter aviation accidents in 1992 compared to 8 in 1991. The number of fatalities aboard commuter airplanes dropped to 21 in 1992 from 77 in 1991.

Part 121 carriers registered only four fatal accidents and 33 deaths in 1992 compared with the same number of accidents and 49 deaths the year before. Air taxis accounted for 74 accidents and 66 fatalities in 1992 compared to 88 accidents and 73 fatalities in 1991. The air taxi crashes constituted the fewest since NTSB began compiling air taxi records in 1975.

Considering that corporate aviation operates in an environment that is more conducive to accidents vis-à-vis the air carriers, the accident rate of corporate aviation is consistently better than general aviation and very closely rivals the airlines.

Corporate pilots do not have the operational support that their airline counterparts enjoy. They are their own dispatchers and their own weather guessers; they often have to fly unknown routes and land at airports that they have never seen before. Airline pilots are in constant contact with their companies and can receive advice or help any time they need it.

Corporate pilots have to rely on their own judgment and make their own decisions.

Management must recognize contributing elements to an effective safety program such as:

Employee/management relations (respectful and fair treatment of personnel)

Personnel morale (maintain confidence, cheerfulness, discipline)

Duty/flight time schedules (do not exceed duty/flight time limitations)

Financial planning, etc. (capital resources to achieve safety goals)

The holistic approach to aviation safety requires that the flight operation manager or chief pilot be conscious of the consequences of an accident. Further, it must be instilled in each employee that errors will not be tolerated.

Remember, if low safety standards are tolerated, people will work toward that standard. Consider three consequence "arousers":

1. *Cost-benefit.* Here, safety is related to cost efficiency, or the cost of a comprehensive maintenance program versus the cost of a maintenance-induced accident. In other words, does the potential loss of a human hand warrant the installation of a safety device on the company's bandsaw? Cost-benefit is the potential use of capital resources to achieve certain safety goals whose benefits outweigh the cost of an accident.

2. *Human life value.* Human life value varies with different societies. Consequently, the acceptance of fatalities varies from society to society. Human life value also varies with a person's level in society and earning power, an unfortunate twist of values. Nevertheless, it still appears to be true.

All financial and human loss consequences of an accident must be considered, plus the fact that insurance premiums are adjusted to liability settlements. That is a statistical fact. But, how do you measure the loss of a human life to a loving family or to a company? Consider that the injury or death may irrevocably affect the company's functioning, to say nothing of the family's. And what bearing will the accident have on the acceptance of similar mishaps in the future? A case in point is the space shuttle tragedy, which shut down America's shuttle program after seven astronauts perished. That same year, over 300 persons died in airline accidents, but the airlines continued to fly.

3. *Inculcate in employees a positive attitude toward safety.* The holistic approach says that every activity and function has a bearing on safety. There-

fore, every person involved with the performance of those functions and activities must be made to appreciate how valuable their contributions are. Their presence has a direct impact on safety, both for the operation and the safety of the aircraft and people involved.

It can be said that humans possess self-destructive behavior. The proof is everywhere, from high-wire walkers to everyday drivers on the highway. Conversely, we also possess a self-preservation instinct or mode of behavior that reduces the potential for self-inflicted harm. With his or her built-in instincts, humans can control some risks. The question is, under what conditions will the self preservation instinct prevail vis-à-vis destructive behavior? The probability is that surrounding circumstances can control the instinct or behavior of each individual. For that reason, management has to be aware of each individual's behavior pattern and act according to it.

Accident Vocabulary

When referring to accidents, the words that most frequently arise are safety, safe, risk, danger, hazard, and luck. The six words must be defined and distinguished in order to explain adequately the required tasks necessary for the successful implementation of accident prevention.

1. Safety: Maximum freedom from injury or risk. *Safety* is an abstract idea at best. It has no quantitative meaning for employees. How would you differentiate between too much safety and too little safety? The term *safety* cannot mean total freedom from injury or risk as there is no such thing.

2. Safe: Secure from liability to injury or risk. Consider that a pilot reduces the liability to injury or risk if he or she abides by safe operational practices and procedures. Likewise, a baseball player is safe on base as long as he remains there, while his moving away from base makes him liable to be tagged.

3. Risk: Exposure to the chance of injury or loss. *Risk* implies that *exposure* to injury or loss is ever present. The *chance* implies that the exposure can be controlled or managed.

4. Danger: Liability to harm or injury. The possibility exists that harm or injury may result in the execution of a *dangerous* exercise.

5. Hazard: Something that causes danger. There is an element of hazard in the flying of an aircraft or in the lighting of a gas grill.

6. Luck: The force that seems to operate for good or ill in one's life.

When a star basketball player shoots ten consecutive baskets in a game, few would call that luck. However, if a novice were to accomplish the same thing, it would certainly be called *luck*. In the same vein, if a novice pilot has an accident and survives, it is luck. But if a professional pilot has an accident, he or she survives because of his or her skill. Is there a relationship between skill, chance, and tolerance for error? (See Daniel C. Dennett, *Elbow Room* [Cambridge: MIT, 1984].)

In distinguishing the six definitions, it is found that risk has a relative value that can be identified, evaluated, managed, and controlled. Therefore, for operational purposes, *risk management* is a term that can be rationally accepted. (See Jerome Lederer, "Economics and Air Safety," *Flight Safety Foundation Safety Digest* [May 1987].)

Risk management is the control of risk through the application of skill, knowledge, and sound operational practices. The skill necessary to achieve the reduction of the hazard is acquired through study, practice, and experience. Knowledge is possessing and understanding all operational functions. Sound operational practices are those strategies that have been proven effective in reducing risk. When instituted, these practices result in the acceptable reduction of a given hazard.

In order to organize for risk management, two types of accidents must be considered by management: 1) the industrial-type accident, and 2) the accident that occurs during the operation of an aircraft. In an industrial-type accident, a person might be injured or perhaps killed in the workplace in the performance of duties. In yet another case, equipment might be damaged while it is being worked on. Witness these cases:

The injury to an individual who fell off a ladder might have been the result of a poor ladder or the ladder not being properly positioned. A mechanic was crushed to death when attempting to repair the landing-gear system on an airplane without first jacking the airplane. The gear retracted, killing the mechanic and damaging the airplane. Another case involved an airplane jacking operation in which the jack was misplaced, which caused it to go through the wing.

Once the aircraft leaves the chocks, an accident that occurs during the operation of the aircraft becomes the responsibility of the pilot. Again, accidents are the result of multiple incidents that occur in a sequential manner to produce the eventual mishap. "Accidents don't just happen, they manifest themselves in a series of incidents." Any number of accident reports will attest to the validity of this statement. For example, there was a taxi accident where a pilot shut down the engines and relied on the accumulator

pressure for brakes. Unfortunately, lack of pressure in the accumulator resulted in the airplane's colliding with a fuel truck.

It should be noted that many accidents are maintenance induced,
e.g., the Japan Airlines Boeing 747 that was lost due to incorrect pressure-
dome repair.[1] The pressure-dome repair was necessary because a previous
tail-dragging accident had damaged the pressure-dome. An American
Airlines DC-10 crashed in Chicago in 1979 as a result of the left engine's
becoming loose from its mount and dropping onto the runway. The loss
of hydraulic pressure on the left side of the aircraft created an asymmet-
rical control condition that the pilot could not cope with. It can be seen
from the actual accidents how the sequential series of incidents can cause
accidents.

The three elements in risk management are:

1. The human element
2. The element of anticipation
3. The operational element

1. THE HUMAN ELEMENT

The majority of accidents are attributed to the human element, and
rightly so. By virtue of human psychological makeup, there are many factors that are bound to affect employee performance. The figure 12.1 matrix indicates the human element areas to be considered.

A. The psychological element encompasses two human behavior areas.
1) management must accept the responsibility for minimizing risk situations, as well as nurturing the employee's self-preservation instinct; and
2) each person must learn to identify his or her own psychological behavior patterns, in order to control those tendencies that are potentially
dangerous—compulsion, complacency, carelessness, incompetence, inatten-
tion, haste, etc.

B. Ergonomics: The interface of man and machine. And what of the interface
of man and machine? Ergonomics, as it relates to our discussion of risk management in aviation states that an aircraft, its flight characteristics, and operating systems should not increase the normal accident-risk potential. Management should therefore be confident that operating systems and cockpit
configuration are state-of-the-art. They should also be easy to operate, easy
to understand, and as similar as possible to other airplanes operated by the
company.

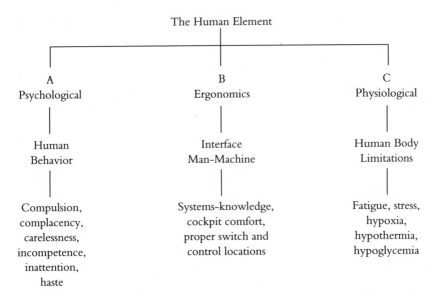

Figure 12.1. Human elements matrix. *Source*: AIMS, Inc., Upland, CA

C. Physiological human body limitations. The human body is limited to deviations from the normal environment: 1) Fatigue and stress compounded by lack of nutritious food can cause degraded pilot performance. 2) Hypoxia, the inadequate amount of oxygen, is incapacitating and is conducive to headaches, loss of consciousness, and fatigue. 3) Hypothermia is an abnormal drop in body temperature below the normal 98.6 degrees F. A person becomes confused and uncoordinated. If the body temperature drops below a level of around 80 degrees, a person may die. 4) Hypoglycemia is the indication of an inadequate level of glucose in the body. It can cause faintness, weakness, and nervousness, among other symptoms. The above conditions must be "self-recognizable" by the pilot; however, management must be aware of these situations and prevent working conditions or schedules that can cause a deviation from normal body limitations.

2. THE ELEMENT OF ANTICIPATION

If every act and procedure could be planned so that all possible risks would be anticipated, then once a problem arose, an alternate plan to meet all possible contingencies could be constructed. A safe alternative to the problem would be provided or the flight would be canceled. By this definition, anticipation becomes a functional part of risk management.

3. The Operational Element

The operational element is in coordination with the human element to implement a program that will diagram an airplane's flight. Starting with the flight schedule, the plan flows through the whole flight and is concluded when chocks are in place and paperwork completed.

Operational areas that require risk management attention:

Hangar and shops
A.   Hangar cleanliness
B.   Stands and ladders
C.   Flammable liquids
D.   Fire prevention
E.   Shop machine safety guards and glasses
F.   Aircraft towing procedures
G.   Markings for position of safety equipment
H.   Condition of rolling stock

At the ramp
A.   Passenger boarding, deplaning, and emergency evacuation.
B.   Safety of vehicles around aircraft
C.   Ramp personnel, pilot coordination, and signals
D.   Proper positioning of aircraft
E.   Safety of personnel in aircraft circle
F.   Removing baggage and cargo
G.   Clear engines for starting

Taxi and take-off procedures
A.   Alert to taxi instructions
B.   Proper taxi procedures
C.   Alert to take-off instructions
D.   Proper take-off procedures

Flight
A.   Proper rest, mental, and physical condition
B.   Crew qualifications and current physical
C.   Adequate schedule and passenger information

D.   Aircraft mechanical condition
E.   Proper weather briefing
F.   Proper flight planning
G.   Required fuel quantity
H.   Crew coordination
I.   Abide by standard operating procedures
J.   Attention to passenger requirements

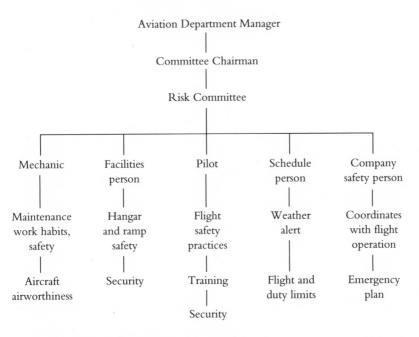

Figure 12.2. Risk management committee.

In order to involve every department in risk management, a committee must be formed. The risk-management committee should include the persons as presented in the following matrix (figure 12.2).

The objective of a risk-management program is to establish the groundwork for action that will prevent and eventually eliminate accidents. Every person in the organization must be involved in the risk program.

The four basic elements of a risk management program are:

1.   Education
2.   Communication
3.   Inspection
4.   Investigation and prevention

1. EDUCATION

The purpose of the education element of risk management is to teach aviation department personnel methods for identifying accident-causing factors, increase personnel awareness of such factors, and condition people to think risk prevention.

2. COMMUNICATION

From the communication standpoint, operational information for risk management should be networked among all departments as well as aircraft manufacturers, the Flight Safety Foundation, and the United States National Transportation Safety Board. Flight Safety, as well as crew and maintenance safety, literature should be made available to all personnel. The risk committee is the forum for planning all risk-management requirements.

3. INSPECTION

The inspection element of a risk program includes continual review of all operations and inspection of all facilities to determine if they meet Occupational Safety and Health Administration (OSHA) and company safety requirements. All employees will be encouraged to report problem areas for corrective measures. The reports should use the following format:

A.   Gather data and information
B.   Analyze data
C.   Define the problem
D.   Draw conclusions
E.   Develop recommendations
F.   Follow corrections

4. INVESTIGATION AND PREVENTION

The purpose of accident and incident investigation is to determine causal factors and then attempt to prevent a recurrence. This investigation

procedure should be used solely for the purpose of enhancing risk management and not for disciplinary action toward individuals. It must be kept in
mind that risk management is largely dependent upon human judgments
and reactions. Consequently, people are the driving force behind any risk-
management effort. In fact, they are the *paramount* factor in any risk-management program. When all else fails, it is people who must compensate.
Human performance is really the controlling factor in risk management.
Ironically, human performance presents the most difficulty because it cannot be predicted, nor can it be programmed to be fail-safe with duplication
or even triplication.

NOTE

1. Excerpts from safety bulletins, 1988 to 1993, Flight Safety Foundation, Inc., 2200 Wilson Blvd., Arlington, VA 22201.

13

Corporate Aviation Security

The objective of this chapter is to impress upon the aviation department manager the need for a precautionary security program, as well as to present methods for setting up a precautionary security program for a corporate flight operation.

SECURITY AWARENESS

Humans, not being predators by nature, are likely to be the most trusting of all species—the least likely to be suspicious. The secure feeling prevails and most of the time we are *complacent* because we know that nothing is going to happen as the security system is adequate. Only when an incursion occurs are we aroused to consider security measures.

Everyone involved in the transportation scheme has to be aware of the security risks that surround all activities. The average aviation person does not feel he/she will ever be involved in a security matter and thus cannot effectively become interested in a *precautionary program*. It is of paramount importance to establish awareness of security needs. Everyone in a flight

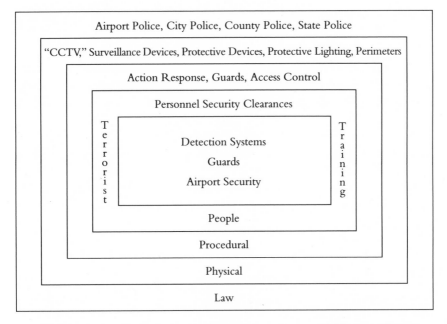

Figure 13.1. Strategy for a security program. *Source*: AIMS, Inc., Upland, CA

operation must change the complacency that exists at all levels when it comes to security matters.

Until now, terrorist activity directed at general aviation has failed to materialize as predicted by experts. Corporate aviation with no orderly schedule, changes of itineraries, and low-profile identification has a built-in security factor. An executive is more prone to security risk while being chauffeured to the airport than when being flown in the corporate aircraft. Vandalism and theft have been the largest threat to corporate aircraft.

STRATEGY

Security is not provided by one or two measures but by a combination of measures that provide in-depth security and that pose the intruder considerable difficulty.[1] Figure 13.1 proposes a strategy that may be used in developing a precautionary security program.

Precautionary Security Program

Although the probability of a security emergency in corporate aviation is quite remote, having a *precautionary security program* is essential to insure awareness and preparation for the possibility of such an incident's occurring. A precautionary security program must include standards and recommended practices that can make security function effectively.

The first consideration when contemplating a security program should be the exposure to security intrusion incidents. The development of preventive measures hinges on the exposure potential that a particular operation may encounter.[2] In order to prevent security lapses, the service that the aviation department offers to company personnel must be portal-to-portal transportation.

Security Chain of Events

The exposure areas encompass the whole operation, starting from the time the passengers leave home or office to the time they arrive at their final destination.[3] Everyone involved in the transportation scheme has to know that a security program is in effect and has to be aware of the security risks that surround activities, starting with passenger pick-up and following the chain of events to the final destination, as depicted in the flow chart figure 13.2.

Crew trip security is controlled by the conditions that surround the hangaring or parking of the aircraft. If the aircraft is hangared or parked with a fixed base operator, the FBO must have adequate hangar area security that will protect his/her customers in the areas that the FBO controls. If the corporate operator has his/her own hangar, it is the responsibility of the operator to develop and implement a security program that will fit operational requirements.

In any case, trip security starts with crew arrival at the hangar area entrance gate, going through the chain of events to check that the airplane has not been tampered with, followed by the exterior and interior preflight inspection, with emphasis on wheel wells, engine intakes, and any opening that could be accessible to unauthorized persons. All services—fueling, maintenance, and cabin service—should be supervised by a crew member.

At the ramp, the main cabin door should be locked any time that authorized persons do not require access. When the main cabin door is open

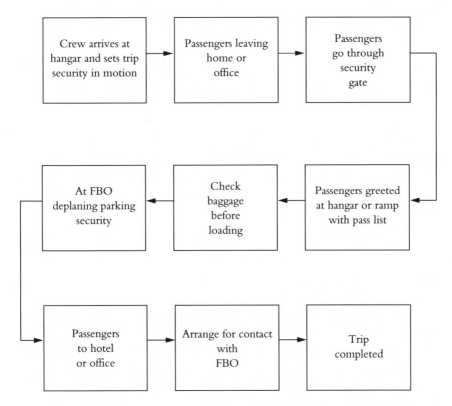

Figure 13.2. Security chain of events. *Source*: AIMS, Inc., Upland, CA

prior to passenger boarding, a no admittance sign and chain should be placed across the steps.

Passengers leaving home or office should be monitored in order to be informed as to the person or persons who are going to chauffeur them to the airport. Passengers should have the names and check the ID cards of the chauffeurs to preclude the risk of kidnapping by change of drivers. From time to time, routes between home, office, and airport should be changed. Knowing which passengers are driving their own cars to the airport is important in order to permit their access to the airplane and to park their cars in a secure location identified by code rather than by name.

Passengers going through a security gate should be identified by the guard. If there is an electronic gate in lieu of a guard, passengers should be iden- tified by the person controlling the gate.

Passengers greeted at hangar or ramp should be verified against the passenger list.

Checking baggage before loading is important, especially if the baggage is sent ahead of passengers. Baggage should never be loaded until it has been positively identified. Packages or parcels should be identified by the sender or person knowledgeable as to the contents.

At FBO, deplaning and parking security means one of the crew members should deplane first, not only from the standpoint of security but also from the safety standpoint, to guide the passengers in the proper direction. After the passengers have departed, the airplane should either be hangared or parked in a well-lighted, secure open area so the aircraft or anyone approaching the aircraft may be seen.

Passengers going to hotel or office should be anticipated, if possible, and arrangements made for their transportation. The transportation company and drivers should be known to the flight operation, the passengers, or the FBO. The captain should inform the passengers of his or her whereabouts by means of a preprinted card.

Arrange for contact with FBO as to where the crew will be billeted, including provision of telephone numbers.

Corporate aircraft operators have to consider four items in the process of developing precautionary measures to avert a possible incursion into the protected area:

1.   Exposure
2.   Precautions
3.   Protection
4.   Training

1. Exposure

Company personnel, equipment, and facilities are exposed to kidnappers, hijackers, bombers, and extortionists. The methods and motives of those persons should be studied in an attempt to anticipate their tactics and to develop the necessary safeguards. The limousine, airplane, hangar, and ramp parking area are exposed to possible incursions. How incursions could occur are assumptions for consideration. The following "Exposure Awareness Conditioning" matrix (figure 13.3) should be posted on the bulletin board as a reminder of exposure possibilities.

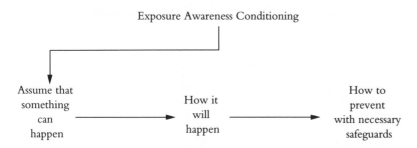

Figure 13.3. Exposure awareness conditioning. *Source*: AIMS, Inc., Upland, CA

In today's environment it is imperative that all crew members and Aviation Department employees be constantly alert to and guard against any situation that might be conducive to acts affecting the security of the aircraft and passengers.

Examples:

1.   Failure to close aircraft door(s)
2.   Parking in dark, remote areas of the airport
3.   Permitting unauthorized persons on board the aircraft
4.   Failure to properly identify luggage and cargo
5.   Failure to conduct thorough preflights of all compartments, gear wells, etc., for foreign objects
6.   Failure to properly identify passengers, checking them against the passenger manifest
7.   Improper security in the hangar, main entrance, and all doors leading to hangar floor
8.   Poor security of hangar complex periphery, such as ramp, entrance gate, etc.

2. PRECAUTIONS

There are a large number of flight departments that have instituted security programs, but there are others that refuse to believe that they could be targets and don't think precautions are necessary. Lax security not only invites intruders and thieves but also violates Federal Aviation Regulation Part 107, which governs airport security.

The first precautionary security line of defense is privacy and anonymity. Ostentation begets attraction, which points intruders to high-priority targets that may be worthwhile attacking, kidnapping, or robbing.

Checking the credentials of anyone entering the hangar and ramp areas should be a routine procedure, and verification of passengers and baggage control is necessary to ascertain that each bag or package belongs in the airplane. In a remain-overnight trip (RON) the crew should check its aircraft every day. Avoiding hazardous situations and using reasonable precautions can reduce security risks.

3. PROTECTION

The precautionary security program must include procedures, regulations, protective anti-intrusion systems, and security-aware employees.

The procedures must not only include precautionary instructions but also ways to cope in the event of trouble. Regulations and procedures must be written to fit the operational requirements of each section considering geographical areas covered by the flight operation.

An anti-intrusion system is necessary for the protection of the hangar area and to identify and monitor possible intruders. A silent-alarm protective system should be considered to provide a means of warning to crew members from a distance of any breach in aircraft security.

4. TRAINING

Increased emphasis is being placed on electronic detection equipment and anti-intrusion systems, but the human element is still the most critical factor. Training is of major importance not only to develop awareness and eliminate complacency but also to develop and implement workable procedures that are less susceptible to security threats.

FAA regulations that apply to security are: FAR Part 107, which provides for passenger security rules as documented in a security program and applies to air carrier airports. Security requirements for airports served by small air carrier aircraft are defined in FAR Part 108. The security program is designed to protect passengers from acts of violence and aircraft piracy.

NOTES

1. Pat Howgill, *Airport Security Operations* (London: Sterling Publications, 1992).

2. Benjamin Netanyahu, *Terrorism: How the West Can Win* (New York: Farrar, Straus & Giroux, 1984).

3. Excerpts from Management Aids, National Business Aircraft Association, Inc., Washington, DC.

14

Emergency and Pre-accident Plans

This chapter explains the reason why every flight operation should have comprehensive emergency and pre-accident plans to eliminate chaos, delineate responsibility, and provide set procedures should an emergency or accident occur.[1]

Emergency definition. "An Emergency is a sudden unforeseen occurrence or incident requiring immediate action." An emergency can be comprised of incidents or accidents that require immediate attention in an organized sequential manner. Examples are: fire, fuel spill, employee accidents, damage to equipment, damage or work stoppage due to weather, security incursions, aircraft air accidents.

Reason for emergency and pre-accident plans. It is imperative that every flight operation have plans that employees can follow in the event of an emergency. Emergency and pre-accident plans present forms and methods for coping with emergencies that require immediate response. The forms outline the methods of planned response and how to proceed with required reporting.

Emergency plan distribution. The emergency plan should be part of the operations manual, but it should also be published as a separate document to be posted in conspicuous areas and distributed to safety committee members as well as all involved supervisors. All department personnel should be familiar with the plan. Individuals on the immediate and secondary response lists should have a current copy at home. The plan should be reviewed and updated on a regular basis.

Purpose of emergency plan. The plan is a checklist to be used in conjunction with the airport's emergency plan and the company's pre-accident plan. The plan is written to outline the actions to be taken by company personnel in the event of an incident or emergency within the area of responsibility of the company Flight Operations.

The Action Plan is to be used in coordination with the airport emergency plan and the company's pre-accident plan.

Be familiar with the plan!

Use *pencil* to record names and phone numbers.

KEEP THIS PLAN IN PLAIN VIEW

Remember, there is no substitute for good judgment.

Immediate Response

The individual noting the emergency is responsible for:

1.   Notifying Airport Operations #_____

                                                        or

    Notifying Central Dispatch #_____

                                                         or

    Local Emergency Dispatch Center.

2.   Take immediate action to prevent further damage or injury.

3.   Only after the emergency has been satisfactorily controlled, proceed with *Secondary Response Action.*

Secondary Response

The individual on the scene of the emergency is responsible for initiating communication with company Flight Department management and acting as coordinator until management personnel arrive.

All contacts are to be made in accordance with the following sequence:

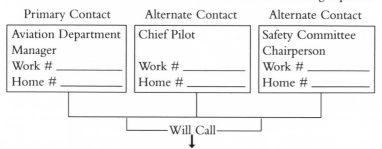

Primary Contact	Alternate Contact	Alternate Contact
Aviation Department Manager Work # _____ Home # _____	Chief Pilot Work # _____ Home # _____	Safety Committee Chairperson Work # _____ Home # _____

——Will Call——

Executive in Charge of Flight Operations

Work #_____   NTSB #_____

Home #_____   FAA #_____

Public Relations	Insurance	Legal Dept.
Work #_____	Work #_____	Work #_____
Home #_____	Home #_____	Home #_____

The following is a ready reference list of Emergency contacts which may be useful in an Emergency.

Additional Assistance Phone Numbers

Phone numbers checked on: (date)_____

Fire Departments

#_____   #_____

#_____   #_____

#_____   #_____

Ambulance Departments

#_____   #_____

#_____   #_____

Pre-accident plan. The pre-accident plan uses the emergency action plan format, but it goes beyond the geographical area of the flight operations responsibility. The pre-accident plan is mainly concerned with aircraft accidents. It outlines reporting procedures to company management and government agencies and the use of forms provided for that purpose.

Organizing procedures to be put into effect by manager, chief pilot, or safety committee when an accident occurs
1.   Responsibility and authority
2.   Medical assistance
3.   Guarding the wreckage
4.   Inform top corporate executive with the latest status report.
5.   Photographic coverage
6.   Locating witnesses

7.   Maintenance will proceed to accident site or dispatch mechanic to provide pertinent information regarding state of aircraft.

8.   Manager or chief pilot will assemble all flight records, training records, and other information that the government agencies may require. Records to be released only to authorized persons or agencies.

9.   Maintenance will assemble all maintenance records, log book forms, all maintenance records of maintenance performed by outside contractors. Records to be released only to authorized persons or agencies.

10.   All personnel in the aviation department will cooperate with government agencies assigned to the investigation.

11.   Maintenance will prepare a repair and recovery plan to be submitted to the manager or chief pilot.

12.   Members of the aviation department will confine statements regarding the incident/accident to the proper agencies only.

13.   The Safety Committee will proceed with the accident investigation.

Company Incident and Damaged Airplane Report Form

1.   Location of accident:_____
2.   Pilot-in-command:_____
3.   Second-in-command:_____
4.   Type airplane and registration #: _____
5.   Date and time damage occurred: _____
6.   Location of crew and passengers and all necessary phone numbers
7.   Location of airplane when damaged
      Ground: _____
      Air: _____
8.   How was airplane damaged (taxi, weather, hail, etc.)?
9.   Give brief description of events leading to damage.
10.   Give as much detail describing damage to airplane, engines, and equipment.
11.   Was all equipment operating properly?
12.   Did crew or passengers sustain any injuries? (Give names.)
13.   Names of any other persons involved in accident
14.   Damage to other property
15.   Names of witnesses, if any

Handling the Media, What Information to Give
      Do give:
            Routing and takeoff time (if available)

Type of aircraft
Number of seats
Number of crew
Destination
How to reach company Public Relations people
Other information to authorities only—NTSB, FAA
Do not:
Speculate on cause of accident
Identify passengers or crew
Comment on any other accidents of company
Identify next of kin
The sources of information:
Local police
State police
FAA
Air Traffic Control
At the scene:
Identify yourself as member of the company
Require credentials
Don't touch anything[2]

Accident response variables. The immediate response to a reported emergency has to be identical whether the emergency is at the airport or outside the airport or whether there are fatalities or no fatalities. The accident circumstances dictate the procedures to be used after the secondary response is initiated.

Emergency Phases
Phase I
Nonfatal airport accident
Phase II
Fatal airport accident
Phase III
Nonfatal outside of airport accident
Phase IV
Fatal outside of airport accident

Decide what phase the emergency is classified in:

I.	Proceed with immediate response and secondary response contacts.	Secure: description of trouble crash location pilots intentions

injuries if any
Contact tower and
request permission
to proceed to
accident site.
Contact company
medical department
and follow
instructions.

II.   Proceed with
immediate response
and secondary response
contacts.
Secure: description of
trouble
crash location
injuries
Contact company
medical department;
advise and take
instructions.
Contact tower and
proceed to crash site.

III.   Proceed with
immediate response

and secondary response
contacts.
Secure: crash location
from authorities at
crash site; get
description of
trouble; learn pilots'
intentions; find out
about injuries, if
any; use grid map to
locate crash site;
contact company
medical department.

IV.   Proceed with
immediate response and
secondary response
contacts.
Contact company
medical department.
Secure: crash location
from authorities at
crash site; use grid
map to locate crash
site; contact involved
company personnel.

Most municipal airports have special requirements for allowing an outside ambulance on the airport. Those requirements should be part of the pre-accident plan. The company aviation department manager or safety committee must comply with NTSB and FAA accident reporting requirements and instructions as specified in the summary section of this chapter.

Federal government requirements. The independent National Transportation Safety Board (NTSB) began operating on April 1, 1975. The primary function of the NTSB is to promote safety in transportation. The following discussion will focus upon the role of the NTSB in aviation safety and aircraft accident investigation.

The rules pertaining to aircraft accidents are published by the National Transportation Safety Board and are contained in Safety Investigation Regulations, in Part 830. They are published, in part, in the *Airman's Information Manual.*

Part 821, "Rules of Practice in Air Safety Proceedings," governs all air safety enforcement proceedings before a law judge involving a review or appeal of an action by the FAA Administrator and upon appeal to the board (NTSB) from any order or decision of a law judge.

Part 830 is "Notification and Reporting of Aircraft Accidents or Incidents and Overdue Aircraft, and the Preservation of Aircraft Wreckage, Mail, Cargo, and Records."

Part 831 is "Aircraft Accidents/Incident Investigation Procedures."

Definition of pertinent terms (NTSB Part 830)

A.   "Aircraft accident" means an occurrence associated with the operation of an aircraft which takes place between the time any person boards the aircraft with the intention of flight until such time as all such persons have disembarked, and in which any person suffers death or serious injury as a result of being in or upon the aircraft or by direct contact with the aircraft or anything attached thereto, or in which the aircraft received substantial damage.

B.   Substantial damage:

1.   Except as provided in subparagraph (2) of this section (B), substantial damage means damage or structural failure which adversely affects the structural strength, performance, or flight characteristics of the aircraft, and which would normally require major repair or replacement of the affected component.

2.   Engine failure, damage limited to an engine, bent fairings or cowling, dented skin, small punctured holes in the skin or fabric, ground damage to rotor or propeller blades, damage to landing gear, wheels, tires, flaps, engine accessories, brakes, or wingtips are NOT considered "substantial damage" for the purpose of this part.

Reporting requirements—general (NTSB)

A.   Any "Aircraft Accident" as defined above will require NTSB notification.

B.   Minor accidents or incidents wherein there is not "Substantial Damage" as defined above, nor any fatal or serious injury will not require NTSB notification.

C.   The operator of an aircraft shall immediately, and by the most expeditious means available, notify the nearest National Transportation Safety Board, Bureau of Aviation Safety Field Office, if reporting is required.

D.   The notification required above shall contain the following information, if available:

1.   Type, nationality, and registration marks of the aircraft
2.   Names of owner and operator of the aircraft
3.   Name of pilot-in-command
4.   Date and time of the accident
5.   Last point of departure and point of intended landing of the aircraft
6.   Position of the aircraft with reference to some easily de-fined geographical point
7.   Number of persons aboard, number of fatalities and number seriously injured
8.   Nature of the accident, the weather and the extent of damage to the aircraft, so far as is known
9.   A description of any explosives, radioactive materials, or other dangerous articles carried

Manner of notification. The most expeditious method of notification to the National Transportation Safety Board by the operator will be deter-mined by the circumstances existing at that time. The National Transpor-tation Safety Board has advised that any of the following would be consid-ered examples of the type of notification that would be acceptable:

A.   Direct telephone notification
B.   Telegraphic notification
C.   Notification to the Federal Aviation Administration which would in turn notify the NTSB by direct communication, i.e., dispatch or telephone

Note: Flight Operations conducting flights in foreign countries should have their crews become acquainted with accident or incident no-tification and reporting procedures of the countries in whose air space they are flying into.

Summary. When a company airplane is involved in an accident, it is imperative that the company determine who is involved, the cause of the accident, the nature and extent of all injuries, and the extent of damage to company property and other property. The company investigation should be conducted regardless of the extent of personal injuries and whether or not others are conducting a similar investigation.

The company that owns the airplane is legally required to cooperate with the investigation of the selected insurance carrier. The immediate in-vestigation of the accident by the safety committee using the proper guidelines and/or check list can be critical in the collection of material that may disappear or in gathering information that may be forgotten before the insurance investigator can arrive. A thorough investigation with documentation, files, and pictures for future use will greatly assist the insurance investigator and can expedite the settlement of claims.

As aircraft incidents are not investigated by federal agencies other than to determine if a violation took place, it is very important that the company have a complete file of the incident and *that an aviation attorney be hired in the event that the FAA starts violation proceedings against the company and/or crew*. A separate investigation by an outside consultant working with the attorney will save days of investigation time that can be of great value to the company.[3]

Corporate aviation insurance. An aviation insurance contract is especially tailored to fit the requirements of the specified insured. In doing this, it sets forth the circumstances and territory under which the corporation agrees to operate the aircraft, crew requirements, home base, etc. By tailoring the policy to fit the normal flight operations of the corporation involved, the insurance coverage is limited to operations in these parameters and thus allows for lower premium.

Obtaining coverage. Insurance coverage is normally obtained as follows: the corporation goes to an insurance broker who collects the necessary information and submits it to several aviation insurance companies and/or aviation underwriting groups (general agents for various insurance companies) and asks for quotes (bids). The difference in these quotes can be surprising. An underwriter may bid high or even refuse to bid not because he or she thinks the risk is a bad one but because he or she already has too many of that model aircraft on the books or because he or she is reaching a saturation point in the reinsurance contract. Underwriters, like bookies, do lay off a percentage of their risks (bets) with reinsurance companies, both foreign and domestic.

In any event, providing the coverage is equal or similar, the broker will then recommend to the corporation that a certain quote be accepted. The policy is then written. If time is of the essence, a new airplane being delivered or the previous policy expiring, the underwriter can issue a "cover note" to insure the airplane until the policy can be written.

Industrial aid insurance. In the parlance of insurance, corporate aircraft are referred to as "industrial aid" aircraft. This, to the industry, denotes an airplane flown by a professional pilot or pilots and used principally for company business. Business aircraft, on the other hand, are airplanes flown by an officer or employee of the company whose primary job description is something other than "pilot." The risk to the insurer differs between the two operations.

Industrial aid risks are looked on with great favor by underwriters and their policies will extend a number of coverage perks that are only available to other types of risks by payment of an additional premium. For the purpose of this chapter, we will deal only with the industrial aid risk. To quality for industrial aid coverage, the corporation must employ a professional pilot or pilots that have received ground and flight training at a school approved by the aircraft manufacturer.

The underwriter looks for and prefers a well-managed flight operation with good pilot and mechanic training programs. The pilot training program should include ground school and simulator training to preclude the possibility of flight training accidents. Mechanics should be scheduled for annual recurrent factory training. When a policy is written or renewed the underwriter will require that this training was within the last twelve months. This information is normally transmitted to the underwriter by means of the "Pilot Experience" section of the insurance application form that will be completed by the flight department.

If maintenance is performed in-house, the director of maintenance or the chief mechanic should be a graduate of the aircraft manufacturer's factory school. If not, the shop should be one approved for work on the model involved.

The information supplied by the insurance application will enable the underwriter to determine the policy premium and will also, in certain ways, limit the use of the airplane. If, for instance, the application indicates that the aircraft will always be flown by an Airline Transport Pilot (ATP rated) and this is made a part of the policy's "Pilot Clause," then any flight in command of a pilot with a Commercial ticket, regardless of his or her experience, may void the insurance coverage as far as that particular flight is concerned. Just because the flight is legal under the FARs does not mean that insurance coverage will be provided if the policy provisions have not been adhered to.

If the airplane is flown with some regularity to foreign countries, then the application should so indicate. If only an occasional trip is made outside the continental United States, then it may be possible to arrange for insurance coverage on an individual trip basis by means of a policy endorsement issued before the trip is made. This would result in some saving of premium. In fact before any flight is made outside the parameters of the policy (a flight under a ferry permit for instance), a representative of the insurance carrier should be consulted. Almost any type of flight can be covered by endorsement on a one-time basis. In addition to the insurance application, the broker will also supply the underwriter with a verbal review of the risk including: average flight profile, number of passengers carried and their corporate identities, i.e., employees, contractors, or guests.

Coverages available. Hull: This is normally written as "All Risk, Ground and Flight" and covers all damage to the aircraft excluding "wear and tear." It also covers engine FOD (Foreign Object Damage). While deductibles are called for in other classes of hull insurance, most underwriters do not require a deductible on an industrial aid policy. The coverage is written on an "insured for and valued at" basis, which is normally the market value of the airplane at the time the policy is written.

If there is a total loss, i.e., where repairs are not economical, the insurer would pay the insured the value of the aircraft and then sell the salvage on its own account. If there is a partial loss, the insurer will pay the reasonable cost of repairs less depreciation only on those items that have a measured time/life, i.e., engines, tires, etc.

Engine mechanical breakdown. This coverage is available but not often selected by the insured. It carries a sizable deductible, as much as $25,000 per engine. When the insured adds the deductible to the additional premium required and compares it with the cost of engine work, he or she often opts to accept this risk himself or herself. Engine longevity is so good today that the risk is not all that great.

Medical payments. This is written on a "per seat" basis and covers medical expenses for the occupants, usually including crew members, who are injured in or while boarding or alighting from the aircraft. It covers all related medical expenses up to a specified limit per seat regardless of fault or other medical coverage available to the injured party.

Guest voluntary payments. This is akin to "no fault" insurance in that in the event of an injury to a guest-passenger the insurer will negotiate a settlement with the injured party up to the limit specified regardless of the degree of fault of the corporation and its employees.

This coverage is written on a "per seat" basis and is usually a sizable amount, running up to $500,000 per seat. This coverage does not normally apply to corporate employees who may be passengers.

This type of coverage has fallen into disuse because of the present litigious nature of our society. There seems to be little reason to spend the extra premium for this coverage when experience shows that most claims will be in the hands of an attorney before the dust settles. It is rare that an injured party agrees to release the corporation and its employees from all other claims that may result from an accident.

Non-owner hull and liability. This is designed to extend coverage for the use of a rented or borrowed aircraft while the insured airplane is undergoing maintenance or repairs. It is considered excess to specific insurance that is written to cover the other airplane. The hull portion of the coverage is actually a property damage coverage and protects the corporation from any legal liability for damage while the airplane is in its care, custody, and control.

Property damage. This covers the legal liability of the corporation and its employees for damage to the property of others caused by the use of the aircraft.

General liability. This protects the corporation and its employees from claims due to the injury or death of persons other than occupants of the aircraft.

Passenger liability. This protects against claims for injury or death of passengers while in, boarding, or deplaning the airplane and is usually written on a "per seat" basis.

Single limit liability. Most industrial aid policies today are written with this coverage, which combines property damage, general liability, and passenger liability into one package written for a stated amount without a specific limitation on any of the above-listed coverages.

In these policies, the amount usually runs from $50 million for turboprops to $100 million for jets, however greater limits are available. While these large figures may seem like overkill, the object of liability insurance is to protect the assets of the corporation.

Excess liability. This is a separate policy (not an aviation policy) written as umbrella coverage to cover a catastrophic liability claim made against the corporation for any of its operations. Most excess liability policies exclude coverage for aircraft operations, and it will be necessary to have the policy properly endorsed to remove this exclusion.

Hangar keepers liability. This coverage is designed to protect the legal liability of a hangar owner/lessee who acts as a landlord and rents space to others. The landlord is known as the bailee and the tenant as the bailor. Unless the corporation has nonowned aircraft in their hangar, this coverage will not be needed.

Shopping for insurance. Many corporations have their own in-house insurance departments, now sometimes euphemistically known as risk-management departments. Whatever they are called, they are charged with placing all of the many insurance coverages necessary for the operation of the business. Aviation insurance may be a foreign field for them and, in any event, it should be the duty of the aviation department manager or chief pilot to work closely with these departments to see that the proper insurance protection is obtained.

The aviation insurance market is limited in size to a handful of companies and underwriting groups that provide aviation insurance. Only a fraction of this handful has the financial capacity and expertise to write industrial aid coverage. Because of the relatively few aviation policies written (as compared to auto insurance for instance) the law of large numbers does not apply.

Rates are fluid and relate to a number of variables including type of aircraft, crew experience, average yearly hours of use, average flight profile, etc. When one gets right down to the nitty-gritty, it is the knowledge, experience, and gut-feeling of the individual underwriter that sets the rate, which can vary from operation to operation. In the event there is no corporate insurance manager or he or she lacks experience in aviation insurance and the corporation's insurance broker of choice has no aviation department, it would be wise to suggest that the broker request quotes through one of the wholesale aviation insurance brokers who are specialists in the field. They have the contacts and are familiar with the various policies and coverages available. They will work as the broker's representative and not as an agent representing the insurer. The wholesale broker will obtain the necessary quotes and submit them to the corporation through the corporation's broker, with their recommendations.

Notes

1. Excerpts from MARCOR aviation department operations manual.
2. *Air Accidents & The News Media*, Aviation/Space Writers Association, 17 S. High St., Suite 1200, Columbus, OH 43215.
3. Conversations with Fred M. McGowan, aviation insurance consultant, Amitec, Inc., P.O. Box 686, Mt. Laurel, NJ 08054

15

Training the Entire Department

This chapter covers the reasons for training all sections of the corporate aviation department and also outlines methods that can be used to develop training programs.

Corporate aviation department training can be separated into management training and aviation-related and non-aviation-related training. Personnel who receive the various types of training are outlined as follow:

MANAGEMENT TRAINING	AVIATION TRAINING	NON-AVIATION TRAINING
Corporate aviation manager	Chief pilot, captains	Secretaries
Chief pilot	First officers	Accountants
Maintenance manager	Schedulers	Schedulers
Training officer	Cabin attendants	
	Maintenance manager	
	Maintenance technicians	
	Training officer	

Training to develop and maintain skills. When training is mentioned, the thinking is in terms of flight crew training without considering that every person in a flight department should be trained to perform his/her job competently. The objective of recurrent training is to keep all employees at a specified level of proficiency, with the understanding that knowledge infrequently used is soon forgotten.

One of the key functions of the corporate aviation manager is maintaining a properly trained staff. A corporate flight department requires many skills, and an attempt is usually made to hire individuals with the desired skills. However, in many cases, those skills are not available or upgrading from within is preferable. The expertise can be developed by training the individual or individuals to be upgraded.

Skills have to be maintained. Therefore, training becomes the key factor in the employee's understanding of accountability and responsibility. Accountability is the obligation to carry out the duties of a position. Responsibility is the obligation to perform work correctly and on time and to see that established schedules are met. Personnel in an aircraft operation must possess a high degree of discipline, reliability, and moral obligation for the passengers well-being and safety.

An Airline Transport Pilot (ATP) certificate or a degree in engineering does not necessarily make a manager. Management training is needed. A mechanic with seniority and an airplane and powerplant (A & P) license aspiring to a maintenance manager position may find that without management skills his or her job as a manager becomes a disaster.

The significant factors of a corporate training program must include pilot and mechanic proficiency, communication skills, leadership, decision making, work organization, delegation of responsibility, acceptance of responsibility, and assertiveness. The employee must have the initiative and take advantage of company-provided training. Regardless of the number of airplanes that a company may be operating, a training program for a corporate flight operation should be structured to fit the unique requirements of that particular flight operation.

Examples:

1. An aviation department manager must be in constant training to keep up with the state-of-the-art of management. New management methods that can improve the operation should be explored. This can be accomplished by attending development programs and seminars in organization and management.

2. A company operating flights overseas should have crew members trained in all aspects of overwater flight and emergency procedures. Crew

members should be versed in communication terminology and procedural differences.

3. A company operating in and out of Aspen, Colorado, should train crews with emphasis on high altitude airports, mountain terrain flying, crosswind takeoff and landings, and Aspen airport approach and departure procedures.

4. Maintenance personnel should be trained on the equipment they are to work on. Also they should be trained to integrate maintenance with the flight schedule in order to maximize aircraft utilization.

Basic training requirements. The basic training requirements for a corporate flight operation are:

A.   Management training
B.   Pilot initial and recurrent training
C.   Maintenance personnel initial and recurrent training
D.   Survival and first aid training for all personnel
E.   Safety, security, and emergency plan for all personnel
F.   Scheduler initial and recurrent training
G.   Office personnel initial and recurrent training

Source: *Flight Safety Digest 1990*

A. MANAGEMENT TRAINING

Management training is the training a corporate aviation manager must undergo to maintain management skills and keep up with state-of-the-art management. Management training is addressed to those concerned with effective management and efficient operation of corporate flight departments.

Corporations are entering the most challenging management period in their history. The 1990s will be marked as the period when the corporate aviation department faces many of the constraints that other corporate departments are facing. Corporate aviation can only be as good as the company it serves, and managers must remain flexible to changes in the economy.

The corporate aviation management methods of the seventies and eighties have become obsolete. Corporations are becoming "leaner and meaner," and the "money is no object" contention is no longer valid, with the consequences that management training and education must be future oriented. "Development" is the concept to be used, a combination of productive training and positive experience.

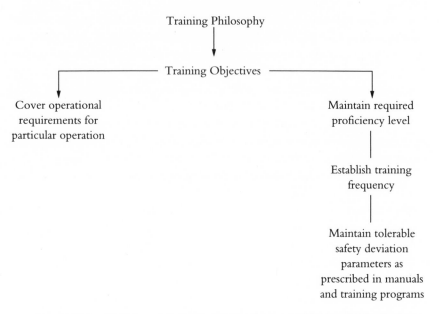

Figure 15.1.   Training philosophy matrix. *Source*: AIMS, Inc., Upland, CA

In many of the aviation magazine articles on management, the corporate aviation manager talks about the programs he or she has instituted for his/her employees but no mention is made of his/her own training. This leads one to assume that he/she does not require training because he/she has all the answers. "When a manager is finished learning, he is finished;" "managers fail the test of reality by bad management practices and when they do not satisfy the needs for respect and recognition of the ability of employees" (*Flight Safety Digest 1990*).

B. Pilot Initial and Recurrent Training

Programs should be based on the training objectives whose philosophy can best be demonstrated with the following matrix depicted in figure 15.1

Crew training must cover all the unique operational requirements of flight operations. An emphasis must be placed on operational procedures. A proficiency level must be attained and a means of maintaining that level must be prescribed through frequent training sessions. Tolerable safe deviation from prescribed standard operating procedures must be defined.

In order to accomplish a viable interface between man and machine and optimum crew coordination, the main means is through discipline and the ability to transfer classroom and simulator training to the actual airplane cockpit. It would be impossible to achieve crew coordination without the implementation of standard operating procedures that would integrate individuals into the formation of a disciplined crew. Such goals are accomplished by training that will maximize human performance and provide better application of present training knowledge, while also making optimum use of flight simulators.

The salient training objectives can be categorized as follows:

1. Proficiency
2. Standard operating procedures
3. Crew coordination
4. Systems emergencies
5. Preparedness for other-than-normal flight situations

These five objectives, properly realized and combined, should assure operational safety emphasizing that a training program must be developed to suit the requirements of each individual flight operation.

1. Proficiency as it applies to flight training is: A) The general knowledge of how a task should be performed, and B) The ability to perform the specific task in a competent and skilled manner.[1]

The two meanings must be distinguished. A person can be knowledgeable in the theoretical sense but may be incompetent in the performance of a task. For example, one can be knowledgeable because of knowing how an airplane should be flown but cannot be competent or adept because of not having flown an airplane for some time.

There is a level of skill beyond which one has more than is necessary to be competent or adept at a given task. Beyond this level, one must isolate the aspects of one's skill directly relevant to the tasks at hand and apply them straightforwardly to their accomplishment. Otherwise, irrelevant aspects may interfere so as to breed complacency or ineptitude and generally thwart accomplishment.

2. Standard operating procedures are essential to the basic foundation of a training program. This cannot be overemphasized. Standard operating procedures include the discipline in the use of all checklists, which is essential to ensure that all specific tasks are properly followed and carried out according to procedure as outlined in the flight and operation manuals.

Every pilot has certain ideas or idiosyncracies as to how a cockpit should be managed or an airplane flown; also, because of specific airport or route operating conditions, deviation from the standard cannot always be avoided. However, the deviation should be within tolerable safety parameters as prescribed and not in conflict with standard flight operating procedures. The captain then must be sure to brief the crew as to the reason for deviation.

3. *Crew coordination* is the harmonious interaction and cooperation between crew members and a key factor in the safe operation of an aircraft. Under no circumstances can there be room for conflicts of personality or individual traits that may impede cooperation in the cockpit. The complexity of the modern aircraft and the work load imposed by the Air Traffic Control System make team work imperative. Therefore, it should be understood that errors made by a crew member will be brought to his or her attention.

4. *Systems emergencies* have to be taught to ensure that information is presented in a logical and objective manner, with less emphasis on engineering aspects and more emphasis on operating techniques. We have to teach intelligent action.

Maintaining currency in the handling of systems emergencies requires constant review. Experience shows that knowledge infrequently used is soon forgotten, especially when not practically applied.

Systems must be taught in three diverse groups: first, "Need-to-know," second, "Nice-to-know," and third, "Where-do-you-find-it." "Need-to-know" are the essential items on the checklist that have to be as practical as possible and relevant to the job in the cockpit. "Nice-to-Know" is an augmentation that assists in the understanding of the subject matter. "Where-do-you-find-it" consists of diagrams and other aids that can be used to provide additional information. The emergency checklist must be presented in such a manner that it will minimize the amount of "memory items."

5. *Preparedness for other-than-normal flight situations*, such as unexpected invert, wind shear, tuck under, wake turbulence, heavy rain impacting an aircraft, and ice formation on airframe and engines can be discussed and analyzed both in the classroom and simulator. The simulator will make pilots aware of the existence of such situations, how to cope, and under what conditions to expect them.

The previous five objectives, properly achieved and combined, should assure operational safety. Safety encompasses the application of skill and knowledge to a given situation of risk that results in a satisfactory reduction of the hazard. If every act and procedure could be planned in such a manner as to anticipate all possible emergencies, a safe alternative could be provided to meet all contingencies.

The advent of the true simulator brought about pilot training relevant to the job in the cockpit and the cockpit environment. Emergencies and unusual flight situations can be practiced without the danger of a training accident. The simulator is an ideal vehicle for developing skills, learning flight procedures, practicing and implementing standardization procedures, crew coordination, cockpit management, and discipline. The simulator instructor has an excellent opportunity to determine the tolerable deviation from prescribed procedures, within allowable safety parameters.

All phases of simulator training should be specifically presented in such a manner as to guarantee the transference of knowledge and skill learned in the simulator to the actual cockpit. Training methods and procedures must take human factors into account. Objective criteria must be conscientiously applied to determine if sophisticated training aids and techniques have physical limitations and what aspects are missing in the training procedures that permit human-error accidents to occur.

C. Maintenance Personnel Initial and Recurrent Training

The ever-increasing sophistication of machine and circuitry demands that technicians be trained properly and thoroughly, way beyond the tinkering capability offered by the old vocational school. Consequently, the technician's education must go beyond basic technical training to include the ability to read, understand, and translate into final work operation complex aircraft technical manuals. The technician must also be able to absorb condensed airplane factory training courses, thereby becoming an expert on a particular type of aircraft. A technician as an artist must have some definite traits, aptitude (whether innate or acquired), dedication, and professionalism. For those who strive and have the ability to become managers, knowledge of managerial arts and their application is a must.

Maintenance personnel training can be divided into four sections.

1. Initial training by aircraft type on airframe and powerplant maintenance procedures. This training to be provided by the aircraft manufacturer-designated training agency. Training sessions once a year at a minimum. Simulator or training aids to acquaint the technician with the proper operation of the aircraft.

2.   Recurrent training by aircraft type or, if qualified, on two aircraft
       types alternate training every six months but no less than every year.

3.   An in-house program for "on-the-job-training" (OJT) for ap-
       prentice technicians and technicians who have not had initial
       training on a particular type of aircraft.

4.   Participation by the chief of maintenance in maintenance man-
       agement seminars or courses to enhance his or her maintenance
       managerial skills.

D. Survival and First Aid Training for All Personnel

In many instances, only a minimal amount of training is provided personnel in areas of survival and first aid for in-flight and ground emergencies. The lives of crew and passengers may very well depend on the training
and preparation that have been done in advance when one is faced with the
stark possibility of ditching or having to land in a remote area.

Survival training for crew members should be contemplated regardless
of the area of operation. There are many areas in North and South America
where ditching or landing in a wilderness area can be a real possibility.

The value of first aid training has applications both on and off the aircraft not only in order to help others but in many instances in providing
first aid for one's own injuries.

First aid training can include cardiopulmonary resuscitation (CPR),
the performance of the Heimlich Maneuver, and training in the immediate
and temporary care given a victim in case of accident or sudden illness.

Survival training can be obtained from several training agencies that
specialize in this type of training.

First aid training can be obtained from such organizations as the
American Heart Association, the local fire department, and the training department of the local hospital.

E. Safety, Security, and Emergency Plans for All Personnel

Organizing for safety, security, and emergency plans commences with
the development of programs and then the establishing of groundwork for
action and instruction to meet the necessary objectives. Danger lurks in all

the activities of a twenty-four-hour day. Safety and security are the business of every employee in the flight operation; therefore, training in awareness of threats to safety and security has to be on a continuous basis. An emergency plan should be established as an outline for procedural actions to be taken in the event of an emergency.

Flight operations personnel have to be familiar with the action plan as discussed in chapter 14. This plan has to be reviewed and kept up to date. The emergency plan has to meet the requirements of the particular flight operation. Instruction on procedures can be conducted on an in-house basis by company or outside personnel familiar with the subject.

The training manual. The aviation department training manual is the curriculum that outlines training methods and procedures for the entire aviation department, covering management training, aviation training, and non-aviation training.

The manual should start with the flight operation training philosophy and define the objectives of each training subject and the areas of study to be emphasized (i.e., ground training, flight training, mechanic's training, safety, security, etc.). The course outline with the number of hours required for each subject of initial and recurrent training, proficiency and line check guides, together with grading forms should be included.

To minimize crew manpower loss and to maximize crew training effectiveness a three-phase pilot training program can be developed as per the example in figure 15.2.

Maintenance training can be programmed in the same fashion as pilot training. The training phases can be broken down into power plant and airframe components to make sure that the technician is not overburdened with too much training at one time.

Regardless whether the training is performed in-house or by a contract training agency, the training manual is essential to the company flight operation training requirements. It is the responsibility of the manager or chief pilot to see that the training conforms with flight operation training programs. The training manual need not be part of the operations manual, but the operations manual should mention the existence of a training manual.

Contract training agency. If a contract training agency has been selected for phase II and III of the company training program, the training program should be specifically designed for the company's requirements. The training agency should be instructed to use the company training curriculum and company aircraft checklists when the company pilots are in training. The training agency has the obligation to conduct the training as

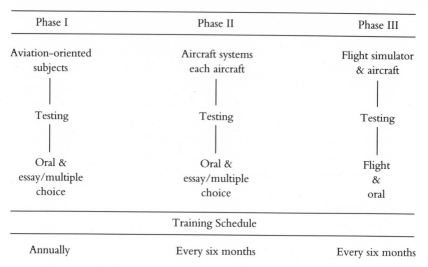

Phase I	Phase II	Phase III
Aviation-oriented subjects	Aircraft systems each aircraft	Flight simulator & aircraft
|	|	|
Testing	Testing	Testing
|	|	|
Oral & essay/multiple choice	Oral & essay/multiple choice	Flight & oral

Training Schedule		
Annually	Every six months	Every six months

Figure 15.2. Three-phase pilot training program. *Source*: AIMS, Inc., Upland, CA

outlined in the company training manuals, and the trainees are responsible to see that the training agency conforms with the company training program.

Training has to maintain pace with the ever-increasing sophistication of machines and procedures in order to prevent the possibility of future human-error accidents. Safety of flight is the overriding concern of those who use airplanes as a mode of transportation. Confidence is the mainstay of the system; projecting an image of incompetence is not the way to promote aircraft use.

The following training manual outline may be used as a suggested outline to develop a training program suitable for the training requirement of the particular flight operation.

Pilot training manual. The training manual is a pilot-training program which covers most phases of pilot training:

PHASE I	PHASE II	PHASE III
In-house training	Training Agency	Training Agency
Subjects that all pilots need to know regardless of the aircraft he or she pilots	Aircraft systems	Simulator and aircraft flight

Training Manual Contents

Introduction
Training phases
Training agency
Phase I training
Phase II training
Phase III simulator training (#1 aircraft type)
Phase III simulator training (#2 aircraft type)
Phase III flight training
Flight proficiency and line checks—applicability
Line checks—general
Proficiency and line check guide
Takeoff procedures

TRAINING PHILOSOPHY

Introduction

Crew training objectives can be defined more realistically in the interface of man and machine to the point where "human error" accidents can be minimized or eliminated entirely. All phases of training must be relevant to the job in the cockpit or in the cockpit environment to assure transference of classroom instruction and simulator training to the actual airplane cockpit.

It would be impossible to achieve crew coordination without the implementation of standard operating procedures that will integrate individuals into the formation of a disciplined crew. To accomplish these goals, the salient training objectives, as stated earlier, must be categorized: Safety means the application of skill and knowledge to a given situation of risk that results in a satisfactory reduction of the hazard.[2]

Training Phases

To minimize crew manpower loss and to maximize crew training effectiveness, a three-phase training program can be programmed.

Phase I	Phase II	Phase III
In-house	Training Agency	Training Agency
Aviation =	Aircraft systems	Flight
oriented	# 1 aircraft type	simulator and
subjects	# 2 aircraft type	aircraft
		#1 Aircraft type
		#2 Aircraft type

Testing		
Oral	Oral	Flight
&	&	&
Essay	Essay	Oral

Training Agency

The training agency is contracted for Phase II and Phase III of the company aviation department training program. This training program is specifically designed to company requirements. The training agency can be instructed to use the company training curriculum and the company aircraft checklists when company pilots are in training. It is the pilot's responsibility to see that the training agency conforms to the company training program.

Phase I—Ground Training— Aviation-oriented Subjects

General. Subject matter and lesson plans for each subject presented will be reviewed at least once each year for currency of material and for "need-to-know." Revisions will be made as necessary.

Testing. A written and oral test will be given to each pilot during or at the completion of Phase I. Test grades will be made a part of the invididual pilot's training file.

Records. The chief pilot will be responsible for keeping all records current and properly filed. An individual record of Phase I will be kept in each pilot's training file, indicating the date each subject was completed. A consolidated record will be kept to indicate the overall status of Phase I training.

Initial training. Each newly hired pilot will be required to complete training in the following subjects before he/she is assigned as a flight crew member on a company airplane.

Initial and Recurrent Training

General. Each line pilot will be required to complete Phase I training by the end of each fiscal year (Dec. 1 through Nov. 30). Subject matter presented will be "need-to-know" based upon the individual pilot's previous training record. Subject matter and annual requirements may be changed at the discretion of the manager, chief pilot, or ground instructor.
Emphasis required:

Balanced field requirements
Hydroplaning
Cabin safety
Crew coordination

PHASE II—TRAINING—TRAINING AGENCY—
AIRCRAFT SYSTEMS

Initial Training. The following pilot personnel will complete Phase II ground training, as applicable to type to airplane, before being scheduled as a flight crew member on a company airplane:

A.   A newly hired pilot
B.   A copilot assigned to another type airplane
C.   A pilot assigned to another type of airplane for the purpose of obtaining a type rating
D.   A copilot upgrading or training to obtain a type rating

Recurrent training. The following flight crew members will complete Phase II ground training:

A.   A pilot assigned and scheduled to fly only one type of airplane: Every six months.
B.   A crew member assigned and scheduled to fly more than one type of airplane: One each year for each type of airplane.
      Note: No company pilot is to be assigned to more than two types of airplane.

Systems outline. Phase II ground training consists of airplane systems. An outline of systems to be covered should be made for each airplane by type and a copy of the Phase II training record form is to be used to record the training received by each person in each type of airplane.

No. 1 Airplane Type—Phase III Simulator
Training, Period 1, Duration
3 or More Hours

1.   Briefing
2.   Checklists
3.   Engine start failures:
     A.   Discontinuing a start
     B.   Hot start
     C.   Fire during start
     D.   Starter dropout failure
     E.   Failure to start—blowout procedures
4.   Crew briefing
5.   ATC clearance and copying (to be done at a minimum)
6.   Radio setup
7.   Taxi:
     Brake fire during taxi
8.   Takeoff—normal ATC clearance to fix
9.   Entering the holding pattern
10. Engine failure, such as loss of oil pressure, during holding
11. Air start
12. ILS approach
13. Missed approach
14. Clearance to fix after completion of missed approach procedure
15. Engine fire-single engine ILS
16. Single-engine missed approach
17. Single-engine Omni approach
18. Debriefing

No. 1 Airplane type—Phase III Simulator
Training, Period 2, Duration
3 or More Hours

1.   Briefing
2.   Checklists
3.   Engine (normal and hot)
4.   Crew briefing
5.   ATC clearance and copying (to be done at a minimum)
6.   Radio setup

7.   Taxi
8.   Takeoff—normal ATC clearance to fix at high altitude (19,000 ft.)
9.   Door open during holding
10.   Emergency descent after depressurization
11.   Unpressurized flight
12.   Radio hot light
13.   ILS approach with radio failure
14.   Circling minimums to land from ADF approach (2-engine)
15.   Missed approach (2-engine)
16.   At missed approach fix generator hot light after series of generator trippings
17.   Normal takeoff
18.   Clearance to fix at 19,000 feet
19.   Inverter failure during climb
20.   Smoke (electrical) at 19,000 feet during holding
21.   Electrical fire checklist—first main and then essential bus
22.   Smoke evacuation and emergency descent
23.   Double generator failure after normal airplane
24.   ADF approach and landing
25.   Debriefing

No. 1 Airplane Type—Phase III Simulator Training, Period 3, Duration 3 or More Hours

1.   Briefing
2.   Clearance to fix at 19,000 feet
3.   During climb:
      A.   Alternator failures with accompanying icing problems.
      B.   Windshield problems
4.   At 19,000 feet:
      A.   Smoke from blower
      B.   Runaway propeller
      C.   Manual feather failure
      D.   Including auto-feather
      E.   Both manual and auto-feather failure
      F.   Slow speed emergency descent with runaway propeller landing after unable to feather
      G.   Land with runaway propeller problem—ILS approach
5.   Engine failure before V_1

6. Engine failure after V_1
7. Hold (1 engine) at fix
8. APU fire during holding
9. Single-engine ILS approach
10. Single-engine missed approach
11. Single-engine VOR approach
12. Normal takeoff
13. Failure to pressurize
14. Radio hot light
15. After normal pressurization, blower hot light
16. Single-engine ADF approach
17. Single-engine missed approach
18. Single-engine VOR approach
19. Single-engine landing
20. Debriefing

No. 1 Airplane Type—Phase III Simulator Training, Period 4, Duration 3 or More Hours

1. Briefing
2. Checklists
3. Engine start (normal)
4. Crew briefing
5. ATC clearance and copying (minimum)
6. Radio setup
7. Taxi
8. Takeoff—failure to retract landing gear
9. Radar vector for ILS approach
10. Missed approach (from landing configuration) with inability to retract gear
11. Loss of engine with gear down and single-engine missed approach with inability to raise gear
12. Single-engine landing from radar vector ILS
13. Normal takeoff
14. Clearance to fix
15. Main hydraulic failure (total loss of fluid; refill reservoir and again lose it)
16. ILS approach with:
    A. Gear extension—emergency
    B. Flap operation—emergency

      C.   Brake operation—emergency
      D.   Landing and taxi without tiller and decelostats
      E.   Total loss of foot brakes after landing

17. Takeoff—normal; clearance to fix
18. APU failure
19. ILS approach, single-engine
20. Debriefing

No. 2 Airplane Type—Phase III Simulator Training, Period 1, Duration 3 or More Hours

1. Briefing and completion of TOLD card—emphasize use of checklists
2. Start using GPU
3. Takeoff checks—normal takeoff—emphasize proper rotation
4. Climb to 17,000 feet
5. Steep turns
6. Approaches to stalls
7. Unusual attitudes
8. Runaway trim, all configurations
9. Fuel system management
10. Engine shut down due to low oil pressure-fuel problems repeated on one engine
11. Airstart procedures—hazards in using wrong procedures
12. Normal descent—turbulence penetration and ice protection management
13. VOR/DME holding—emergency procedures—maximum speed limitations
14. VOR/DME approaches and missed approaches
15. Engine fires during VOR approaches
16. ILS approach to normal landing
17. Localizer back course approach
18. Change seats and repeat as time permits
19. ADF-bearing intercept to ADF approach
20. Debriefing

No. 2 Airplane Type—Phase III Simulator Training, Period 2, Duration 3 or More Hours

1. Briefing and completion of TOLD card—emphasize use of checklists
2. Battery starting—start malfunctions including low oil pressure, hot starts, engine fires, battery runaway
3. Aborted takeoff
4. Takeoff—engine failure at V_R
5. Single-engine ILS approach and landing
6. Takeoff—engine failure between V_1 and V_R
7. Single engine climb to 5,000 feet with area departure
8. Normal relight
9. Engine flame out—immediate and normal relight procedures
10. Generator malfunctions, overheats, and failures
11. Flight instrument failures during approaches
12. Inverter failures
13. Double generator failure—systems lost
14. ILS approach—runaway horizontal stabilizer on missed approach
15. Engine fire during landing
16. Takeoff and complete ADF approaches—normal and single-engine
17. Wind shear problem during approach
18. Change seats and repeat as time permits
19. Debriefing

No. 2 Airplane Type—Phase III Simulator Training, Period 3, Duration 3 or More Hours

1. Debriefing and completion of TOLD cards
2. Takeoff from flooded runway; engine failure before V_1-aborted takeoff
3. Takeoff from slush-covered runway; Use of engine anti-ice
4. SID
5. Climb through 10,000 feet in icing conditions; fast climb to FL350 after 10,000 feet
6. Cruise procedures at FL350

7. Cabin pressure failure—slow—use of emergency pressurization
8. Cabin press fail—fast—emergency descent and oxygen use
9. Fast-rate climb back to FL350; AFT fuselage hot—use of emergency pressurization—right engine flameout—emergency descent
10. Restart engine below 15,000 feet after emergency descent
11. Continue descent through 10,000 feet in icing conditions
12. Thrust reverser problems
13. Fuel system problems
14. Hydraulic pump failure; emergency extension of gear; use of speed brake dump
15. VOR approach and landing with hydraulic emergency—use of emergency brakes
16. Tire failure on takeoff and return for landing
17. Ditching
18. Landing with gear retracted and emergency evacuation
19. Review all systems as time permits
20. Change seats and repeat as time permits
21. Debriefing

Phase III—Flight Training, Training Agency Instructor

Training Procedures

1. For the purpose of standardization, all flights, flight training, flight proficiency checks, and line checks will be accomplished in accordance with the appropriate guide by airplane type, which is contained herein.

2. Each line pilot is required to fly all normally scheduled flights using the procedures outlined in the guide for the type of airplane or airplanes in which he or she is assigned to fly. If this is accomplished with the proper spirit and intent, flight safety and standardization of flight operations will automatically be achieved and flight checks, when due, will be routine.

3. The instructor-pilot will conduct all training and flight checks with the goal of attaining the highest degree of standardization, proficiency, and crew coordination.

Flight Training

1. Flight training will depend upon airplane availability. Priority will

normally be given to company-scheduled flights. Dispatch will provide airplane and schedule training time.

2. The flight operations manager and chief pilot will approve flight training for:

A.   A pilot needing an additional type rating
B.   A copilot upgrading to pilot status who has an Airline Transport Pilot Certificate and requires a type rating
C.   A copilot who is selected to obtain an ATP certificate and type rating

3. Newly hired pilot and copilot personnel will complete the flight training required by Federal Aviation Regulations, as applicable, before being assigned line pilot duties.

PHASE III—FLIGHT PROFICIENCY AND LINE CHECKS—APPLICABILITY

1.   Each pilot will successfully complete a proficiency and line flight check every twelve calendar months.
2.   The proficiency check may be completed in the aircraft or in a simulator.
3.   Each pilot will successfully complete a proficiency flight check every twenty-four calendar months in an airplane in which he or she is rated and scheduled to fly.
4.   The check may be partially completed in the simulator.
5.   If a pilot is required to fly more than one type of airplane, he or she will be given proficiency and line checks, one each year alternating by airplane type.
6.   The following is an example of how proficiency and line checks may be accomplished.

Pilot with one airplane type rating or copilot assigned to one type airplane:

JAN.	JUNE	JAN.
#1 Proficiency	Line	Proficiency

Pilot with two airplane type ratings or copilot assigned to two airplane types:

JAN.	JUNE	JAN.
#1 Proficiency	Line	Line
#2 Line	Line	Proficiency

General

The instructor-pilot will be as objective and impartial as possible in administering flight-proficiency checks. Flight checks may be terminated at any time at the discretion of the instructor-pilot if, in his or her opinion, the pilot receiving the flight check cannot successfully complete the check and rquires additional flight training.

PHASE III—FLIGHT TRAINING GUIDE

The flight maneuvers and procedures contained herein are for use by the instructor-pilots and pilot-trainees as a guide in achieving standard methods of operation. Maneuver outlines are considered basic, and further elaboration should be at the discretion of the instructor-pilot.

Preflight

Reporting policy. The trainee and instructor pilot will report to operations one hour prior to flight time. (This time may be adjusted at the discretion of the instructor.) This period shall be termed *briefing* and will include the following:

A.   Weather briefing
B.   Preparing performance data, flight planning, etc.
C.   Review of maneuvers to be performed
D.   Discussion of emergency procedures
E.   Discussion of systems

Post-flight Critique

A post-flight critique will be conducted at the completion of each flight by the instructor. This period shall be termed the *debriefing* and will include the following:

A.   Complete trainee's flight progress records
B.   A critique on all phases of the trainee's performance

C.   An outline of the directed study for the next flight

Note: During the briefing or debriefing period, the instructor may test the trainee's knowledge of procedures, maneuvers, and aircraft systems.

PHASE III—FLIGHT PROFICIENCY AND LINE CHECKS APPLICABILITY

1.   A captain who fails a proficiency flight check will:
      A.   Be placed in training status
      B.   Be assigned copilot duties until he or she satisfactorily completes the proficiency check
      C.   Be given the flight training necessary before being scheduled for a recheck
2.   A copilot who fails a proficiency flight check will:
      A.   Be given the flight training necessary before being scheduled for a recheck
      B.   Will not be scheduled for passenger-carrying flights

PHASE III—LINE CHECKS—GENERAL

1. Each crew will be required to complete successfully a line check in the type of airplane or airplanes in which it is assigned to fly on a specific trip.

2. The observer-pilot conducting a line check will observe the crew in action from the time the crew arrives at the airport to the time the airplane is secured at the end of the flight. He or she will observe if the operation is conducted according to procedures as specified in the operations manual, training manual, and maintenance manual. At the appropriate time he or she will critique the flight and fill out the line check grade form on the square marked *L* if applicable. Line checks can be conducted with or without passengers on board.

3. A captain or copilot who is considered marginal in the performance of his or her duties or who fails a line check may, at the discretion of the instructor-pilot, be recommended for:

A.   A recheck within ten days
B.   A proficiency flight check
C.   Training status and proficiency flight check

Proficiency and Line Check Guide

Preflight acceptance check (walk-around). The exterior and interior familiarization consists of a complete visual inspection of the aircraft. During the walk-around, make a general inspection of all surfaces (fuselage, empennage, wings, etc.), windows, antennas, engines, external lighting, etc., checking particularly for damage, intake duct blockage, fluid leakage, and secure closure of all access panels and doors.

Passenger cabin inspection will include cabin furnishings and equipment for general condition and security, proper location, use of all emergency equipment and exits, and completion of companionway checklist.

Cockpit familiarization. The trainee is to become thoroughly familiarized with the seat belt, shoulder harness, and all seat adjustments. This is to ensure complete freedom of movement for full aileron, rudder, and elevator control, as well as total visibility to ensure ability to read all flight instruments. The trainee should determine the most favorable seat position early in his or her training and adjust the seat accordingly thereafter.

In addition, the trainee should be familiar with the operation of the rudder pedal adjustment, cockpit windows, cockpit lighting, and location of all switches, controls, etc., so that he or she will be able to locate any switch or control immediately. Additionally, the instructor-pilot should discuss and familiarize the trainee with all of the radio equipment, integrated flight systems, instrument crossover systems, autopilot system, stall protection systems, anti-icing systems, use of emergency brakes, etc.

Checklist management. The trainee should study the checklists and expansions, both normal and emergency, prior to entering flight training. While it is not expected that a pilot will memorize the checklists, a good working knowledge of them is very desirable and will enhance the pilot's performance of both the normal and emergency procedures.

The first officer will read the challenge portion of the checklist and the pilot-in-command will respond with appropriate action except for those items on the right side of the cockpit. In this case, the first officer will respond vocally with the pilot-in-command making a visual check to ascertain that the items were accomplished. Adherence to company checklist procedures is mandatory.

Starting engines. Prior to starting engines the pilot will complete the before start checklist. Compliance with established starting procedures and limitations is mandatory. After both engines are started, complete the after start checklist.

Taxiing and pre-takeoff checks. The instructor will provide the runway information and air traffic control clearances. While the aircraft is being taxied to the runway, the before takeoff checklist will be completed using the "challenge and response" method. Appropriate "V" speeds and engine power settings will be computed by the trainee.

TAKEOFF PROCEDURES

A. Pilot at Controls:

1.   Will apply thrust with power levers as specified in airplane flight manual.
2.   On airplanes requiring nose-wheel steering with "tiller" or "wheel," the pilot at controls will take over yoke when airplane has reached rudder-control speed.

B. Pilot Not at Controls:

1.   Will adjust power levers to the proper thrust as specified in airplane flight manual.
2.   Will hold yoke until airplane has reached rudder control speed.
3.   Will monitor all engine instruments and will keep all instruments within takeoff parameters.
4.   Call out:
      A.   Maximum recommended steering speed
      B. V_1
      C. V_r
      D. V_2
      E.   Any other speed requested by the pilot at controls

NOTES

1. Raoul Castro, "Transferring Skill from Classroom to Cockpit," *Air Taxi/Commuter Safety Bulletin* (March/April 1984).

2. Raoul Castro, "Safety," *Flight Crew Magazine* (July 1988).

Part Four
Conclusions

16

The Future of
Corporate Aviation

The purpose of this chapter is, first, to describe the future of corporate aviation through a discussion of related Federal Aviation Administration forecasts. Then a discussion of a range of important issues affecting the regulation, operation, and management of corporate aviation will be presented. Even though corporate aviation can be considered one of the healthier branches of general aviation, it faces a challenging future in many ways.

The Federal Aviation Administration publishes its FAA Aviation Forecasts annually. The latest version, entitled *FAA Aviation Forecasts: Fiscal Years 1992–2003* (February 1992), presented some interesting information about corporate and business aviation-related trends as part of its general aviation forecast.

Throughout the 1980s there was a restructuring of general aviation which has affected corporate aviation. This restructuring has to do with declining general aviation new aircraft shipments since the late 1970s. This decline in shipments, shown in table 16.1, has affected both general aviation and corporate aviation aircraft deliveries and has occurred for many reasons:

1.   An overproduction of corporate aircraft compared to industry

TABLE 16.1.   ANNUAL SHIPMENTS OF NEW UNITED STATES
GENERAL AVIATION AIRCRAFT, 1981–1992

Year	Units Shipped	Factory Net Billings (in millions)
1981	9,457	$2,919.9
1982	4,266	$1,999.5
1983	2,691	$1,469.5
1984	2,431	$1,680.7
1985	2,029	$1,430.6
1986	1,495	$1,261.9
1987	1,085	$1,363.5
1988	1,143	$1,918.0
1989	1,535	$1,803.9
1990	1,144	$2,007.5
1991	1,021	$1,968.3
1992	899	$1,836.2

Source: General Aviation Manufacturers Association

needs in the 1970s, due in part to lower interest rates and better tax advantages available then.

2. The success of airline deregulation in providing improved service at stable prices in many domestic hub locations, thus negating some of the need for corporate aircraft. (Note: This factor has also worked the other way by making it more difficult to reach certain domestic nonhub locations by airline, thus enhancing the need for corporate aircraft in these specific circumstances.)

3. Purchase price cost increases for corporate aircraft. As shown in table 16.2, purchase prices for both key types of corporate aircraft have almost doubled since 1981.

4. Increases in maintenance and operating costs for corporate aircraft. As shown in tables 16.3 and 16.4, the maintenance and operating costs have almost doubled since 1981.

5. Changes in tastes and/or management philosophy relative to owning a corporate aircraft. This may occur due to a change in the management team, the CEO, or some other influential top executive who is influential in such decisions and is not favorably disposed toward corporate aviation (*FAA Aviation Forecasts,* pp. 110–17).

These, and other reasons, have provided numerous roadblocks to growth in corporate aviation in the 1980s. Even though this resulted in de-

TABLE 16.2. CORPORATE AIRCRAFT PURCHASE PRICE COST INDICES, 1981–1992

Year	Turboprops	Turbojets
1981	182.7	216.7
1982	189.9	240.4
1983	204.3	251.8
1984	213.0	266.2
1985	236.2	287.4
1986	247.5	299.0
1987	251.8	309.3
1988	295.6	328.2
1989	318.4	326.9
1990	343.1	363.9
1991	357.2	370.0
1992	380.1	411.4

Source: Federal Aviation Administration

clining annual turbine aircraft (turboprop and turbofan/jet) and turbine helicopter shipments, the overall size of these fleets grew during the 1980s. For example, the turbine-powered aircraft fleet grew from 6,200 aircraft in 1980 to 9,500 aircraft in 1989. This is a net increase of 3,300 aircraft or 53.2 percent. It is also an annual average increase of 5.3 percent in turbine aircraft fleet size during the 1980s. The FAA also notes that there was an average increase of 1.1 percent in the use of general aviation for business (in terms of hours flown) (*FAA Aviation Forecasts*, pp. 109–19).

TABLE 16.3. CORPORATE AIRCRAFT MAINTENANCE COST INDICES, 1981–1992

Year	Turboprops	Turbojets
1981	169.6	187.1
1982	180.2	198.7
1983	187.5	206.7
1984	194.7	214.7
1985	201.3	221.3
1986	205.3	225.7
1987	209.1	229.9
1988	215.0	236.4
1989	221.3	243.3
1990	228.9	251.7
1991	236.1	259.6
1992	241.6	265.6

Source: Federal Aviation Administration

TABLE 16.4.   CORPORATE AIRCRAFT OPERATING COST INDICES, 1981–1992

Year	Turboprops	Turbojets
1981	403.8	403.8
1982	420.8	420.8
1983	434.7	434.7
1984	434.7	434.7
1985	429.9	429.9
1986	384.8	484.8
1987	384.8	484.8
1988	384.8	484.8
1989	384.8	484.8
1990	422.4	422.8
1991	465.1	465.6
1992	458.0	458.4

Source: Federal Aviation Administration

The *FAA Aviation Forecasts* reveal that turboprop and turbojet general aviation aircraft will grow at an average annual rate of 4.3 percent. These percentage share increases are accompanied by sizable increases in the numbers of turbine powered aircraft and turbine rotorcraft, as reflected in table 16.5.

Turboprop aircraft will increase by 2,300 aircraft by the year 2003, and turbojet aircraft will increase by 2,400. Overall, turbine powered aircraft will grow from 10,400 in 1993 to 13,700 in 2003. Turbine rotorcraft will grow from 4,500 in 1993 to 8,000 in 2003. All of this growth in aircraft will also produce an increase in hours flown in turbine powered aircraft of 1.3 million or 0.77 percent per year. Turbine rotorcraft hours flown will increase at a rate of 0.54 percent per year. These increases will create a number of growth-related issues pertaining to the regulation, operation, and management of a larger national fleet of turbine aircraft and rotorcraft. These issues will be discussed in the next section.

ISSUES FACING CORPORATE AVIATION

The future of corporate aviation includes the distinct possibility of steady growth through the year 2000, according to the Federal Aviation Administration. This, in turn, means that there are all the usual problems of corporate aviation—regulatory, operational, and managerial. A discussion of these issues follows.

TABLE 16.5. FORECASTS OF ACTIVE CORPORATE GENERAL
AVIATION AIRCRAFT TYPES, 1993–2003

Year	Turboprops	Turbojets	Turbine Rotorcraft
1993	5,800	4,600	4,500
1994	6,000	4,700	4,800
1995	6,200	4,800	5,100
1996	6,400	4,900	5,500
1997	6,600	5,000	5,700
1998	6,800	6,100	6,000
1999	7,000	5,200	6,400
2000	7,200	5,300	6,800
2001	7,500	5,400	7,200
2002	7,800	5,500	7,600
2003	8,100	5,600	8,000

Source: Federal Aviation Administration, *FAA Aviation Forecasts: Fiscal Years 1992–2003*

1. Growth-related issues. Growth in corporate aviation will present many issues, including:

A. Improving access to airports for corporate aircraft in the face of increasing airline traffic will be a problem. Also, the tendency of some airports, as well as federal slot rules, to restrict corporate and general aviation in favor of airlines, has placed even greater pressure on corporate operations at major metropolitan airports.

B. Complicating the access issue for corporate aviation at metropolitan airports is the aircraft noise issue and related airport-sponsored noise-abatement issues. These issues include aircraft operating restrictions such as flight track limits, aircraft type restriction, curfews, ground noise restrictions, and the like. Corporate aviation, because of its nonscheduled nature, can be viewed as the noise villian at many airports simply because of the wide range of its operating times (e.g., early morning and late night). If these operations grow, there is a potential for more complaints.

C. The development of new aircraft to meet new needs, particularly those related to the increasingly global nature of the economies of many businesses, will be difficult. This development will be an especially difficult issue with new corporate aircraft sales having slumped for much of the last decade. It will be difficult to convince aircraft manufacturers to respond to such needs.

D. The provision of adequate numbers of well-qualified personnel to meet the future needs of corporate aviation will be a problem, especially with the parallel growth of airlines and their related personnel needs. Pilots and airframe and powerplant mechanics will continue to be in demand in all segments of aviation throughout the 1990s, especially those with turbine experience. This personnel problem will place both a cost (wage-related) and a placement/hiring effort pressure on corporate aviation.

2. *Regulatory issues.* These issues relate to the future federal, state, and local aviation-related regulatory and/or legal changes facing corporate aviation. Some possible areas to watch for include:

A. Changes in regulations or laws which affect the economics of corporate aircraft operations. These changes include possible federal tax law changes related to the depreciation of aircraft purchases or the use of corporate aircraft. Changes in the 1980s made it generally more expensive both to purchase and operate corporate aircraft.

B. Changes in aviation safety regulation affecting corporate aviation will most likely include aging aircraft and human factors/training type regulatory revisions. These areas have been the subject of much debate in the aviation industry in general. In corporate aviation, the use of older turbine equipment in response to higher new turbine aircraft prices leaves some portions of corporate aviation open to impact from aging aircraft regulatory initiatives. Potential human factors and training-related regulatory changes stem from the general belief that this is the one area where major progress in aviation safety can still be achieved. Much research is being devoted to this subject with the distinct possibility of regulatory reform as an end result.

C. Environmental law and regulatory change will also affect the future of corporate aviation. Every year individual local airports enact new, or revise existing, noise abatement procedures. These local environmentally based regulatory initiatives create a maze of operating rules for corporate flight departments to know in addition to their normal flight-related operating procedures. Future revision will be tied to a federal decision to establish new aircraft noise emission guidelines at the source (e.g., the aircraft and its engines). Also, as many metropolitan "fringe" airports are improved to enable them to accept corporate turbine equipment, local airport environmental regulations are sure to follow.

3. *Operations management issues*

A. *Changes in United States business:* Heading the operations/management issue list has been the continuing restructuring of business in America today and its parallel effects on corporate aviation. For example, a number of seemingly excellent corporate flight departments have been dismantled with impunity in recent years.

Many of these changes were brought about by ownership changes in the parent company, including such practices as mergers, leveraged buyouts, hostile takeovers, and the like. A by-product of this process is the fate of the corporate flight department. This trend can be expected to continue. Also affecting the restructuring topic is the trend toward contract-managed corporate flight department. Those businesses wishing to have the benefits of corporate aircraft, but not wishing to involve themselves in the direct management of corporate aircraft, can turn to contract-managed aircraft.

B. *Costs:* Another major operation/management issue is the high purchase and operating costs of corporate aircraft. As noted earlier in this chapter, these costs are way up over the 1972 base costs. These increased costs have focused more corporate attention to the high-cost flight department, sometimes simultaneously with the restructuring of the company itself. Those companies with the "Royal Barge" concept of running the corporate flight department are, at this point, extremely vulnerable to cost-conscious managers who may see little corporation-wide benefit derived from the flight department. In these cases, internal policies regarding the use of corporate aircraft must be liberalized to create a more effective corporate executive user base for the flight department.

C. *Good management practices:* Using the corporate airplane wisely is of great importance to establishing a well-run flight department. Corporate aircraft use policies can include:

1. Assignment of aircraft to high-volume, high-frequency shuttle routes. Kimberly-Clark, Xerox, and GTE, among others, operate such internal corporate airlines to great advantage.

2. Broad availability of corporate aircraft to as many levels of employees as possible within the corporate overall travel cost, marketing, and planning objectives. *Advertisement* of this availability to get the broadest exposure possible of the flight departments' services is also necessary.

3. Consideration of both *internally owned* and *contracted* flight department strategies. There are numerous contract operators available for corporate aircraft, especially in the larger cities. Contract operators offer both advantages and disadvantage to corporations. Some corporations are able to use contract operators to add services during peak periods. Others use contract operations as a way to get into corporate flight operations without making a commitment to hiring pilots, etc.

4. *International issues.* Corporate aviation, like all aviation, has entered

a truly international era. Corporate aircraft such as the Gulfstream IV have intercontinental range and this capability brings corporate flight department into an important arena of activity and growth. Among the various international issues facing corporate aviation are:

A. Continued competitive offering of foreign-built corporate aircraft has made inroads into the United States aircraft fleets. This is especially true of European manufactures such as Dassault (makers of the Falcon 50, 100, 200, and 900) and British Aerospace (makers of the BAe 1000).

B. Corporate flight departments must be sensitized to the variables of international flying operations, including flight planning and preparation, arranging for fuel (and other onboard, enroute services), language barriers, customs clearance issues, passport/immigration requirements, and other issues.

C. Corporate flight departments with significant overwater operations must prepare for the specific conditions and requirements affecting these operations.

The future of corporate aviation is linked to global economic stability.

The near future will see an upward trend in corporate aviation stimulated by improving worldwide economic conditions that will precipitate capital investment and boost sales of turbine fixed wing corporate aircraft and helicopters.

New business ventures emerging from the improved global economy will create a new demand for corporate jets and helicopters in the United States, Europe, Central and South America, also the Pacific Rim and Asian countries. By the year 2000 the Pacific Rim and Asian region will be second to Europe as the largest market for corporate aircraft jets.

After sustaining the economic downturn of late 1991 and the first half of 1992, corporate aviation will begin an uphill recovery. A forecasted improved economy together with the need to replace aging aircraft and the need for fast short-range transportation will spur helicopter sales.

The Cessna CitationJet and the Swearingen SJ-30 are to be certificated and will begin deliveries in 1992–93. These fast small size jets will compete favorably with turboprop aircraft in price and performance providing corporate aviation entrant companies with high-performance aircraft.

In order to meet future technical engineering and financial challenges, new consortiums will be formed such as the cooperation between helicopter manufacturers Bell and Boeing and Aerospatiale of France and MBB of Germany. Cessna Aircraft is up for sale and Gulfstream Aerospace has been looking at possible acquisitions, the trend having started with General Electric and Snecma followed by General Motors Allison and Allied Signal Garret developing the LHTEC T800. Buyouts and mergers will occur, such as Canadair and Lear.

Most corporate aviation manufacturers and suppliers are bullish on the future of corporate aviation. However, they admit that there is going to be a close, careful examination before a company decides to enter into corporate aviation or buy a new airplane. Most corporate aviation departments will be required to operate in a business manner, efficiently, economically, and reliably. Acquiring a corporate aircraft is considered a capital expenditure, and corporations will not consider buying new equipment unless the economy is in good health.

Emerging new Aircraft

Low-priced Small Aircraft

Small low-price ($2,500,000 to $2,700,000) jet entry-level aircraft such as the Swearingen SJ-30 and the Cessna CitationJet will do much to stimulate corporate aviation. Many companies that have been reluctant to purchase a six- to ten-million-dollar corporate jet will have a good opportunity to enter into corporate jet operation at a relatively low investment cost. Four customer owned Cessna CititationJets have entered service after completing the certification process. Cessna expects to deliver fifty CitationJets in 1993.

Long-range Aircraft

Canadair Global Express is a 75,000-pound intercontinental corporate jet with a designed range of 5,600 nautical miles. Powered by two 14,000 to 16,000 pound thrust turbofans, the Global Express will have a new-technology wing, six flat-panel displays, a Heads Up Display (HUD), and pilot/copilot side stick controlers. Cabin length is equal to that of the Canadair Regional Jet whose cabin height is 6.25 feet. Power plant proposals are presently being evaluated. Refundable $250,000 deposits on the $25 million (green) aircraft are being taken by Canadair for deliveries in 1997.

Gulfstream V is an 80,000 to 90,000 pound gross weight twin-engine jet. The aircraft IFR range with 7,000 pound payload is over 5,000 nautical

miles at 0.8 Mach. Gulfstream and engine maker Rolls-Royce are performing design and market studies with the goal of beginning flight testing in
1994.

Midsize Corporate Aircraft

Dassault Falcon 2000 is a mid-size cabin corporate jet that began flight
tests in March 1993. The $14 million aircraft has external dimensions as
follow: length, 63.4 feet; height, 22.9 feet; wingspan, 63.4 feet. It is powered by two 5,725-pound thrust General Electric CFE 738 turbofan engines. The aircraft will be equipped with Collins Pro line 4 avionics including an EFIS and a Category III autopilot and digital flight control system.
The aft fuselage of the Falcon 2000 is one of the most complex curved and
area-ruled aerodynamic shapes ever created for use on a corporate jet aircraft. The Falcon 2000's low drag is the reason why the airplane will have
an IFR range (with NBAA reserves) of 3,000 nautical miles at Mach 0.8
with eight passengers.

Cessna Citation X is a stretched version of the Cessna corporate jet line
using a 60-foot-long supercritical wing and powered by two 6,000 pound
thrust Allison GMA 3007C engines for 0.9 Mach max speed making it the
fastest corporate jet. Range with full fuel at max gross weight of 31,000
pounds is 3,300 nautical miles with a payload of 1,215 pounds. The Citation X will be equipped with the Honeywell Primus 2000 avionics package, which includes AFCS, EFIS, and EICAS. The $13 million jet will have
a full-length dropped aisle and 600-cubic-foot heated and pressurized baggage compartment located adjacent to the cabin.

Helicopters

McDonnell Douglas MD Explorer helicopter features eight energy
absorbing seats, the Douglas Notar anti-torque control system, five blade
bearingless main rotor, and integrated glass cockpit. Two power plants
are being offered: the 593-shaft horsepower Pratt & Whitney 206B and
the 605-shaft horsepower Turbomeca Arrius-2C. The Explorer's gross
weight is 5,800 pounds; empty weight, 3,080 pounds; useful load, 2,250
pounds; max cruise speed, 150 knots; range 363 nm, with a service ceiling
of 20,000 feet.

The *Sikorsky S-92* cabin is six feet wide and six feet tall and more than
nineteen feet long. Gross weight is 22,220 pounds; empty weight is 13,730

pounds. The helicopter will be able to cruise at 160 knots and travel up to 400 nautical miles. In airline configuration, it will seat 19 passengers. No official price has been given, but it is estimated at $11 million.

Kaman K-Max is a new single turbine utility helicopter using the Kaman intermeshing main rotor, no tail rotor system. The K-Max is designed to lift 5,000 pounds on the hook to 8,000 feet out of ground effect. Powered by a Lycoming T5317A 1,800 shaft/horsepower engine derated to 1,500 shp, the K-Max has an empty weight of 4,100 pounds and a gross weight of 10,500 pounds.

Appendixes
Selected Bibliography
Index

Appendix A
Job Descriptions

Job descriptions play an important role in identifying the tasks to be performed and can be used as a guide in recruiting, interviewing, reviewing, and promoting. The following are job descriptions containing the position basic function, duties and responsibilities, and the training and background expected.

Job Title: Aviation Department Manager

Reports To: Company President

Basic Function: Broad authority and responsibility to supervise all phases of the Aviation Department. Supervises Flight Operations, Maintenance, and Scheduling.

Duties and Responsibilities

1. Responsible for maintaining maximum standards of safety through proper maintenance, pilot proficiency, and flight schedules.
2. Keeps fully informed on FAA regulations pertinent to operations.
3. Recommends the standards to be followed in procurement, operation, and maintenance of aircraft.
4. Develops and maintains flight operations manual, training manual; incorporates FAA flight regulations; creates flight operating specifications, company flight rules, pilot proficiency

checks, periodic inspections of aircraft, and necessary flight
logs and records.

5. Coordinates with Maintenance Chief on inspection and maintenance of aircraft and engines.

6. Coordinates with the Chief Pilot on the training of pilots and maintaining pilot proficiency.

7. Prepares reports required by Company, FAA, or other governmental agencies.

8. Responsible for preparation of budgets, auditing of all charges for maintenance, equipment, fuel, and other operational expenses.

9. Keeps abreast of latest information on the development and availability of aircraft and aircraft equipment to be used as a basis for recommending improvements to be incorporated on Company airplanes.

10. Prepares or delegates authority to prepare flight schedules to meet needs of company travelers to obtain maximum aircraft utilization.

11. Provides for licensing and registration of airplanes.

12. Acts as pilot on relief basis.

13. Responsible for comfort and convenience of passengers.

14. Represents the company as directed in national organizations relating to operation of company aircraft.

15. Makes summary appraisals at specified times of department personnel outlining individual weaknesses and suggestions for correction. Appraisals to be kept as part of personnel file.

16. Performs or delegates line or proficiency checks.

17. While the operation of the aircraft is governed by Federal Aviation Regulations and company standard operating procedures, it is the Manager's responsibility to maintain adherence to these regulations, as well as to prohibit implementation of arbitrary policies by the flight crews. This function shall be coordinated with the Chief Pilot.

18. Corollary responsibilities include scheduling and flight control procedures, flight crew recurrent training procedures, aircraft operational procedures, aircraft utilization, etc.

19. Coordinates personnel rules, policy, and wage evaluations for Operations, Maintenance, and Ground Personnel, to optimize departmental efficiency.

20. Is concerned with passenger, aircraft, and facilities security at home base.

21. Insures that all publications are revised and current.

Job Specifications

1. Education (check level required):
   High School _____ College _____
   or equivalent experience.
   Technical training (specify area): Maintenance or Engineering.
2. Knowledge and Skills: Five thousand hours in command of turbine aircraft preferably in type of aircraft operated by the Company. Management training or management experience.

Job Title: Chief Pilot

Reports To: Aviation Department Manager

Basic Function: General management of pilots; including flight scheduling, training, and regulations. Assists the Manager in all duties involving the operation of Company airplanes.

Duties and Responsibilities

1. Acts as Manager during Manager's absence.
2. Coordinates with Schedule and Maintenance to ensure efficient aircraft utilization and that each aircraft scheduled to fly has been properly released for flight.
3. Coordinates with Federal Aviation Agency personnel and other Company representatives in matters that pertain to the operation or evaluation of the pilots, mechanics, aircraft, or equipment.
4. Assures that all flight personnel are properly qualified and trained for duties to which they are assigned.
5. Develops programs to promote safety and standardization in all flight activities.
6. Develops control procedures for manuals, including Aircraft Flight Manual, Training Manuals, and Flight Operations Manual. Assures revisions are made to Operations Manual and Aircraft Flight Manual.
7. Acts as coordinator between Flight Department and Contract Training Agencies, arranging school, simulator and flight training: arranges type ratings and pilot proficiency checks to ensure timely completion of required items. Develops in-house flight training programs. Ensures that the latest operating procedures and changes are made available to each pilot as soon as possible. Is responsible for scheduling pilots for flight and ground train-

ing. Maintains flight training folder for each pilot that will include copies of pilot certificate, medical certificate, schools completed, simulator and flight training records, type ratings, PPE check, and other material deemed necessary.

8.   Initiates programs to ensure that each pilot is familiar with aircraft emergency equipment, including use of emergency exits, fire extinguisher, oxygen, and first-aid equipment.

9.   Supervises the activities of the flight crew personnel to ensure that the overall flight operations are conducted as safely and efficiently as possible.

10. Ensures that each flight crew member has valid certificates, as follows:

A.   An appropriate and current Airman Certificate.

B.   Current Medical Certificate.

C.   Radio Telephone License (if required).

D.   Any other documents or certificates required for special flights.

11. Provides current material or publications in an appropriate form. This is not limited to, but will include:

A.   Airplane checklists (normal and emergency), in accordance with the Airplane Flight Manual.

B.   Aeronautical Charts: High and Low Altitude; Terminal, Approach, and other charts, as necessary.

C.   Airmans Information Manual

D.   Federal Aviation Regulations: Parts 61, 91.

E.   Approved Airplane Flight Manual.

F.   Operating manuals for each piece of equipment installed in aircraft.

12. Ensures that each flight crew member scheduled to fly will not exceed flight and duty limitations.

13. Develops and maintains training manuals, incorporating FAA flight regulations, manufacturer's flight operating specifications, Company flight rules, pilot proficiency checks, and necessary flight logs and records.

14. Keeps abreast of latest information on the development and availability of aircraft and aircraft eqiupment, to be used as a basis for recommending improvements to be incorporated in Company airplanes.

15. Makes reviews of flight personnel outlining individual weaknesses and suggestions for correction.

16. Is concerned with passenger and aircraft security away from home base.

17. Designates a Captain and a Second-in-Command for each scheduled flight.
18. Acts as Captain to maintain proficiency on no more than two types of aircraft.

Job Specifications

1. Education (check level required):
   High School _____ College _____
   or equivalent experience
   Technical training (specify area):
2. Knowledge and skills:

Job Title: Captain

Reports To: Chief Pilot

Basic Function: Responsible for all phases of the operation of his or her aircraft with major emphasis on safety. Maintains strict adherence to all applicable FARs, Company policies, and published safety standards.

Duties and Responsibilities

1. Responsible for the airworthiness of the aircraft he or she is assigned to and for the safety of passengers on aboard. Responsible for maintaining maximum standards of safety through pilot proficiency.
2. Keeps fully informed on FAA regulations pertaining to operations.
3. Keeps informed of latest information on the development of aircraft and aircraft equipment.
4. Maintains assigned flight manuals and charts in current condition.
5. Completes the Company Daily Flight Log for each flight, together with all required trip records.
6. Insures that his or her airplane is properly cleaned and stocked prior to flight, and restocked after flight in accordance to published directives.
7. Remains alert to any activities that may affect the security of Company aircraft.
8. Assures safety and security of aircraft by use of engine covers, chocks, tie-downs, control locks, door locks, hangaring, or any other measures available.
9. Arranges necessary transportation or lodging for passengers in

the event of flight cancellation due to weather or mechanical problems.

Job Specifications

1.   Education (check level required):
     High School _____ College _____
     or equivalent experience
     Technical training (specify area):
2.   Knowledge and skills:

Job Title: First Officer

Reports To: Chief Pilot

Basic Function: The First Officer is second in command, administratively responsible to the Chief Pilot, and is functionally responsible to the Captain on the flight to which he or she is assigned. The First Officer is considered to be in training for upgrading to Captain status and is to take full advantage of the Captain's experience. The First Officer must be highly knowledgeable of the Operations Manual, FAA Regulations, Operations Specifications, Flight Manuals, Instrument Procedures, and other instructions pertinent to his or her duties.

Duties and Responsibilities

1.   Assists pilot in planning flight, determination of fuel requirements, weight and balance, weather, flying conditions, preflight checks.
2.   Arrange for fuel and catering services.
3.   Coordinates with the captain for proper storage and protection of aircraft, including hangars and tie-down, when necessary.
4.   Responsible for the cleanliness and stocking of aircraft in accordance with published directives.
5.   Maintains current certificates and ratings applicable to performance of duties.
6.   Performs other duties as prescribed by Chief Pilot.
7.   Assists in the storing of baggage in the aircraft.

Job Specifications

1.   Education (check level required):
     High School _____ College _____

or equivalent experience
Technical training (specify area):
2.   Knowledge and skills:

Job Title: Flight Attendant

Reports To: Chief Pilot

Basic Function: Serves as flight attendant, performing all necessary functions to take care of passenger needs. Sees that airplane is in good state of cleanliness.

Job Specifications

1.   Education (check level required):
       High School _____ College _____
       or equivalent experience
       Technical training (specify area):
2.   Knowledge and skills:

Job Title: Flight Mechanic

Reports To: Chief Pilot

Basic Function: Serves as flight mechanic on all flights performing external preflight and internal preflight up to circuit breakers; also performs post-flight check. Attends cabin performing all necessary functions to insure the comfort and safety of passengers. Performs duties as floor mechanic when schedule permits.

Duties and Responsibilities

1.   Assures that airplane is mechanically ready for flight and properly cleaned externally and internally prior to each flight.
2.   Responsible for external preflight.
3.   Responsible for internal preflight up to circuit breakers in companionway.
4.   Responsible for ordering catering or any other cabin services as required. Takes care of stocking airplane.
5.   Sits at jump seat and monitors takeoff and landing.
6.   Attends to passenger needs, keeps passenger cabin in orderly and clean condition at all times in flight.
7.   Helps load and unload luggage.
8.   Performs postflight check at end of flight.

Job Specifications

    1.   Education (check level required):
             High School _____ College _____
             or equivalent experience
             Technical training (specify area):
    2.   Knowledge and skills:

Job Title: Secretary/Dispatcher

Reports To: Aviation Department Manager

Basic Function: Broad authority and responsibility for maximum aircraft utilization; selects best aircraft for the mission, considering number of passengers, distance of trip, and runway requirements.

Duties and Responsibilities

1. Coordinates with Flight and Maintenance departments for best aircraft schedules and maximum aircraft utilization.
2. Keeps schedule information up-to-date, in order to inform promptly concerned personnel of aircraft situation concerning location and availability.
3. Coordinates with Aviation Department Manager and Chief Pilot regarding operational limitations.
4. Notifies crews of flight, training, and other duty schedules.
5. Schedules Pilots' duty and flight time according to Operations Policy Manual.
6. Coordinates with Transportation Department for necessary ground transportation.
7. Develops and makes necessary reports on aircraft utilization.
8. Performs necessary secretarial work as time permits.

Job Specifications

    1.   Education (check level required):
             High School _____ College _____
             or equivalent experience
             Technical training (specify area):
    2.   Knowledge and skills:

Job Title: Receptionist/Secretary

Reports To: Aviation Department Manager

Basic Function: Reception, entrance security, telephone communications, and general secretarial.

Duties and Responsibilities

1. Performs duties of receptionist, meeting and guiding visitors.
2. Maintains entrance security, screening persons seeking entrance to Company Hangar.
3. Controls telephone communications, allocating lines to proper call recipients and taking telephone messages.
4. Performs duties as secretary, handling correspondence, filing, appointments, etc.
5. Prepares necessary Maintenance records.
6. Prepares necessary Purchasing paperwork and maintains necessary files of such.
7. Disseminates employee information.

Job Specifications

1. Education (check level required):
   High School _____ College _____
   or equivalent experience
   Technical training (specify area):
2. Knowledge and skills:

Job Title: Accounting and Records Secretary

Reports To: Aviation Department Manager

Basic Function: Responsible for all accounting functions; keeps costs records for each aircraft; maintains log books, keeps all employee records, handles correspondence for the accounting department.

Job Specifications

1. Education (check level required):
   High School _____ College _____
   or equivalent experience
   Technical training (specify area):
2. Knowledge and skills:

Job Title: Standardization and Procedures Coordinator

Reports To: Aviation Department Manager

Basic Function: Responsible for ground and flight training as outlined in the Training Manual; keeps abreast of latest training aids and developments; develops training programs to improve pilot skills.

Duties and Responsibilities

1. Establishes curriculum for ground school and revises material as necessary, so that subjects presented by training agencies are current.
2. Schedules and conducts semiannual flight proficiency tests of Company pilots, in accordance with applicable current Federal Aviation Regulations and Company standards, to insure highest level of crew coordination.
3. Maintains current file for each Company pilot containing records of training and other related recurrent training.
4. Maintains library consisting of audiovisual materials, airplane manuals, Federal Aviation Regulations, and other publications relative to flight operations.
5. Performs P.P.E. flight checks.
6. Maintains personnel records.

Job Specifications

1. Education (check level required):
    High School _____ College _____
    or equivalent experience
    Technical training (specify area):
2. Knowledge and skills:

Job Title: Chief of Maintenance

Reports To: Aviation Department Manager

Basic Function: Has broad responsibility and authority for safe and efficient aircraft maintenance operation.

Duties and Responsibilities

1. Ensures that only aircraft in airworthy condition are operated/scheduled and that safety is the first consideration in all maintenance operations.
2. Schedules aircraft maintenance so as to provide for maximum availability with minimum downtime.

3. Ensures compliance with FAA and Company regulations and policies affecting maintenance.

4. Maintains liaison with the FAA, and manufacturers technical representatives in matters of maintenance and coordinates with the Aviation Department Manager or Chief Pilot.

5. Coordinates plans and activities in the Maintenance Departments with other Company departments, i.e., Schedule and Flight.

6. Promotes the morale and general efficiency of all Maintenance Personnel.

7. Ensures that all Company aircraft meet the current empty weight and center of gravity requirements established by the aircraft specifications.

8. Insures that all Maintenance Personnel are adequately and properly trained for their duties and responsibilities.

9. Insures that Maintenance irregularity requirements of the FARs are complied with in their entirety.

10. Evaluates new equipment and procedures; coordinates with manufacturers and suppliers in developing more effective maintenance operations.

11. Insures that current maintenance information is passed on to the following shift by use of a turnover form.

12. Insures that outside (contract) maintenance agencies have adequate facilities, personnel, and experience to maintain company aircraft.

13. Administers functional record-keeping system, as outlined in Maintenance Manual and FAA regulations.

14. Administers inventory control of parts, equipment, and supplies in stockroom and airplanes.

15. Ensures that applicable maintenance manuals are up-to-date and that mechanics are fully versed and cognizant of procedures and changes.

16. Receives all purchase requests and coordinates with Aviation Department Manager or Chief Pilot on parts and materials requirements.

17. Initiates Purchase Orders and Repair Orders to obtain parts, materials, and repair/overhaul of components.

18. Follows up with vendors to assure timely shipment of required materials.

19. Checks incoming materials for proper identification, certification, and freedom from shipping damage.

20.   Administers packing and shipping of outgoing components and parts.

21.   Makes recommendations to the Aviation Department Manager or Chief Pilot for parts and materials needed to facilitate the maintenance of aircraft.

22.   Provides Mechanics, Scheduler, and Aviation Department Manager with "time since" overhaul figures and forecasts "time due" of various maintenance activities.

23.   Coordinates with contract agencies providing computerized data and records for aircraft.

24.   Reviews component removal/installation reports for accuracy. Makes sure data is mailed to contract agency for input.

25.   Audits data processing reports for accuracy and makes corrections, if required, on information transmitted to them.

26.   Maintains records of borrowed parts transactions.

27.   Maintains historical files and log books of all aircraft, powerplants, and props.

28.   Edits for legibility all completed maintenance forms, work packs, and other maintenance records transmitted to the Company for records purposes.

Job Specifications

1.   Education (check level required):
High School _____ College _____
or equivalent experience
Technical training (specify area):

2.   Knowledge and skills:

Job Title: Maintenance Foreman

Reports To: Chief of Maintenance

Basic Function: Setting up of maintenance systems for proper maintenance schedules and FAA approval. Insures quality control of work assigned to mechanics by inspection of jobs completed, as required.

Duties and Responsibilities

1.   Leading, directing, and assigning work to other employees and performing all tasks necessary for safe and efficient maintenance of Company-owned aircraft.

2.   Utilizing all employees working under his or her direction and

assisting the Maintenance Secretary in timekeeping duties, inventory control, and parts procurement.

3. Signing for his or her own work and possibly that of others under his or her supervision. Seeing that all appropriate log book entries are made and signed for by his or her signature or that of the mechanic performing the work.

4. Keeping the Maintenance Supervisor informed as to work progress, problems incurred, and any impending problems that he or she is able to foresee.

Job Specifications

1. Education (check level required):
   High School _____ College _____
   or equivalent experience
   Technical training (specify area):

2. Knowledge and skills:

Job Title: Mechanic

Reports To: Chief of Maintenance

Duties and Responsibilities

1. Performs all routine maintenance on Company aircraft consistent with available tools and knowledge of job to be completed.

2. Performs duties under direction of Maintenance Foreman, being constantly aware of his or her own responsibility to meet and exceed requirements of airworthiness and safety.

3. Makes constant use of all maintenance manuals, computer worksheets, and recognized sources of information for proper maintenance of Company-owned aircraft.

Job Specifications

1. Education (check level required):
   High School _____ College _____
   or equivalent experience
   Technical training (specify area):

2. Knowledge and skills:

Job Title: Maintenance Clerk

Reports To: Chief of Maintenance

Basic Function: Responsible for all maintenance records and secretarial and accounting functions, as designated by Chief of Maintenance. Types all required reports and correspondence.

Duties and Responsibilities

1. Logsheets—checks, corrects, posts, makes copies and end-of-month records.
2. Purchase Orders—completes, dispatches, and posts.
3. Shipping—makes out packing slips and copies, labels, R&R tags, and inventory-out slips.
4. Worksheets—makes out, transfers items, and updates maintenance systems.
5. Debriefing Sheets—files and transfers items to worksheets.
6. Time Cards—fills out, copies, records overtime records, shift differential records; keeps records of outside labor used by Company.
7. Handles computer systems and works with Chief of Maintenance on inspection changes to submit for FAA approval.
8. Revises manuals when necessary.
9. Handles all correspondence for the Maintenance Department.
10. Accounting—handles all maintenance invoices, makes copies for file, and has them approved by Chief of Maintenance and Aviation Department Manager.
11. Maintains all Maintenance Department files and answers telephone for Maintenance Department.
12. Maintains established inventory of commissary supplies for all aircraft. Reorders items as necessary.
13. Maintains a current inventory record of aircraft parts and tools in Company stock.
14. Monthly—prepares all maintenance records/reports.

Job Specifications

1. Education (check level required):
   High School _____ College _____
   or equivalent experience
   Technical training (specify area):
2. Knowledge and skills:

Appendix B
Operations Policy Manual

Management Responsibilities
Distribution
Operating Philosophy

SIGNATURE FILE COPY

I hereby certify that I have read, understand, and concur with the Company Aviation Department Operations Policy Manual.

_____   _____

Date   Signature

MANUAL # _____

Note: This manual is the property of the Company. It is to be used solely by company personnel. The manual is to be returned upon leaving Company employ.

To be part of personnel file

REVISION RECORD

Revision No.	Date of Issuance	Date of Incorporation	Initials of Incorporator

Revision Control Sheet

Manual Holder: _____ Affected Publication:

Manual No.: _____ [   ] Operations Manual

Revision No.: _____ [   ] Maintenance Policy and Pro-
                                              cedures Manual

Issued Date: _____ [   ] Training Manual

Please revise your manual in accordance with the following instructions:

Remove Pages	Incorporate Pages	Initial Completion

I hereby certify that I have read and understand the above numbered revision(s), inserted the revised pages in accordance with the instructions, and recorded the revision on the revision record form in the manual.

_____   _____
        Signature   Date

Upon completion of the Revision, sign and date this form and return it to your supervisor.

Risk Management

The Company Operations Policy Manual and Aircraft Flight Manual set operational guidelines that are to be abided by as closely as possible. As professional aviation personnel, we have to develop discipline consonant with safety and good judgment.

The only safety is in care, which is a must, and competence, which is skill developed through study, practice, and experience.

None can say they are masters of all emergencies. Pilots who stop their progress toward an ultimate mastery of the air are deluding themselves and placing themselves in positions in which their operations cease to be safe.

All hazards can be combated by good operational practices, proper training, and good maintenance.

We all realize that there can be no compromise with safety. Therefore, there will be no compromise with safety under any circumstances, as it shall be our keynote of all operations.

The aircraft used in this operation were designed and built to be the safest possible vehicle for transport by air. The maintenance has been planned to maintain the highest degree of mechanical perfection possible. The procedures used will be those established as a result of years of flight experience and no element of the operation will be left to chance.

A pilot's ability and proficiency are tested when an emergency occurs. In order to prepare a pilot to cope with any emergency, a ground and flight training proficiency program has been instituted. We realize that the most important contribution to a safe operation is made by the pilot; to aid him or her, management will cooperate to the fullest extent.

Letter from Management

This manual is for the purpose of outlining certain rules and regulations in the Aviation Department to assure maximum safety for our customers and employees.

Company aircraft shall be assigned with consideration given to number of passengers, distance of trip and runway requirements.

Pilots have the responsibility of providing safe, dependable, and efficient transportation for the passengers. Federal Aviation and Company regulations must be followed at all times. When emergencies arise, the pilot-in-command must use his or her best judgment consistent with safety.

The pilot-in-command has complete responsibility for his or her aircraft and passengers from the time of takeoff until landing. All passengers are expected to comply with any reasonable request of the crew while aboard the airplane. The pilot-in-command must be sole judge as to whether conditions warrant concluding a trip or stopping short of destination. This means that his or her judgment is final and that he or she cannot be overruled in these matters.

We believe the purpose of these instructions is clear and that there need be no deviation from this policy.

_____
Management Signature

INTRODUCTION

The Aviation Department Policy Manual is the instrument established to provide flight operations personnel with the general policies and regulations of the Company and concerned governmental agencies.

Good judgment should be the basis of operations at all times. Should deviation from prescribed operating procedures become necessary under extenuating circumstances, be prepared to substantiate the compelled action with sound reasoning.

The Aviation Department Operations Policy Manual is the property of [Company] Aviation Department and is subject to recall at any time. This manual is restricted to the use of [Company] personnel and is not to be made available to any other persons or agencies unless so stipulated by [Company] Management.

Manual holders will be issued revision pages as necessary and it shall be the responsibility of said manual holder to revise and keep current his or her Aviation Department Flight Operations Policy Manual at all times.

The Aviation Department Operations Policy Manual shall be placed in each airplane, accessible to the crew.

It shall be the responsibility of all personnel to make available, on management's request, his or her Aviation Department Operations Policy Manual in a current and revised state for management's review.

The Administration and Maintenance Chief or the Chief Pilot must be notified if the manual is inadequate in meeting operational requirements.

MANAGEMENT RESPONSIBILITIES

The development of the aviation department within the corporation is clearly the function and responsibility of management. It is important that the aviation department be accepted as an integral part of the corporation.

The management of the aviation department is responsible for a safe, efficient, and economical operation of Company aircraft. There is also a responsibility to develop operations, flight training and maintenance manuals, as guidelines for conducting the operation.

Federal Aviation Regulations (FARs) are rules of the Federal Government with which all operators of aircraft must conform. FARs should be regarded as foundations upon which sound precepts of practice and judgment can be based. It is the concern and duty of management to be familiar with the safe, conservative principles of aircraft operations. Management should determine that these principles are carried out by the personnel in charge. Truly effective policies guiding management, operation, and maintenance of a corporate aircraft aviation department go beyond the basic requirements of the FARs.

DISTRIBUTION

Copies of manuals will be issued to and maintained by the following:

1.   Chairman and Chief Executive Officer: Operations Manual
2.   Senior Vice President: Operations, Maintenance, and Training Manuals
3.   Maintenance Chief: Operations, Maintenance, and Training Manuals
4.   Chief Pilot: Operations, Maintenance, and Training Manuals
5.   All pilots: Operations and Training Manuals
6.   Lead Technician: Operations and Maintenance Manuals

THERE WILL BE ONE OPERATIONS MANUAL PLACED IN EACH AIRCRAFT.

Operating Philosophy

A. Anticipation

Safety of flight may really be summed up in one word—*anticipation*. If every act and procedure could be planned in such a manner so as to anticipate all possible emergencies, we should either have provided a safe alternative to meet all possible contingencies or we would not fly. Could this be accomplished, accidents would cease.

B. Dependability

Second only to safety, dependability is the operating factor of greatest importance for providing a reliable and predictable transport service.

C. Passenger Comfort

The practices that will contribute to the comfort of the passengers also materially contribute to the dependability and safety of the operation.

Smooth operation on the ground as well as in the air will result in passenger comfort. It is not expected of the crew to impress the passengers with cabin service or other practices that will distract the crew from their duties or that will take up time which should be spent on maintenance, weather, or other matters that are in the interest of safety.

D. Efficiency

Efficiency of operation is construed to mean two things:

1. The efficient utilization of the aircraft. This is accomplished by proper scheduling and routing of the aircraft.
2. It also means the efficient operation from the standpoint of cost. Proper maintenance and operational planning will contribute to an economical operation.

E. Speed

The aircraft, when operated in a normal manner, meets the requirements of speed without undue haste on the part of the crew, whether in rushing through the pre-flight check or checking weather. In short, speed is the least important of all factors considered above.

F. Regulations

While the FAR 91 regulations apply to most operations, there are occasions where more restrictive regulations need apply. In these cases 135, 121, or Company regulations will be complied with.

G. Writing the Manual

The manual should be a handy book giving information and offering guidelines that are easy to interpret. It may prove difficult to get most of the personnel in the operation to read and understand the contents of the text.

The language should be appropriate to what has to be said, eliminating rhetoric but making sure that the aviation meanings are clear. The book is a technical manual that requires the diction to be highly specific, so the meaning is clear and unequivocal. The book is not a novel or biography.

Your company realizes that you were hired as manager or chief pilot, not as a writer. Therefore, we are sure the Company does not expect you to have expertise in disciplines such as *translating the spoken word into written language, using the proper writing style, and developing the proper format style*. You are however, expected to provide the inputs to an expert writer so he or she may develop a book or manual.

Writing Style must be consistent throughout the whole manual, almost always there are three or more *styles* used in the manual. The use of *I* or *We* in a manual is entirely inappropriate. Such usage will lead to a manual full of *I*'s and *We*'s.

Deficiency in writing skills makes the task of writing an operations manual usually difficult for the aviation manager or chief pilot. It is difficult to translate aviation knowledge and skills into the written word. It is always better to have an expert who can compile the manual in the proper language and proper format.

Format is the organization and style of a book or manual. To be a good writer you must know your audience, its purpose, and knowledge. You must think about the purpose of your audience in reading what you write. The purpose of an operations manual is to define operational guidelines for the safe operation of the company airplanes. Therefore, the manual must be addressed to: employees of the flight operation, the FAA, the NTSB, and a lawyer in the event of litigation. Consider how these agencies or persons are going to interpret the text.

In order to obtain an operating certificate, an airplane or air taxi has to submit to the FAA for approval the necessary manuals relevant to their particular operation requirements.

No corporate flight operation should start without having the necessary manuals that provide a supplement that go beyond FAR Part 91. This supplement can be derived from FAR Part 121 or FAR Part 135 or certain company regulations that are as comprehensive as the regulations mandated to airline operators.

An operations manual establishes common administrative and flight operations procedures that ensure that strong measures of standardization are conveyed to the pilots. The operations phase has a direct bearing on the safety of the mission so every phase from flight preparation through parking at the ramp must be as detailed as possible.

Contents of an operations manual may vary in order to meet the needs of each operation. Therefore, the manual should be tailored to the operational requirements to include coverage of the following subjects:

- Signature File Copy. I hereby certify that I have read, understand, and concur with the Company Flight Operations Manual.
- Revision Record. Revision Record Form.
- Revision Control Sheet. A control sheet to indicate that revisions have been read and inserted in manual.
- Manual Distribution. Copies of manuals will be issued to and maintained by the following:
- Letter from Upper Management. Affirming the rules and regulations in the operations manual.
- Introduction and/or Preface. The reason for the manual and the need to adhere to the contents.
- Company Management Responsibilities. The Flight Operations is accepted as an integral part of the corporation.
- Operating Philosophy. Who can use the airplanes, dependability, passenger comfort, efficiency, speed, regulations.
- Safety. The manual should not belabor the word *safety* to the point that it becomes trite by repeated use. The chapter on safety should tell about the safety program and how it is going to be managed. Refrain making employees paranoid with the use of the word. They may not want to do anything for fear of being unsafe.

- Structural Format. The structure chart should show the chain of command and let employees know who they are reporting to.
- The Seven Key Factors of Corporate Aviation Operation.
  1. Administration: The administrative functions can be divided into three areas:
     A. Activities of the aviation manager or chief pilot: These are the activities required of the manager or chief pilot in the administrative process. The activities may vary depending on the number of airplanes operated and the complexity of the operation.
     B. Resources, Human, and Physical facilities: Number of personnel required and skills required. Job expectations and conduct of employees. Crew members in a corporate flight operation are expected to be self-sufficient and perform efficiently as individuals. This section should list activities expected to be carried out by individuals or crew members. Physical facilities required: hangar, offices, etc.
     C. Interdepartmental coordination: The coordination of activities where all departments are involved to achieve unity of purpose in the operating plans.
  2. Passenger Service: Schedule of passengers and all passenger services.
  3. Training: It should only be mentioned that there is a training program with a short explanation of the program. Then refer to the training manual.
  4. Maintenance: Explanation of maintenance programs and the responsibilities of crew members to maintenance at base and away from base. Refer to maintenance manual.
  5. Safety: Safety program and how program is administered.
  6. Security: Security program and how it is administered.
  7. Emergency and Pre-Accident Plans: Emergency and pre-accident plan format.

In summary:

- Use the proper language. By using the proper language and eliminating rhetoric, many pages can be eliminated from the manual.
- The writing style must be consistent throughout the whole manual.

- Get to the point of what has to be said in as plain a language as possible using a minimum of rhetoric. The manual is not a novel or biography. Make the manual manageable so it can be carried. Pilots do not need to carry maintenance and training manuals.
- Consider how other persons are going to interpret the text, especially a lawyer, FAA inspector, or the NTSB. Make sure the personnel will abide by the manuals and that the manuals do not become so restrictive that you fail to give flexible service to the airplane users.
- Sectionalize the manual according to the seven key factors or to company needs.
- Avoid being redundant. Don't go out of the section or chapter.
- Do not compromise the Federal Aviation Regulations. Adapt as much as possible to the format and text of Part 121 or Part 135 of the FAA manuals.
- The aviation department organization structure should be well presented to let employees know who they are reporting to and what their responsibilities are.
- The text is intended for professionals. Don't use basic instructions and insult their intelligence.

Appendix C
Aviation Department
Maintenance Manual

Index

Forms and Records
Aircraft Maintenance Log
Aircraft Log Sign-off Procedures
Deferred Maintenance Items
Aircraft Records
Record Retention Requirements
Component Tags and Procedures for Use

Index

Maintenance Planning and Control Procedures
Approved Maintenance Procedures—Compliance Policy
Functional Test Policy After System or Component Repair or Replacement
Maintenance Postflight Checks
Scheduled Maintenance Control
Completed Work Records Review
Release of Aircraft from Maintenance
Crew Turnover Activity Reports
Engine Run-up Requirements
System Deactivation Tag
Warranty Control Procedures

Index

Material Control Procedures
Approved Aeronautical Replacement Parts
Receiving Inspection of Incoming Parts
Borrowed Parts Procedure
Other Operators "Loaner" Parts
Shelf Life Limitation
Storage and Handling of Critical Items

Index

Inspection Procedures
Required Inspection Items and Buy Back Policy and Procedures
Inspection Prior to Close Up of Critical Areas
Calibration and Testing of Precision Tools
Receiving Inspection of Incoming Materials
Inspection of Emergency Equipment and First Aid Kits

Inspection Procedures at Contract Agencies
Fuel Quality Control Procedures

Index

Index
Aircraft Ground Handling
  Aircraft Parking and Ground Safety
  Aircraft Security
  Maintenance Run-ups
  Cold Weather Procedures
  De-Icing Procedures
  Hangar Fire Safety
  Mechanics Run-up and Taxi Training

Index
Airworthiness Directives and Service Bulletin Control
  Airworthiness Directives
  Service Bulletins
  Service Letters and Instructional Data

Index
Safety, Health and Miscellaneous
  Electrical System Safety
  Static Electricity Precautions
  Weather Radar and X-Ray Safety
  Use of Personnel Safety Equipment

Restricted Use Items

Appendix D
History

1900–1920

Contrary to popular belief, corporate aviation began with advertisement, not executive transport. In fact, the first aircraft built for use in the furtherance of business was the airship *Gelatine*. Built for Charles B. Knox, this aircraft made its first flight on September 16, 1905. Drawing a crowd, the aircraft advertised Knox Gelatine to thousands of people who watched as it flew over Portland, Oregon. During this period of aircraft development any machine in the sky was a sight to see. Thus, aircraft displaying a company name or advertisement was noteworthy to the onlooker (Whempner, 1982).

Charles B. Knox was not the only one to use aircraft as a tool of advertisement. In 1920, for example, the James Heddon Company, developers of the wooden fishing lure, used three open cockpit de Havilland biplanes to market its innovative products from Dowagiac, Michigan, to various other locations in the upper Midwest. The Heddon Company had the edge on most of its local and regional competition simply because the de Havillands has a greater range than the competitions' Pullmans and Packards (Baran, 1990).

The first aircraft to come off the general aviation assembly lines with business as the target market arrived in the late 1920s. Technology in the area of passenger comfort had not yet developed to the point where companies were willing to purchase aircraft. Early models produced by Waco,

Spartan, and American Eagle could carry two passengers at approximately 80 miles per hours (mph), but they were noisy open-air cockpit designs held over from the days of the barnstormers. Such lack of comfort prohibited these aircraft from being sold in large numbers for strictly executive transport, although many were ordered in company colors and logos and used as flying billboards for marketing purposes.

1920–1930

One of the most important developments in aviation history came in 1926 with the introduction of the Ford Trimotor. The affectionately nickname "Tin Goose" was produced by the Ford Motor Company. The Trimotor rumbled through the sky at 115 mph with three 300 horse power (hp) engines. While the airplane had a range of only 500 miles, its most remarkable achievement was that it could carry 13 passengers in relative comfort. Although it was most appealing to airlines, the Trimotor also found its place in business aviation. Large corporations such as the Richfield and Standard Oil companies found the Ford an ideal airplane for transporting high-level executives and important customers in a style previously unknown to air travelers.

In 1928, numerous manufacturers introduced aircraft that caught the eyes of corporate executives. Travel Air introduced the Travel Air 6000, which was a six-seat commercial cabin high-wing monoplane. The 6000 came with a 220 hp engine propelling the aircraft over 125 mph for a range of almost 700 miles. Fairchild also produced a high-wing taildragger during the same year. The seven-seat Fairchild 71 was equipped with a 410 hp Wasp radial engine, which topped-out at nearly 140 mph. The extra power enabled the Fairchild to travel at a higher altitude than the Travel Air: 17,000 feet versus 15,000 feet, respectively. Cessna also entered the market with its first production airplane, the Type A. While few of the four-seaters were built, it became the predecessor to a long line of Cessna aircraft.

Perhaps the greatest hindrance to the growth of business aviation during the late 1920s was not the capabilities of the aircraft but the quality and quantity of ground-support services. Landing facilities at large cities could usually accommodate ground service needs of based and transient aircraft, but those needs were difficult to satisfy when companies wanted to travel to less populated areas. Reliable air navigational devices were also in short supply in the 1920s. Despite the infancy of corporate aviation, 34 nonaviation companies were operating business aircraft in 1927. By 1930 the number had grown to 300, and manufacturers such as Stinson, Travel Air, Waco, and Fokker were cultivating the market.

1930–1940

The 1930s brought numerous new aircraft choices to businesses of all sizes. Producers included the likes of Stinson, Beechcraft, Lockheed, Spartan, Bellanca, and Cessna. The Stinson Reliant became a popular business airplane prior to World War II. Early models of the high-wing aircraft had four seats, with an additional seat added in the latter half of the decade. The Reliant cruised at 130 mph with a 225 hp Lycoming radial engine, and was affordable enough for a moderately sized business at $5,000 to $10,000.

One of the most well-known airplanes produced in the post-WWI era was the Beechcraft Model 17 (Staggerwing). The Staggerwing was a five-seat cabin biplane produced for sixteen years from 1932 to 1948. The Model 17 was luxuriously appointed, but its most attractive feature to business travelers was its 200 mph speed and nearly 1,000 mile range. With a price tag ranging from $12,000 to $24,000, however, only those large companies not suffering financial setbacks during the Great Depression could afford an aircraft as fine as the Staggerwing.

After shutting down operations for three years, Cessna reentered the light airplane market in 1934 with an aircraft targeted for the business pilot, the C-34 Airmaster. The C-34 was able to use a smaller, more economical engine through the employment of a cowled engine, streamlined wheelcovers, and a cantilevered wing. With only a 145 to 165 hp engine, the Airmaster still managed to cruise at over 150 mph at ranges of up to 700 miles. The early models sold at an amazingly low $4,995, a price that made it very popular among small- to medium-sized companies.

Another high-performance single-engine airplane built before WWII was produced by the Spartan Company. With the high-flying corporate elite in mind, the aircraft was duly named the Spartan Executive 7-W. The all-metal low-wing Executive whizzed through the sky at nearly 200 mph, with a 450 hp Pratt and Whitney Wasp Junior radial engine. The aircraft was appointed with armrests, ashtrays, dome lights, soundproofing, and even window curtains for its passengers. With a ceiling of 24,000 feet and range of nearly 1,000 miles, the Spartan Executive was aimed at the upper end of the business spectrum much like the Beechcraft Staggerwing. With a price approaching $20,000, not many companies could justify the aircraft as a necessary business expense.

As the severity of the Depression began to decrease in the latter part of the decade, two manufacturers introduced high-priced twin-engine aircraft. Cessna came out with the T-50 in 1939. The T-50 was a fabric-covered airplane equipped with two 245 hp Jacobs radial engines, but could cruise at only 165 mph with six people on board. Beechcraft, on the other hand introduced a magnificent twin-engine two years earlier. The Model 18 was originally planned to be used as a feeder aircraft for airlines in the United States, much like its Lockheed look-alike, the Electra. The Beech 18 utilized a special heat-treated all-metal skin, which enabled it to endure high amounts of stress while simultaneously reducing weight. Most of these aircraft were equipped with two 450 hp radial engines, which propelled six passengers at 200 mph for nearly 1,000 miles. Despite selling in the mid $30,000 range, nearly $10,000 more than its Cessna counterpart, the Twin Beech still managed to find a home in the business market. One insurance executive from Oregon, named Henry K. Coffey, used a Model 18 to visit his widely dispersed branch offices in the Pacific Northwest. A Puerto Rican sugar growing and refining firm flew a Twin Beech around its various island operations in the Caribbean; another business aircraft owner was a Canadian department store chain run by John D. Eaton. The Model 18 continued on to the longest airplane production run in aviation history, lasting thirty-seven years until 1969.

1940–1950

The early 1940s saw little growth for the corporate sector of general aviation. Virtually all aircraft produced in the United States from the start of the decade until 1945 went to the government for use in the military for WWII. Most civilian aircraft that were still flying on business trips in the United States during this time were only for those companies that were involved in the war effort.

With the end of the war in 1945, business aviation experienced a tremendous expansion. This boom was largely attributed to the government's selling of thousands of military aircraft to the business community to be converted into executive transports, including Beech 18s, Cessna T-50s, and even 28-passenger Douglas DC-3s.

When tens of thousands of military personnel began coming back from the war in the mid-1940s with pilot's certificates, aviation experts predicted enormous increases in the amount of aircraft that would be sold to ex-servicemen for personal flying. This factor, combined with the influx of ex-military multiengine aircraft, led manufacturers to concentrate their efforts on small pleasure aircraft rather than the business market. Only a few manufacturers produced aircraft with business in mind as a customer.

The Beech Bonanza Model 35 was one of the few. The four-seat low-wing aircraft, commonly referred to as the V-tail for its distinctive V-shaped vertical stabilizer, featured full flight and navigational instruments necessary for day or night VFR cross-country flights, fully retractable landing gear, and even a two-way radio as standard equipment. The Bonanza was a popular plane among businesses throughout its lengthy thirty-year production lifespan.

Cessna also introduced new aircraft aimed at the business market during the mid-1940s. The Cessna 190/195 series of 1947, along with the slightly smaller 170 series of 1948, were popular among business people needing efficient transportation in the 500 to 700 mile range. Nearly 4,000 of these aircraft were built between 1947 and 1956.

When the predicted post–WWII general aviation pleasure flying boom did not materialize into anything near the hopes of airplane manufacturers, most went out of business. Only those manufacturers who had aircraft seating four or more people on their production list had realistic chances for survival. Three of the larger companies that managed to pull through the 1940s, albeit not unscathed, were Beechcraft, Cessna, and Piper. Sales to corporate aviation played an important part in keeping these three companies alive.

1950–1960

After general aviation sales hit an alltime low in the early 1950s, airplane manufacturers began looking toward the business community as the aviation market with the greatest potential for growth and profit. While they did not abandon single-engine, four-passenger aircraft, manufacturers viewed high-priced, twin-engine business-oriented airplanes as their salvation. Some of the single-engine aircraft built during this time found their way into business aviation included the Beech Bonanza, Cessna 170, 172, 175, 180, and 182, Piper Pacer, Mooney Mark 21, and Aero Commander 200.

Beechcraft added a twin version of its Bonanza to be sold alongside the Model 18. The twin Bonanza seated six passengers in comfort. Not only did the new Beech have a high useful load capacity for plenty of luggage, but it also offered executives an outstanding range of 900 miles.

A striking high-wing twin came to the market called the Aero Commander 560. The 560 carried five to seven passengers at a speed of 230 mph for over 1,700 miles. President Eisenhower popularized the Aero Commander by using it as his personal short-haul transport. Cessna and Piper introduced four-place twins in 1945 called the 310 and Apache, respectively.

By the close of the decade, businesses finally had a wide range of aircraft choices to accommodate a variety of corporate needs. Small aircraft like the Piper Pacer would be ideally suited to a company that did a considerable amount of business 100 to 300 miles from its base of operations, while a Twin Beech or Aero Commander 560 could transport executives to faraway destinations in style and comfort.

1960–1970

As the number of businesses operating aircraft began to increase, so too did the size of available airplanes. While manufacturers continued to meet the needs of small- to medium-sized companies with high-performance singles and light twin aircraft, airplane producers set their sights on the transportation needs of the largest of corporations. These needs were for larger and faster business planes.

The Grumman Gulfstream I addressed these corporate desires directly. The G-I cruised at nearly 300 mph and could carry from ten to fourteen passengers. The Grumman was also the first business aircraft certified to cruise at 30,000 feet. The G-I with its turboprop engines and pressurized cabin set the standard for the new heavy-twin category of aircraft.

Beechcraft and Cessna also went after the large business market, but with scaled down versions of the Grumman G-I. Beechcraft introduced its Queen Air and King Air series, which featured comfortable seating for six to seven passengers. The Queen Air traveled at 230 mph and had a range of just over 1,000 miles. The Cessna 401/402 series arrived in the mid-1960s with seating capabilities and performance characteristics similar to those of the Queen Air.

The 1960s also brought the reality of applying jet transport technology to corporate aviation. The first business jet on the market did not come from the big three general aviation manufacturers but from Lockheed. The Lockheed Jetstar was truly an executive airplane with airliner performance. It featured a walk-through cabin, a complete lavatory, and thrust reversers. The biggest advantages of this pioneer aircraft were in its range and speed: over 1,900 miles at 550 mph. The first delivery of the Jetstar went to Continental Can Company, but many companies could not afford the lofty $1.5 million price tag.

The Jetstar was not the only executive jet offered in the early 1960s. The North American Sabreliner, a twin jet also seating ten passengers, was made available for civilian use in 1963. While the Sabreliner was less expensive to maintain than the Jetstar, the twin jet had lower performance and range capabilities: 525 mph and 2,000 miles.

In 1964 perhaps the world's best-known business jet was introduced: the Learjet. The Learjet carried six passengers over 500 mph at altitudes up to 45,000 feet. The most appealing characteristic of the new jet was it price, which was under $1 million. The Learjet revolutionized corporate aviation by proving the need for executive jets, and it set the stage for business jets that would arrive in the decades to come.

1970–1990

Throughout the last two decades, general aviation manufacturers have been in pursuit of the perfect business airplane. There were a few new single-engine models introduced in the 1970s, such as the Cessna Cardinal RG, Cessna 207 Skywagon, and the Piper Cherokee Lance. Most manufacturers, however, have focused their attention on twin-engine and jet aircraft in trying to attract business customers.

New twin-engine aircraft were developed by each of the big three during the 1970s. Beechcraft came out with the low-priced Duchess Model 76. Cessna produced a variety of new airplanes called the 340, Titan, and Conquest. The three Cessnas ranged in size from six, six to eight, and eight to eleven passengers, respectively. Piper introduced the Seneca and Cheyenne twins. The latter was equipped with 680 hp Pratt and Whitney turboprops.

In the early 1980s, Piper introduced two new twin-engine designs, the Seminole and the Aerostar. Although the four-seat Seminole was only produced for two years, 361 were sold. The Aerostar was a six-seat version.

Although Cessna produced the T37 jet under military contract, the Cessna Fanjet 500 was the first civilian jet to be produced by Cessna. The Cessna Fanjet 500 was replaced by the Citation series in 1977. This eight-seat business jet is powered by Pratt & Whitney JT15D-1 turbofans for a range of 1,505 nm at 400 mph. Its special features at the time were a base price lower than most other executive jets and the capability of operating in and out of small airports. The Citation aircraft had become the worlds best-selling business jet (Thurston, 1979).

Improvements to the original Citation came with the development of the Citation II. At a cruise speed of 372 kts, the Citation II is certified for ten passengers and has a range of 1,825 nm. With an increase in fuel capacity the Citation II is also certified for ten passengers. However, the range increased to 2,000 nm with a cruise speed of 405 kts.

The Citation III came out in 1984. Offering the versatility of both domestic and overwater trips, the thirteen-passenger Citation III cruises at 463 kts with a range of 2,500 nm.

Finally, in 1989, the Citation V was added to the business jet market. With a certification for eight to ten passengers, it cruises at 425 kts and has a range of 1,920 nm.

Although Piper came out with no jet aircraft (as Cessna did) during this time period, significant developments were made in the single-engine piston, multiengine piston, and turboprop categories.

In 1977, Piper added the Lance to the Cherokee line of single engine aircraft. The Lance's distinction is that it was the first airplane to make the step from fixed-gear super-hauler (Cherokee 6) to a high-performance retractable. Although the gross weight of the Lance was higher than the original 6 model, Piper was able to increase the useful load by refining the intake and exhaust system, thus achieving more horsepower. This seven-seat aircraft retains a 114 lb. useful load advantage over the Cherokee 6. At 300 hp, the Lance cruises at 182 mph with a range of 1,055 nm.

In 1972, the six-seat Seneca was produced and sold alongside the Twin Comanche until 1973 when the Comanche was discontinued. This six-seat 200 hp multiengine aircraft is full-time turbocharged. Piper had done away with the costly hydraulics waste gate system. At 218 mph cruise, the Seneca has a 900-mile range with a useful load of 1,747 lbs.

Based on the Navajo airframe, Piper's first turboprop was produced in 1975. The Piper Cheyenne is a six-seat plane with a girthy 4,130 lb. useful load and a cruise speed at 309 mph.

In 1978, Piper produced the Dakota, a 235 hp, four-seat, single-engine (piston) plane that cruises at 140 kts. The first Saratoga was delivered in 1980. At 150 kts, this six-seat single-engine became very popular, especially in its upgraded versions, the SP and Turbo SP. In fact, the Piper Company sold a whopping 1,655 between 1975 and 1985.

In 1982 Piper built the first Malibu. This six-seat, single-engine, piston, pressurized, speedstar cruises at 215 kts at a certified ceiling of 25,000 feet. This 310 hp machine was a significant development in that it outperformed (and still does today) many light twins.

Other aircraft developed by the Piper Company during the 1970s and 1980s include the very popular multiengine piston Chieftain, which sold 1,824 between 1973 and 1985, and the not-so-popular T-1020 of which Piper only produced eighteen since its first delivery in 1981.

The aircraft described above are just a small sampling of what was offered to the business/corporate market between 1970 and 1990. This twenty-year period of astonishing development is marked by the fact that there were at that time over forty-one manufacturers (in the United States and abroad) offering over 112 different aircraft for the business world. These aircraft ranged from single-engine piston planes to multiengine jets and helicopters.

Selected Bibliography

BOOKS

Addison-Wesley. *How to Write Effective Reports*. Reading, MA: Addison-Wesley, 1965.

Allen, Louis A. *Making Managerial Planning More Effective*. New York: McGraw-Hill, 1982.

Baran, R. T. *Anatomy of a Flight Department*. Edition 90–2. Washington, DC: National Business Aircraft Association, Mar. 16, 1990.

Davies, D. P. *Handling the Big Jets*. Redhill, Surrey, England: Brabazon House, 1969.

Dennett, Daniel C. *Elbow Room: The Varieties of Free Will Worth Wanting*. Cambridge, MA: MIT/Bradford, 1984.

Fulmer, Robert M. *The New Management*. New York: Macmillan, 1978.

Garrison, P. *Corporate Aircraft Owner's Handbook*. Blue Ridge Summit, PA: Tab Books, 1981.

General Aviation Manufacturers Association. *Financial Benefits and Intangible Advantages: Business Aircraft Operations*. Washington, DC: GAMA, 1990.

Houp, Kenneth W., and Pearsall, Thomas E. *Reporting Technical Information*. Encino, CA: Glencoe Publishing, 1977.

Howgill, Pat. *Airport Security Operations*. London: Sterling Publications, 1992.

Jane's Encyclopedia of Aviation. New York: Portland House, 1989.

Kane, Robert M., and Vose, Allan D. *Air Transportation*. Dubuque, IA: Kendall/Hunt, 1976.

King, Frank H. *Aviation Maintenance Management*. Carbondale: Southern Illinois Univ. Press, 1986.

McGregor, Douglas. *The Human Side of Enterprise*. New York: McGraw-Hill, 1960.

Matson, Katinka. *Psychology Today*. New York: William Morrow, 1977.

Miner, John B. *The Practice of Management*. Columbus, OH: Charles E. Merrill, 1985.

National Academy of Sciences. *Improving Aircraft Safety*. Washington, DC: NAS, Office of Publications, 1980.

National Business Aircraft Association. *Aviation Financial Analysis Package*. Washington, DC: NBAA, 1990.

_____. *Business Aviation Factbook*. Washington, DC; NBAA, 1991.

_____. *Business Aviation Issues*. Washington, DC: NBAA, 1991.

_____. *Business Aviation Management Guide*. Washington, DC: NBAA, 1988.

_____. *Evolution of Business Aviation*. Washington, DC: NBAA, 1986.

_____. *Operating Costs*. Washington, DC: NBAA, 1992.

Netanyahu, Benjamin. *Terrorism: How the West Can Win*. New York: Farrar, Straus & Giroux, 1984.

1992 Planning & Purchasing Handbook. Business and Commercial Aviation, 1993.

Progress in Aircraft Design Since 1903. Washington, DC: GPO, 1978.

Ramsden, J. M. *The Safe Airline*. London: MacDonald and Janes, 1976.

Taneja, Nawal K. *The Commercial Airline Industry*. Lexington, MA: Heath, 1976.

Timm, Paul R. *Managerial Communication*. Englewood Cliffs, NJ: Prentice-Hall, 1980.

Verderber, Rudolph F. *Communciate*. Belmont, CA: Wadsworth, 1978.

Wells, Alexander T. *Introduction to Aviation Insurance*. Malabar, FL: Robert E. Krieger, 1988.

Whempner, B. *Corporate Aviation*. New York: McGraw-Hill, 1982.

Winant, J. H. *Keep Business Flying*. Washington, DC: National Business Aircraft Association, 1989.

Wolfe, Harry P., and NewMyer, David A. *Aviation Industry Regulation*. Carbondale: Southern Illinois Univ. Press, 1985.

PERIODICALS

Aviation Equipment Maintenance. 7300 N. Cicero Ave., Lincolnwood, IL 60646-1696.

Aviation Week & Space Technology. 1221 Avenue of the Americas, New York, NY 10020.

Business & Commercial Aviation. Hangar C-1, Westchester County Airport, White Plains, NY 10604.

Business Aviation Safety. 405 Main St., Parkville, MO 64152.

Interavia: Aerospace World. Swissair Centre, 31 Route de l'Aéroport, PO Box 437, 1215 Geneva 15, Switzerland.

Professional Pilot. 3014 Colvin St., Alexandria, VA 22314.

Rotor & Wing International. News Plaza, P.O. Box 1797, Peoria, IL 61656.

ARTICLES IN PERIODICALS

Alcock, C. "Commuters Find Favor as Corporate Shuttles." *Aviation International News*, Sept. 1, 1991.

_____. "Europe: Trade Barriers Fall While Recession Worries Rise." *Aviation International News*, Mar. 1, 1991.

Bonneau, Bertrand. "Farming Out Business Aircraft." *Interavia: Aerospace Review*, Mar. 1988.

_____. "The Second Hand Market Explodes." *Interavia: Aerospace Review*, Apr. 1988.

Castro, Raoul. "Cost Effectiveness Points." *Professional Pilot*, Aug. 1975.

_____. "Dealing with Bean-Counters." *Professional Pilot*, Dec. 1989.

_____. "How Castro's System Analysis Chose a Falcon and a Lear for Ward's." *Professional Pilot*, Mar. 1968.

_____. "Let's Drop Annual Inspections." *Professional Pilot*, Feb. 1972.

_____. "Paperwork Systems." *Professional Pilot*, Feb. 1969.

_____. "Safety." *Flight Crew Magazine*, July 1988.

_____. "Transferring Skill from Classroom to Cockpit." *Air Taxi/Commuter Safety Bulletin*, Mar./Apr. 1984.

Dennis, S. "There's no Substitute for Business Aviation." *Professional Pilot*, Apr. 1991.

Endres, G. "Distribution of Regional Business Aircraft Fleets." *Interavia: Aerospace Review*, Oct. 1991.

Esler, D. "Phillips' Corporate Flight Department Logs 64 Years from Biplanes to Jets." *Aviation International News*, May 1, 1991.

"Expanding World Markets Offer New Opportunities for Business Aviation." *Professional Pilot*, May 1992.

Glines, C. V. "Executive Jet Aviation: A New Era." *Professional Pilot*, Sept. 1988.

Gromley, M. "Justifying Business Aircraft: A Synergy of Benefits." *Business & Commercial Aviation*, Dec. 1991.

Katz, Robert L. "Skills of an Effective Administrator." *Harvard Business Review*, Sept.–Oct. 1984.

Kolcum, E. H. "Cessna Foresees Large Orders for New $2.4 Million Citation Jet." *Aviation Week & Space Technology*. Oct. 9, 1989.

Lederer, Jerome F. "Fallacies in Aviation Safety and System Management." Los Angeles: Institute of Aviation Safety, University of Southern California, 1988.

McLaren, G. "Baxter Needs Wings at Waukegan." *Professional Pilot*, Dec. 1991.

Nordwall, B. D. "Corporate Avionics Linked to Needs of Traveling Executives." *Aviation Week & Space Technology*, Oct. 28, 1991.

"Operators Hire Management Firms to Reduce Aircraft Costs." *Aviation Week & Space Technology*, Oct. 17, 1988.

Parrish, R. L. "Business Aviation in Today's Environment." *Business & Commercial Aviation*, Nov. 1988.

Rockwood, R. "How to Get More When You Sell and Pay Less When You Buy." *Professional Pilot*, Jan. 1989.

Salerno, J. "Business Aviation within *Fortune*'s 500." *Business & Commercial Aviation*, Dec. 1991.

Schneider, Charles E. "Aircraft Utilization Stressed by Marcor." *Aviation Week & Space Technology*, Nov. 27, 1972.

_____. "Maintenance Key to Marcor's Reliability." *Aviation Week & Space Technology*, Dec. 11, 1972.

Seidenman, P. "Cockpits, Cabins, and Comfort." *Professional Pilot*, Jan. 1990.

_____. "A Global Scan of Current and Upcoming Models." *Professional Pilot*, Nov. 1990.

_____. "Intercontinental Corporate Jet Survey." *Professional Pilot*, Feb. 1988.

Seidenman, P., and Spanovich, D. "Helicopter Business on the Upswing." *Professional Pilot*, Jan. 1991.

_____. "Orders up in Big Aircraft." *Professional Pilot*, Nov. 1991.

Spanovich, D. "1992 Jet Buyers' Guide." *Professional Pilot*, Nov. 1991.

Tippens, M. "Enron's Dynamic Energy." *Professional Pilot*, Mar. 1987.

Index

Raoul Castro is president, Aerospace International Management Systems (AIMS), Inc., which he founded in 1979 as a service organization to provide comprehensive consulting and evaluating services to corporate aviation and related business enterprises. For seventeen years he managed seven aircraft for Marcor flight operations based at Chicago O'Hare International Airport. Other positions include: two years as technical manager and chief pilot for Turbo Flight Inc.; the modification and marketing of a French four-engine turboprop for the American corporate aircraft market; eleven years as captain pilot in charge of maintenance and scheduling for International Harvester Company, four airplanes; two years as chief pilot for Square D Company, Milwaukee, Wisconsin; three years as chief pilot for Globe Steel Company, Milwaukee, Wisconsin; captain pilot for United States airlines flying North and South American routes; and four-engine pilot and engineering officer with the United States Air Force. He has also served as a visiting instructor for Southern Illinois University's bachelor of science off-campus degree program in corporate aviation management, and has published over sixty articles on aviation subjects. Raoul Castro's specialized experience, coupled with the fact that he has actually managed corporate flight operations, enables him to write with authority on the subject of corporate aviation management.